Unconventional Politics

Unconventional Politics

NINETEENTH-CENTURY WOMEN WRITERS AND U.S. INDIAN POLICY

Janet Dean

University of Massachusetts Press
Amherst and Boston

Printed in the United States of America

ISBN 978-1-62534-203-4 (paper); 202-7 (hardcover)

Designed by Sally Nichols
Set in ITC New Baskerville Std
Printed and bound by Sheridan Books, Inc.

Cover art: "Miss Ora V. Eddleman as an Indian Huntress costume, Cherokee, 1903." *Twin Territories: The Indian Magazine Collection,* courtesy Research Division of the Oklahoma Historical Society, #21178.5.79.

Library of Congress Cataloging-in-Publication Data

Names: Dean, Janet, 1965– author.
Title: Unconventional politics : nineteenth-century women writers and U.S. Indian policy / Janet Dean.
Other titles: Nineteenth-century women writers and U.S. Indian policy
Description: Amherst and Boston : University of Massachusetts Press, 2016. | Includes bibliographical references and index.
Identifiers: LCCN 2016012906| ISBN 9781625342027 (hardcover : alk. paper) | ISBN 9781625342034 (pbk. : alk. paper)
Subjects: LCSH: American literature—Women authors—History and criticism. | American literature—Indian authors—History and criticism. | Wakefield, Sarah F.--Criticism and interpretation. | Sigourney, L. H. (Lydia Howard), 1791-1865—Criticism and interpretation. | Callahan, S. Alice, 1868-—Criticism and interpretation. | Eddleman, Ora V., 1880–1968—Criticism and interpretation. | Indians in literature. | Indians of North America—Government relations—History—19th century. | Politics and literature—United States—History—19th century. | Women and literature—United States—History—19th century.
Classification: LCC PS152 .D43 2016 | DDC 810.9/928708997—dc23
LC record available at https://lccn.loc.gov/2016012906

British Library Cataloguing-in-Publication Data
A catalog record for this book is available from the British Library.

For Ed, with gratitude and love

Contents

Acknowledgments

This book examines, among other things, the constraints of popular literary conventions. The scholarly monograph has its own constraints, and they are most acutely felt on the acknowledgments pages. This small space cannot possibly accommodate the gratitude I want to express to the many people, over many years, who have helped bring this book into being.

I am indebted to two wise, patient mentors who guided me at the start of my career and continue to illuminate my path, always checking in at precisely the right moment. Robert A. Ferguson had confidence in my work when I did not. He offered invaluable advice at an early stage and kind encouragement as my writing began to look like a book. Priscilla Wald is an extraordinary teacher and friend, as well as the most generous scholar I know. Her incisive comments on one chapter clarified the entire project for me, and conversations with her over long walks in various cities kept me on the right track. Her example as a teacher-scholar who balances intellectual rigor with genuine good-heartedness serves me every day.

I have been fortunate to find homes in vibrant academic communities full of smart and caring colleagues and intellectually adventurous students. I owe a huge debt of gratitude to my first department chair, Susan J. Wolfe at the University of South Dakota, who arranged the course releases that got the ball rolling on this project. Since then I have had the support of several administrators at Bryant University. Thanks to my department chairs there, the late Nora Barry, Terri Hasseler, Mary Prescott, and Elizabeth Walden. I am grateful to Dean David Lux for granting summer stipends that funded research and to Dean Wendy Samter and Provost Glenn Sulmasy for vital support in the final stages of revision. Thanks, too, to students in my U.S. Protest Literature classes for their willingness to engage tough questions and for sharing their own creative expressions of protest.

In researching this book I spent many happy hours poring over obscure texts and images, and I depended a great deal on their guardians at several institutions. I appreciate the assistance provided by librarians and archivists at my home universities and at the Beinecke Library at Yale University, the Cumberland County Historical Society, the DeGolyer Library of Southern Methodist University, the Dickinson Research Center at the National Cowboy and Western Heritage Museum, the Connecticut Historical Society, the Kansas City Public Library, the Library of Congress, the National Archives, the New York Public Library, the Oklahoma Historical Society, and the Western History Collections at the University of Oklahoma. For images from *Super Indian: Volume One* and permission to reprint, I thank the ever-gracious Arigon Starr.

Many generous fellow scholars have commented helpfully on my writing. Mary Louise Kete and Michael Millner each read drafts of the entire manuscript; I am grateful for their thoughtful engagement with my ideas and for their good cheer. Heartfelt thanks to Thom Bassett, Terri Hasseler, David Kyuman Kim, and Siobhan Senier for incredibly useful responses to drafts of individual chapters, and to Amber Day, Lucia McMahon, and Tom Roach for guiding me to envision the book as a whole. At conferences and meetings I have benefited from the wisdom and encouragement of too many fellow scholars to name here, but I would like to acknowledge in particular Susan Bernardin, Christine Bold, and Augusta Rohrbach for endorsing the project at various stages and for urging me forward.

Earlier versions of the first and third chapters appeared in *American Literature* and *ESQ: A Journal of the American Renaissance,* respectively. I appreciate the journals' permission to reprint, and I thank their readers and editors for advice that sharpened my arguments and expanded my thinking. I am also grateful to Siobhan Senier and Cari Carpenter, readers for the University of Massachusetts Press, whose scholarship I have long admired. They challenged me to consider the broader implications of my analyses, and their insights greatly improved the final product. I thank Siobhan as well for modeling for me and so many others what it means to be an activist in the academy. Brian Halley at the press solicited the book at the American Studies Association Conference. I am grateful to him for seeing merit in the work and for patiently shepherding it through to publication. Thanks also to Carol Betsch, managing editor, and her colleague Mary Bellino; to production manager Jack Harrison; and to others at the press for the care they took with the manuscript. It was my good fortune to have had Margaret Hogan copyedit the book; her expert suggestions elevated my prose and her efficiency and kindness made the process remarkably pain-free.

Friends and family have listened to me, fed me, entertained me, and rooted for me. My late grandmother Leona Coy Richards called me a writer and gave me a room of my own at the very start of the project; I was blessed to have her faith in my abilities and her abiding love. My extended family has an amazing capacity to be both buoy and anchor, lifting me up and keeping me safely moored at the same time. Thanks and love to David and Sylvia Dean, Ginny and Ted Raff, Ruth Dean, John Slobod, Anna Raff, Joel Lowden, Tom and Gena Dean, Jim and Renee Dean, and all the kids. Dear friends have heartened me in my work and, when needed, provided just the right amount of distraction. Thank you Sandra Enos, Carla Ferrari, Diane Hoffman-Kim, Anna Raff, and Nanci Weinberger. Friends in the Narragansett Indian community, fellow members of the Board of Trustees of Tomaquag Museum, and Tomaquag Executive Director Lorén Spears inspire me with their dedication to educating others about Native American history and culture. I am immensely grateful for all they have taught me about hearing and telling important stories.

As this project grew into a book, my children, Caleb and Will, grew into the intelligent, principled, and creative adults they are today. Nothing could make me prouder. Lastly, this book would not be possible without the presence of Ed Raff in my life. His energy, goodness, and love carry me through, and there are not enough pages in the world to express my thanks.

A version of chapter 1 appeared as "Nameless Outrages: Narrative Authority, Rape Rhetoric, and the Dakota Conflict of 1862," in *American*

Literature 77, no. 1 (2005), 93–122. Copyright © 2005 by Duke University Press. All rights reserved. Reprinted by permission of the present publisher, Duke University Press, www.dukeupress.edu. A version of chapter 3 appeared as "Reading Lessons: Sentimental Literacy and Assimilation in *Stiya: A Carlisle Indian Girl at Home* and *Wynema: A Child of the Forest*," in *ESQ: A Journal of the American Renaissance* 57, no. 3 (2011), 201–40. Copyright © 2014 by the Board of Regents of Washington State University. Reprinted by permission of the Board of Regents of Washington State University.

Unconventional Politics

Introduction

Aesthetics, Politics, and Literary Convention

In this book I examine women writers' responses to nineteenth-century U.S. Indian policy and explore the ways their unconventional politics informed and transformed conventional literature. Long before the Women's National Indian Association asserted in 1888 that "the Indian Question must become more and more a woman question," Native and non-Native women had been intervening in public debates about federal actions affecting indigenous people.[1] Women worked together in tribal delegations and reform organizations to influence policy. They circulated petitions and lobbied Congress in response to laws that infringed on Native rights to sovereignty, property, and personhood. And they wrote—letters to politicians, editorials, and polemics, but also conventional poems, personal narratives, novels, and magazine fiction addressing Native issues. In the fight against the oppression of indigenous people, as in the abolition movement and the campaign for women's rights, conventional literary forms often served as platforms for women's political opposition. These forms, with their protocols for consensus and compliance, did not easily accommodate political outrage. Yet the subjects of this book—Sarah Wakefield, Lydia Huntley Sigourney, S. Alice Callahan (Muscogee [Creek]), and Ora V. Eddleman (Cherokee)— found ways to articulate their horror at legal injustices and military assaults on tribes; to condemn programs aimed at dispossessing, exiling, and erasing Native peoples and cultures; and to fight against social attitudes that devalued and threatened indigenous lifeways. Less discernibly, the writer-activists I examine also critiqued literary protocols and stretched the contours of popular forms in order to create new instruments of protest.

In calling my subjects writer-activists, I mean both to resurface their political commitments and to draw attention to a fundamental tension between literary expression and political action for women in the nineteenth century. As protesters, my subjects worked to break down established structures of power and advocate for the radical revision of political and social relations between Natives and non-Natives in the United States. As women writers interested in reaching wide audiences, they were at the same time obliged to work within normative and conventionally feminine genres that tended to reflect and sustain rather than challenge the status quo. By definition, conventional modes are anything but revolutionary: in privileging consistency and answering the requirements of genre, they encourage a fantasy of consensus and cohesion; they placate rather than agitate. The incommensurability of form and intention raises the questions that occupy me here. How did women writer-activists manage the conflict between the modes of expression available to them and their aims of remaking the world? How did they navigate the unmapped shoreline where conventional literature and radical resistance converge?

This book, then, is both a feminist literary-historical recovery project and a study of the elasticity of genre. My subjects entered into debates about federal policies affecting Native tribes and individuals, contesting official decisions about removal, war, capital punishment, assimilation, tribal citizenship, resource distribution, and property rights. They put into service highly popular and commercial forms of expression. Their literary protests involved recognizable tropes like Indian tears and white female vulnerability. To some extent, these writers trafficked in established models of middle-class selfhood and Indian "progress" toward acculturation. But the case studies that follow show how such conformist print instruments could be made to serve an oppositional politics. I argue that women writer-activists contested both oppressive governmental regimes and entrenched dominant cultural traditions. As I hope to reveal, nothing less than a revolution in American women's public expression is evidenced in their writings.

Protest in Unexpected Places

Critics tend to see Wakefield, Sigourney, Callahan, and Eddleman (when they see them at all) as anything but political. Of the four, only Sigourney is likely to be familiar to general readers. Her reputation has been as a prolific elegist whose sentimental poetry made her rich and famous. But she was also an activist, writing on U.S. Indian policies and playing an important role in a major movement protesting Indian removal—activities that figure relatively little in scholarly discussions of her life and work.[2] Callahan has received a flurry of attention since A. LaVonne Brown Ruoff reissued her 1891 novel *Wynema: A Child of the Forest* and named it the first such work published by a Native woman. Entire chapters of the book are devoted to arguments against allotment, and an original publisher's preface identifies the novel as a "protest against the present Indian policy of our government."[3] Still, contemporary critics tend to think of Callahan as more politically compromised than resistant. Kathryn Zabelle Derounian-Stodola identifies Wakefield's memoir of her experience in the Dakota Conflict as "protest literature," but most scholars encounter the text as an example of nineteenth-century Indian captivity narrative.[4] Eddleman is virtually unknown despite her status as the first Native person to edit a widely distributed commercial magazine. She published in a time and place of extreme political upheaval, when the U.S. government instituted allotment and took over tribal enrollment in Oklahoma and the Indian Territories even as the Native inhabitants of these territories campaigned for the creation of a sovereign Indian state. Yet her "Indian Magazine" has not been noticed as a platform of Native political expression.

We have failed to recognize these women writers as activists in part because their protests were less overt than others. *A Century of Dishonor,* Helen Hunt Jackson's 1881 polemic, explicitly condemns the oppression of Native people. The Yankton Sioux (Dakota) writer Zitkala-Ša (Gertrude Simmons Bonnin) argued for Native rights and criticized Christianity, assimilationist education, and the economic exploitation of tribes in the pages of mainstream publications like the *Atlantic Monthly;* her 1923 pamphlet *Oklahoma's Poor*

Rich Indians: An Orgy of Graft and Exploitation of the Five Civilized Tribes—Legalized Robbery, written with an attorney for the American Indian Defense Association and the secretary of the Indian Rights Association, presents damning evidence of systematized government abuse of Native people. The title of Sarah Winnemucca's autobiography, *Life among the Piutes: Their Wrongs and Claims* (1883), advertises its oppositional politics, and its appendix includes a petition to Congress demanding the restoration of Paiute land rights and a request that readers moved by Winnemucca's story circulate the document and collect signatures. These recognizably political works are part of a rich field of print production by women activists in the nineteenth century, one that we should continue to explore. But a central contention of this book is that protest exists in print culture across a broad spectrum of expressive possibilities, from the official to the vernacular, the civic-minded to the commercial, the straightforward to the oblique.

Unconventional Politics is motivated in part by a wish to broaden our understanding of the political commitments of American women writers and the genres and modes they mobilized for resistance. In unearthing the social significance of nineteenth-century women's conventional writing, a generation of literary scholars has focused on a handful of key issues: slavery and abolition, women's and African Americans' rights, U.S. imperialism, the plight of immigrants and the underclass. Scholars have been less attuned to the ways women writers involved themselves in the equally pressing calamity of settler colonialism's threat to Native life, culture, and sovereignty. At the same time, academics have settled on the sentimental novel as the primary form women writers used to enter political debates. The wealth of scholarship on the power of sympathy in nineteenth-century fiction by women has deepened our understanding of the mechanics of ideology and resistance in popular culture, but there has not been enough attention paid to the ways other print forms (popular poetry and the commercial magazine, for instance) and other literary modes (like sensation or irony) relate to political problems. My subjects' activism on behalf of Native people has remained hidden because we have not recognized that many kinds of print conventions accommodate many kinds of political expression.

Women took up conventional print forms to enter debates over Indian policy both because they were compelled by gender norms and because it was a way to make their voices heard in a social climate that constrained them. In the nineteenth century, women had limited access to official political forums, and social pressure and commercial demands pushed them into conventionally feminine, seemingly apolitical forms of discourse. Yet they often found these forms could make their oppositional political messages more legible. On completing *Ramona* (1884), her sentimental romance about a mixed-race Native woman facing discrimination, Jackson declared, "I have sugared my pill, and it remains to be seen if it will go down."[5] The comment suggests that while nineteenth-century women might try to influence Indian policy through treatises like *A Century of Dishonor,* repackaging their arguments in gender-appropriate genres would help them to better communicate their protests.

Similarly, the non-Native women writers I examine here attempted to use official forums to challenge Indian policy, for example by testifying in court, writing to government officials, or circulating petitions. When they found themselves ignored and their appeals distorted by predominant cultural mythologies that changed their meanings, they turned to popular literary forms. For the Native women writer-activists I consider, the pressure to assimilate and the end of treaty-making in the second half of the nineteenth century channeled public expression into didactic and mass-media print genres. Paradoxically, these women discovered greater agency when they shifted away from formally political modes of expression and toward creative popular print genres. All four of my subjects turned to popular print as a side entrance to public debate. Convention was the price of admission, but it also widened the entryway into the political realm.

I concentrate on writers whose challenges to federal Indian policy are not always legible on the surface of their texts; I bring them to light precisely because their expressions of political resistance are found where we might least expect them. Indeed, it is the very conventionality of my subjects' writing, and the clash between the forms they engaged and the oppositional politics they performed, that makes their work so fascinating. The genres my subjects adopted—sensationalistic captivity narrative, nostalgic Indian lament poetry, didactic assimilation fiction, and commercial magazine publication—typically helped sustain U.S. Indian policy. In most incarnations, these genres reinforced popular justifications for federal actions aimed at removing, managing, or annihilating Native people. To repurpose these instruments for protest was to claim political *and* cultural agency.

The idea for this book was born many years ago when I read Wakefield's memoir of her experiences in the 1862 war between Dakota insurrectionists and the United States on the plains of Minnesota. I found *Six Weeks in the Sioux Tepees* (1864) in an anthology of captivity narratives, which makes sense: Wakefield's own subtitle categorizes her story as *A Narrative of Indian Captivity*. It quickly became clear to me, however, that the captivity narrative form ill-suited the kind of pointed protest Wakefield was launching against the U.S. government's military and judicial assaults on the Dakota people. Indian captivity narratives most commonly recirculated the stereotypes of Native savagery and white female vulnerability that underwrote federal Indian policies in the nineteenth century. In registering political protest in her nominal captivity narrative, Wakefield necessarily confronted the limits of the genre. More strikingly, her tale of interracial cooperation directly contradicts dominant histories of rape in captivity that were being used to justify the federal campaign of forced displacement, military assault, and execution against the Native inhabitants of Minnesota. I began to contemplate not just the political significance of Wakefield's writing as a white woman "captive" criticizing the government that arranged her "release" but also the literary implications of articulating protest from within such a politically conservative textual form. Clearly the conventions of the captivity narrative must impinge on the possibilities for protest. But might the expression of dissent, in turn, alter the established conventions of the captivity narrative? With what degree of self-consciousness did Wakefield understand and challenge the literary protocols she took up, and to what extent do her efforts amount to a reinvention of the genre?

These questions led to investigations of works by other women writers who voiced their objections to Indian policy through conventional print forms, especially those writers whose political activism has not been recognized. As it turns out, works by Sigourney, Callahan, and Eddleman raise the same questions about the relationship between protest and literary form as Wakefield's narrative. Many of Sigourney's poems on Native subjects resemble popular Indian laments in their focus on scenes of indigenous mourning. Like the captivity narrative, the Indian lament poem typically supports U.S. Indian policy by evoking readers' emotional responses, in this case producing a satisfying nostalgia for vanishing Indians that papers over the violence of settler colonialism. What happens to the poet's protest against the Removal Act of 1830 when she delivers it through an iconic scene more typically deployed to naturalize Native erasure? And what happens to the fetishized, romantic portrait of Native suffering when it is used to articulate opposition to the specific policies that condition it? Similarly, the plot of Callahan's *Wynema* seems to parallel those of the didactic assimilation novels and stories the author likely read as a Native woman educated in mission schools. How does she remake the assimilationist novel, and to what extent do her adaptations create a frame for Native resistance? Eddleman produced *Twin Territories: The Indian Magazine,* the first nationally distributed commercial magazine created by a Native American, in a moment when mass-media print forms reinforced U.S. policies that categorized, contained, and disempowered indigenous people. Can a form that more typically presents the racist displays sustaining U.S. nationalist projects make space for Native political expression? Can a mass-distributed commercial magazine be an "Indian Magazine"?

In addressing these questions, I make several interlocking claims: that nineteenth-century women writer-activists used conservative print forms to register opposition to U.S. Indian policy; that in doing so, they engaged in a kind of immanent critique of the idioms, styles, and structures those forms involve; and that the commitment to protest and the discernment of discursive constraints could result in revisions or even reinventions of popular genres. Dedication to political change led Wakefield, Sigourney, Callahan, and Eddleman to negotiate boundaries between the universal and historically specific, the public and private, the state-national and tribal, the tribal-national and personal. These writer-activists tested the political efficacy of popular print culture and pressed against the constraints of convention. With sometimes surprising critical distance, they mapped the outer limits of the genres available to them. They also adapted those genres, breaking down conventions with fascinating acts of improvisation, hybridization, and reconfiguration. The writers I examine appropriated popular forms, but they incorporated into them rhetorical devices used in more official discourses, such as eyewitness testimony and editorial address. As they drew on literary conventions like sentimentalism, my subjects simultaneously deployed such seemingly anti-sentimental modes as detached irony and journalistic citation. They adapted forms in order to more effectively dismantle the very social systems that depended on those forms. Their works reveal that normative print conventions are at once more plastic and more politically potent than we have imagined.

Cross-Cultural Comparison and the Difference Race Makes

At first glance, my assemblage of writers may strike some as ad hoc, given the vast differences in life experiences, literary practices, and racial and cultural orientations represented. Two of my subjects were professionals: Sigourney and Eddleman successfully navigated publishing markets and forged new ground as career-women in popular print and other media industries. The other two were amateurs: Wakefield and Callahan each produced only one little-known book in her lifetime, and neither fits the profile of the accomplished author (Callahan's book includes a publisher's preface admitting to "the crudeness and incompleteness of the work," while Wakefield insists in her own preface, "I do not pretend to be a book-writer").[6] Sigourney, Callahan, and Eddleman deliberately involved themselves in public debates on Indian policy, though, as far as I have learned, only Sigourney was part of an organized political protest movement. Wakefield, on the other hand, entered the political fray accidentally, as a collateral victim of war who was compelled to speak out on behalf of the Dakota friends who had protected her. A memoirist, a poet, a novelist, and a magazine writer and editor, my subjects worked in different times and places and concerned themselves with different political issues involving Native people.

Most obviously, these writers present distinct racial subject positions that affect both the political conditions under which they wrote and their uses of conventional print media. *Unconventional Politics* is unusual (though not unprecedented) in bringing together Native and non-Native writers in an examination of Native-centered literary-political expression. Doing so has its risks. A comparative analysis across racial lines could flatten out differences in social privilege and minimize the experiential specificity of both literature and protest. It goes without saying that the stakes in protesting were much higher for Native writers Callahan and Eddleman, whose property and identity were constantly under threat because of U.S. Indian policy, than for non-Natives Wakefield and Sigourney. At the same time, focusing on the ways all four of my subjects engaged dominant-cultural literary forms might be seen as elevating European American traditions over Native representational practices and thereby repeating the violence to Native culture committed by colonization in the first place.

The tendency to privilege European American literary forms and critical perspectives in readings of Native-authored texts has led Native scholars Robert Allen Warrior (Osage Nation), Craig Womack (Muscogee [Creek], Cherokee), Jace Weaver (Cherokee), and others to promote nationalist or Nativist literary criticism, an approach that insists on the primacy of indigenous knowledges and perspectives in any interpretation of Native literary culture.[7] As a non-Native scholar positioned in a critical context outside of Native cultural, intellectual, and creative communities, I cannot interpret through an indigenous perspective. My analysis of the dominant cultural forms my subjects take up risks universalizing white modes of expression. Reading Native writing through a non-Native lens can be, as James H. Cox warns, "an academic version of colonialism."[8] But I remain convinced that we can construct meaningful relational analyses of dominant-cultural literary forms that still focus productively on Native issues, that contribute something to the anti-colonial, anti-racist project underway in Native nationalist literary criticism. We can consider works by Native and non-Native writers in dominant cultural forms and at the same time "tak[e] up Indian concerns as a central rather than peripheral endeavor," as Womack insists we must.[9]

In fact, notwithstanding Womack's identification of his critical practice as literary separatism, Native nationalist criticism is not necessarily, or strictly, about treating Native writing separately from other literary traditions. As Lisa Brooks (Abenaki) writes in her afterword to *American Indian Literary Nationalism,* the nationalist critical paradigm "supports (but does not argue exclusively for) scholarship that draws on theoretical and epistemological models that arise from indigenous languages and literatures, as well as the many, varied, complex, and changing modes in which Native nations have operated on the ground, in particular places, over a wide expanse of time."[10] I take Brooks's description of "operat[ing] on the ground" as indicating the many ways Native people appropriate and indigenize the non-Native discursive practices introduced by colonization. Weaver may have something similar in mind when he argues that the influence of Western literary genres on Native writers does not preclude a Native-centered intention or reading. "Influences are *undeniable,*" he writes, "but influences alone do not define either inclusion or exclusion."[11] Both of these critical positions hearken back to the words of Simon J. Ortiz (Acoma Pueblo), who decades ago celebrated "the creative ability of Indian people to gather in many forms of the sociopolitical colonizing force which beset them and to make these forms meaningful in their own terms."[12]

At the same time, a Native-centered reading practice can illuminate non-Native writing. For Weaver, "American Indian Literary Nationalism is a set of critical strategies, growing out of the concerns and issues of Natives themselves, that is equally as applicable to analysis of Cooper, Faulkner, and Wiebe as it is to Momaday, Silko, and Sherman Alexie."[13] When we make Native issues a focus of critical investigation, we shed new light on dominant literary modes. Native-centered interpretations can reveal the ways settler colonization shapes non-Native creative expression and defines

U.S. literary traditions, but these approaches can also show how non-Native writers who advocate for Native people might chip away at the ideological underpinnings of such traditions.

In describing Native nationalist criticism as a "both/and" rather than an "either/or" proposition, Brooks, Ortiz, and Weaver open up the possibility of a critical approach that is simultaneously relational and Native-centered, one that acknowledges the mutual influence of all manner of creative traditions and political subjectivities. Cox employs just such an approach in *Muting White Noise: Native American and European American Novel Traditions*. He commits to the practice of what Jill Carter (Anishinaabe) has called "red reading," criticism that privileges Native creative and intellectual perspectives and foregrounds issues important to Native people and communities.[14] As a non-Native scholar like me, Cox lacks the tribal knowledge and perspective consistent with a strictly separatist approach. Instead, his "red reading" addresses "the specific strategies that Native novelists use to critique and revise European American storytelling traditions about Native America" as well as the ways European American writers support or critique colonialist imperatives. Native-centered criticism, Cox suggests, requires understanding how writing about Native issues intersects with and affects non-Native literary practices. Taking seriously the charge to maintain an indigenist focus, he finds "there is power in adapting Native stories and ceremonies to the new context that is defined in part by contact and conflict between Native and non-Native worlds."[15] I share Cox's conviction that Native-authored literature is distinguished in part by its strategic revision of colonial genres, but I also follow him in examining the kinds of anti-colonial revisions non-Native authors sometimes undertake. Importantly, Cox finds that among the non-Native writers he considers, "the most radical interrogations of European American colonialism originate with women."[16] Picking up this thread, I identify Native and non-Native women's generic interrogations and revisions as central to their Native-centered protest.

Siobhan Senier, whose *Voices of American Indian Assimilation and Resistance: Helen Hunt Jackson, Sarah Winnemucca, and Victoria Howard* has been a steady influence on this book, provides a model of feminist cross-cultural comparison that keeps Native issues center-stage. Senier capitalizes on Weaver's theory of "communitism," a term that combines "community" and "activism" to designate literature that "has a proactive commitment to Native community, including the wider community."[17] Noting that the "wider community" can extend beyond racial or tribal boundaries while still honoring political and social commitments to Native people, Senier argues that her Native and non-Native subjects participate collectively in "a female tradition of resistance" and share representational strategies that "help us see American Indian culture at the turn of the century as dynamic and intercultural, while also revealing indigenous traditions as bulwarks against and conceivable responses to nationalizing Euro-American traditions."[18] At the same time, Senier keeps careful track of the difference that race makes, emphasizing how Winnemucca and Howard developed distinctly indigenous literary forms that tactically deploy dissemblance and reticence as a means of resisting assimilation.

Cox and Senier eschew interpretations that depend on potentially essentialist measures of "authentic" culture, but they also steer clear of blandly "multicultural" perspectives that erase the specificity of cultural experience. They demonstrate the importance of comparative strategies for illuminating both the synergy of texts across racial and cultural lines and the specific ways racial and cultural identity informs literary production and political activism alike. Following their leads, I bring together texts by Native and non-Native women in an effort to understand how their Native-centered political activism informed their writing in popular, conventionally feminine genres. Reading relationally, I find that all four of my subjects chafed against the constraints of conservative forms. Emphasizing this similarity, however, brings into relief the culturally specific differences in protest writing by Native and non-Native authors. As I suggest, the Native writers in this study deliberated more self-consciously on the limitations of form, and they revised literary conventions more dramatically than did their non-Native counterparts. If Wakefield, Sigourney, Callahan, and Eddleman joined in a collective feminist and indigenist project, if they shared strategies of reimagining popular literary forms, they also reflected the specificity of material experience and racial identity in both creativity and activism.

A Permeable Membrane

In reconsidering the intersection of literature and politics, this book returns to what may seem a fairly old-fashioned question in criticism and theory: what is the relationship between form and content? Or, to use terms deployed by Walter Benjamin in his 1934 essay "The Author as Producer," what is the relationship in politically oriented literature between the artistic "quality" of a text and its ideological "tendency"?[19] For the past several decades—the decades in which I have developed as a scholar—criticism on nineteenth-century American women's writing and Native American literature has suggested that form and content are mutually exclusive categories of analysis. The New Criticism of the 1960s insisted on detaching texts from their historical and social contexts and focusing only on matters of literary technique and style. The development of New Historicism, feminist criticism, cultural studies, and other interpretive models in the last decades of the twentieth century reversed this approach to concentrate on the sociohistorical significance of texts, rather than their aesthetic properties. As important as this shift has been in reshaping canons and elucidating the intricate and pervasive mechanisms of power—developments that make possible the recovery of nineteenth-century women's and Native American literature—it has nonetheless held on to the conceptual binary set in place by the formalist methods of New Criticism. By and large, analyzing the ideological dimensions of texts has required bracketing explorations of the complex ways writers engage with and reimagine particular print forms. The impulse to pit political "tendency" against literary "quality" remains strong in Native American literary criticism and critical approaches to American women's writing. The chapters that follow intervene in both critical practices by emphasizing the complex intersections of the political and the aesthetic.

The critical revival of nineteenth-century women's writing has associated print conventions, particularly literary sentimentality, with the ideological investments and social commitments of authors. Important work on the political significance of sentimental fiction—pursued by scholars from Jane Tompkins to Lauren Berlant—provides a crucial foundation for the present study, and the influence of these investigations is evident in my methodologies and interpretive aims. But this scholarship has tended to present print conventions as ideological instruments rather mechanically wielded. The creative autonomy and formal innovation of individual authors has been seen as beside the point. Inaugurating the revaluation of nineteenth-century American women's popular writing in the 1980s, Tompkins concerned herself with "what made [texts] popular, not what made them art," working on the principle that "a novel's impact on the culture at large depends not on its escape from the formulaic and derivative, but on its tapping into a storehouse of commonly held assumptions, reproducing what is already there in typical and familiar form."[20] Other critics have taken up Tompkins's assumptions about the formal consistency of women's sentimental novels, looking for and ascribing ideological meaning to thematic, rhetorical, and metaphorical patterns across a range of texts identified as sentimental. In this view, nineteenth-century women writers tactically recirculated recognizable tropes—the sanctity of the domestic sphere or the plight of the motherless child, for instance—without much effect on the modalities of sentimentality itself. Lacking the wherewithal to "escape" from the strictures of convention, Tompkins implied, nineteenth-century women writers exerted pressure on the social world but did not change the protocols of literary production. They engaged established forms automatically, rather than interrogating them or creating new, adaptive modes of public expression; they did "work" (if "cultural work"), not "art."

Without doing justice here to the rich and valuable debate that has emerged from Tompkins's reassessment, I would argue that it remains mostly faithful to the idea that what matters about a text is its operation *within* culture, not its contributions *as* culture. The focus on social and historical matters distracts us from the possibilities of writers' creative inventiveness and constructs an opposition between ideological and aesthetic dimensions of texts. As Cindy Weinstein has complained of the critical consensus on American sentimental novels, "it is as if questions of ideology and more conventional matters of literary form were mutually exclusive."[21] Elizabeth Maddock Dillon argues similarly that in academic discussions of conventional nineteenth-century poetry, literary conventions are only examined for their political effects: she laments that "placing *sentimentalism* and *aesthetics* together constitutes something of an oxymoron."[22] Critics like Weinstein and Dillon thus call for more sustained attention to language, style, and formal adaptation in conventional writing by nineteenth-century American women. As much as recent criticism has elevated previously forgotten writers through attention to their political motivations, they suggest, it has also sold them short by failing to recognize the ways they critiqued and reimagined forms, or engaged critically and creatively with readers and reading practices.

The turn away from form and style in favor of the political has a different genealogy in the Native American literary criticism of the past several decades. Scholars of Native American literature have concentrated on the ways texts address authority and authenticity in the context of a long history of assaults on Native sovereignty. They have been less concerned with the aesthetic dimensions of Native writing. Eric Cheyfitz marks a pronounced shift in critical approaches to Native writing since the 1980s, "from ethnographic-formal to the political historical."[23] Critics like Elizabeth Cook-Lynn (Crow Creek Sioux) and Womack assess the tribal dimensions and political commitments of works by Native authors, rather than dwelling (much) on the formal qualities of texts.[24] There is good reason for the suspicion of aesthetics in Native literary studies: as Angela Calcaterra points out, European American aesthetic values have long been used to dismiss texts by Native people as somehow less than literary.[25] The same suspicion drove the larger critical effort to dismantle a canon that once excluded all manner of marginalized writers—women and Native Americans but also African Americans, immigrants, the laboring classes, and others—on the basis of what were presented as universal standards of literary quality, standards rooted in patriarchal, racist, nationalist, and elitist social politics. But scholars of Native American literature also disclaim attention to matters of style and form on the assumption that it necessarily obscures the political implications of texts. Assessing criticism of contemporary works by "mixed-blood" writers, Cook-Lynn insists that focusing on formal dimensions leads us away from the more pressing problem of Native political issues, resulting in an "art for art's sake phenomenon." Notwithstanding this warning, Cook-Lynn does address matters of aesthetics in Native literature, if only to denounce the adoption of European American literary forms as politically corrupting. She cites the use of magical realism in contemporary Native writing as an instance in which a non-Native aesthetic practice moves writers away from specific tribal traditions and political concerns for the sake of winning audiences.[26]

As is the case in literary criticism of nineteenth-century American women's writing, in turning away from matters of style and form, Native American studies scholars may undervalue the creative contributions of writers who participate in and influence Native and non-Native cultural traditions as they fight against oppression. Underlying Cook-Lynn's criticism is the belief that literary traditions are hardened monoliths, their surfaces resistant to any attempts by Native writers to inscribe them. But might writers like Leslie Marmon Silko (Laguna Pueblo) and Louise Erdrich (Ojibwe), who come under attack in Cook-Lynn's critique for their adoption of non-Native literary modes, carve out a distinctly indigenous and politically productive magical realism? Louis Owens (Choctaw, Cherokee) suggests as much in arguing that many Native writers working in Western literary traditions "appropriat[e] the master's discourse . . . abrogating its authority, making the invaders' language our language . . . and turning it against the center."[27] More broadly, readings like Cook-Lynn's take for granted that critical analyses of aesthetics and ideology are mutually exclusive, that we cannot attend to the one without diminishing the other. This false dichotomy inhibits a full appreciation of Native writing. Robert Dale Parker identifies a paradox in the critical recovery of Native American literary traditions: "The current tendency among some critics . . . to set aside literary form and aesthetic taste has the accidental effect of allowing conservative readers to think that noncanonical works aren't terribly interesting as art."[28] In Calcaterra's view, "studies of early native literature might be better served with equal attention to the indigenous grounds for aesthetic imagining."[29] For these critics, reading from a decolonizing perspective need not foreclose appreciation of creative intervention.

Perhaps not surprisingly given trends in feminist literary criticism and Native American studies, what analysis there is of the non-Native and Native women writers I examine in this book tends to underplay not just their political activism but also their "aesthetic imagining," their capacity to interrogate and reinvent forms of expression. Critics characterize Sigourney and Callahan as carefully following the requirements of established literary protocols, whether strategically or as the result of a deficit of political will. Sigourney has been associated, even by her modern-day champions, with determinedly "generic sentimentality" that serves a "republican project," while Callahan's fiction has been deemed so "rigidly formulaic" as to be "bad writing," reflective of her lack of artistry as much as her accommodationist politics.[30] These evaluations treat sentimentality and romance convention as fixed textual components, which Callahan and Sigourney simply took up and recirculated. I find instead that these writers were both cognizant of and willfully insubordinate to the rules of play that shape conventional literature. The inclusion of Wakefield's text in a number of anthologies of captivity narratives makes it seem representative, but even a cursory look at its relation to accounts by other captives in the Dakota Conflict reveals the distinctiveness of its irony, ambiguity, and self-perception. The presumption that commercial print products must be so intractably bound to market demands for formal consistency as to be hostile to true Native expression explains why scholars have failed to notice Eddleman's writing and editing. Yet as I argue, the seriality, multimediality, and heterogeneity of the magazine form can help amplify debates within Native communities that, in turn, confirm their existence as publics. A primary motive for my bringing together four women writing in very different print forms is to liberate their work from critical assumptions that obscure their aesthetic, as well as political, achievements.

This is not to say that we should move too far in the other direction. Debates over the place of aesthetics in Native American literature came to a boiling point after publication of *American Indian*

Fiction: A User's Manual. In that work, David Treuer (Leech Lake Ojibwe) responds to the emphasis on politics and culture in Native American literary criticism by advocating a return to pure formalism, replacing standards of "identity and authenticity" (politics) with emphasis on literary "style" (aesthetics). Treuer contends that it is only when we read Native-authored novels through the narrow lens of language and style, rather than by considering their situation within specific cultures and political contexts, that we understand their value. Contemporary novels by Native writers are poor sources for insight on "authentic" tribal culture in any event, he contends, offering as evidence inconsistencies and inaccuracies in the use of tribal languages in novels by Louise Erdrich and James Welch (Blackfeet, Gros Ventre). For Treuer, the fact that Erdrich "activates her novel using 'Western' literary techniques" indicates that *Love Medicine* is not culturally Ojibwe; rather, the novel is "a portrait of culture" or even just a mark of "the desire for culture." Noting that the novel itself is a Western literary tradition, he comes to the startling conclusion that "Native American fiction does not exist."[31]

This retrograde New Critical perspective has drawn harsh reproach from Native and non-Native critics and writers, many of whom see dismissal of the cultural and political significance of texts as dangerous ("cultural suicide" is what Ojibwe scholar Matthew L. M. Fletcher calls it).[32] It is not necessary to reiterate these criticisms here. Rather, I will simply point out that Treuer essentially reproduces the binary opposition between politics and aesthetics established by Cook-Lynn in relation to Native American texts and by Tompkins in readings of nineteenth-century American women's writing. With Treuer we have another zero-sum game. If we read with any attention to political and cultural contexts, he insists, we cannot possibly appreciate the aesthetic contributions of texts; understanding a text's literary inventions and interventions requires turning a blind eye to political meanings and intentions.

Proponents of aestheticist and political interpretations of literature attempt to separate creativity from protest, but these impulses are never so easily disentangled, nor should they be. As Adrienne Rich reminds us, "There's a permeable membrane between art and society." Rich describes the relationship between creativity and political action as "a continuous dialectical motion. Tides brining the estuary. River flowing into sea."[33] In the fluidity of human expression, creative impulses infuse revolution, and the political transforms art. By missing the ways the aesthetic and the political act on one another, we fail to appreciate fully the contributions made by writer-activists. With this book, then, I join a critical effort to "recalibrate the relation between the literary and the social" that has begun to emerge in both feminist literary criticism and Native American studies, among other areas.[34]

In bringing attention to the formal complexity and innovation of conventional texts that register protest, I argue for a rethinking of the ways aesthetics and politics intersect with and influence one another. I situate conventional writing by women activists in the context of debates over Indian policy and in relation to examples of the official and popular discursive forms available to women and Native Americans. Doing so reveals unexpected moments of proto-feminist and anti-racist protest, as well as fascinating instances of textual critique and innovation. Like Parker, I "read for politics and aesthetics," with the understanding that these two dimensions of texts are always mutually determining.[35]

Recasting Literary Protest

Recognizing the permeability of the membrane between art and society allows us to appreciate the diverse ways American women writers both challenge political authority and reimagine their own opportunities for expression. To further clarify this relationship as it emerges in conventional literature of the nineteenth century, I want to turn briefly to two influential essays of the modern era. Neither Benjamin's "The Author as Producer" nor James Baldwin's "Everybody's Protest Novel" addresses women's or Native American writing or activism. I step further afield here, however, because both essays focus on the kinds of complex interactions between political intention and literary form that I explore in the chapters to come.

In "The Author as Producer" Benjamin sees the relationship

between aesthetic quality and ideological tendency in political literature as impressively and inescapably dialectical. "The tendency of a work can only be politically correct if it is also literarily correct," he insists, and "the politically correct tendency includes a literary tendency." Benjamin argues that a literary work embodying the "correct" politics, which is to say one that springs from and encourages a revolutionary impulse, necessarily involves transformations in the techniques and modes of literature itself. A work's foundation in political dissent engenders the kinds of aesthetic innovations that elevate it beyond bourgeois entertainment and into the realm of art. Ideally, the energies of political and aesthetic production swirl together. True activist writing entails "a mighty re-casting of literary forms," what Bertholt Brecht named *Umfunktionierung* (functional transformation)—in effect, a transformation of author into producer, which amounts to a kind of liberation of the means of (literary) production. At the same time, only texts that advance and innovate literary techniques (Brecht's experimental theater is a prime example) can successfully forward revolution, because "only by transcending the specialization in the process of production which, in the bourgeois view, constitutes its order, is this production made politically valuable."[36] In other words, to be "correct" a text must be both politically and artistically transformative. Its cultural work enables its aesthetic creation, and vice versa.

Written fifteen years after "The Author as Producer," "Everybody's Protest Novel" implicitly corroborates the theory of a dialectical relationship between aesthetic and political intervention. In the essay, Baldwin's complaint about Harriet Beecher Stowe's *Uncle Tom's Cabin* develops into a reproof of a wave of social protest literature and film that emerged in the middle of the twentieth century. For Baldwin, Stowe's novel and works such as *Gentleman's Agreement, The Postman Always Rings Twice, The Best Years of Our Lives,* and Richard Wright's explosive *Native Son* adhere to the formal requirements of simplistic, comforting dichotomies that ultimately undermine the processes of political reform. These works traffic in stereotypes, present spectacles of violence and human suffering, and promote emotional responses that sustain rather than disrupt social hierarchies. Just as Stowe clings to a "medieval morality . . . black, white, the devil, the next world," the social protest novels written by Baldwin's contemporaries repeat "the formula created by the necessity to find a lie more palatable than the truth" of human complexity. These works are "fantasies, connecting nowhere with reality, sentimental." They fail as protest because they do not deviate from the reductive literary protocol of "virtuous rage" and "theological terror" established by Stowe a century earlier.[37]

Baldwin labels twentieth-century social protest novels as "sentimental," but his quarrel is not with sentimentality itself. He is let down, rather, by Stowe's and others' failure to move beyond the simplistic epistemological and moral structures of literary convention. In that sense, the deficiencies he identifies are as much aesthetic as political. Baldwin finds that the spectacular violence in works of twentieth-century social protest fiction is matched by "the violence [their authors] do to language." Stowe's novel, too, is "badly written," in no small part because it privileges "the good of society" above "niceties of style or characterization" (but then "what exactly is the 'good' of society?" Baldwin asks). These criticisms draw a bold line between effective protest art and mere propaganda: Stowe, he contends, "was not so much a novelist as an impassioned pamphleteer."[38]

The problem is that Stowe and her heirs do not make the creative inroads in sentimental convention that would enable that form of writing to do the work of protest. Even in the modern era, social protest novels oversimplify the human condition rather than encourage the critical examination necessary to remake the world. They do not break free of inherited structures and modalities; they do not recast the form of the sentimental novel. The aesthetic impoverishment in such works leaves them politically bankrupt as well: "The failure of the protest novel lies in its rejection of life, the human being, the denial of his beauty, dread, power, in its insistence that it is his categorization alone which is real and cannot be transcended"—that is to say, in its miscarriage of creative production.[39] Baldwin thus joins Benjamin in asserting a "functional interdependency" between literary technique and political tendency, with the insufficiency of one leading to the corruption of the other.[40]

This recognition leaves open the possibility that a work of literature that *does* transcend the categorizations and reductions of literary convention might effectively voice dissent. The characterization of sentimentality as fantasy, as a dishonest "parading of excessive and spurious emotion," leads most readers to see "Everybody's Protest Novel" as a straightforward attack on a literary convention that has become "hard-boiled" in American culture.[41] But as Lauren Berlant demonstrates, Baldwin elsewhere voiced ambivalence about sentimentality and hinted at a buried faith in its capacity to redirect social energy. His own obsessive reading of *Uncle Tom's Cabin* in childhood introduced him to, in Berlant's words, "the sovereign creativity of the artist, the potential relationship of art to revolution, the pleasures of feeling transformed by absorption in an alternative aesthetic space as a way of pre-experiencing a material world that had not yet come into being," among other things. In critiquing Stowe, Berlant writes, Baldwin "abjures the form of the protest novel, but maintains the promise of its refusal to be bound by the normatively real."[42]

Given the strikingly similar demands they make of protest literature, it is surprising that "The Author as Producer" and "Everybody's Protest Novel" have not been discussed in conjunction with one another. Both Benjamin's and Baldwin's essays bear a sense of urgency that reflects the political crises swirling at the moments of their production. Benjamin wrote "The Author as Producer" as a lecture to be delivered at the Paris Institute for the Study of Fascism in 1934, a year after he escaped Nazi Germany. Baldwin fled the racism and homophobia of the United States in 1948; like Benjamin, he composed his essay in exile in Paris a year later. The essays share an objection to the self-serving exploitation of human suffering in cultural products ostensibly aimed at reform. Benjamin condemns the "New Matter-of-factness," the modern trend toward objectivity in photography and literature, for making "the *struggle against poverty* an object of consumption."[43] In Baldwin's view, the "catalogue of violence" in *Uncle Tom's Cabin* only serves to assure readers of their own salvation, and Wright's *Native Son* redoubles the effect. Above all, these essays theorize a process of making print serve social resistance through a revision of literary protocols. Baldwin seems more pessimistic than Benjamin about the revolutionary possibilities of popular literature, but he implicitly holds out hope that a more honest and effective protest might emerge in conventional writing if authors can rise above simplistic reductions of the human condition to "discover and reveal something a little closer to the truth."[44] His essay presses for the self-conscious engagement with forms that Benjamin explicitly prescribes when calling for the author "*to think,* to reflect on his [*sic*] position in the process of production."[45]

Together these essays suggest a way of reconceiving the aesthetic and political missions of proto-feminist, anti-racist conventional texts in the context of nineteenth-century debates over Indian policy. Berlant's reading of "Everybody's Protest Novel" serves her feminist interpretation of one print convention, literary sentimentality, as a reflection of the unfulfilled promise of liberal democracy. For Berlant, Baldwin's essay allows for the possibility of "sentimental radicalism," a performance of resistance that is also a process of formal innovation aimed at politicizing the conventional.[46] But the idea that established forms can be reshaped into vehicles of agency and resistance has equal bearing on other modes of print expression, as I demonstrate in this book. What Barbara Harlow names "resistance literature" not only participates in battles for human rights; it also positions itself as "immediately and directly involved in a struggle against ascendant or dominant forms of ideological and cultural production."[47] It is this doubled struggle, against established political power and the authority of print culture, that animates the works at the heart of *Unconventional Politics.*

Born of crisis, Benjamin's and Baldwin's essays themselves suggest that moments of extreme social and political injustice generate critiques of the discursive protocols that contribute to oppression. In addressing an urgent political issue of their time, the implementation of policies that subjugated the indigenous peoples of the United States, Wakefield, Sigourney, Callahan, and Eddleman performed just such critiques. Their often self-conscious wrestling with the requirements of genre allowed for a reimagining of print culture. I would not go so far as to say that these writers deliberately theorized the interrelation of aesthetics and ideology, as Benjamin and Baldwin would in the next century. Their texts, however, betray a similar preoccupation with the limitations and possibilities of mainstream print for making political change, as well as a faith, albeit fragile and wavering at times, in the revolutionary potential of even the most conventional forms of textual expression. I hope this book goes beyond recovering the political protests in conventional texts by women to contribute to a larger reconsideration of the complex relationships between protest and popular literature.

To understand the distinctive political and aesthetic interventions my subjects make, I contextualize their writing within the public discourses that influenced them and against which they often struggled. For each of my case studies, my first task is to define the mainstream print modes women writers took up to protest U.S. Indian policy. Considering the formal and ideological requirements of literary conventions like Indian lament poetry or assimilationist fiction requires my taking some critical detours, but it allows me to chart the ways my subjects conformed to or departed from protocol. I also build a context in less literary forms of public expression. Popular histories, mainstream media reports, petitions, editorials, souvenir photographs, and other conventional forms represented nineteenth-century Native Americans in ways that supported established power structures. Reading these types of texts reveals how my subjects interrogated and redeployed nonliterary discursive strategies in conventional literary genres. Engagements with these modes of expression constitute another way that my subjects applied pressure to print conventions and developed new ways to protest.

My first chapter examines Sarah Wakefield's repeated attempts to tell her personal story of interracial cooperation in the context of a predominating narrative of the mass rape of white women by Dakota men. That narrative, circulated in mainstream histories, newspapers, and political commentary, impinged on Wakefield's efforts to intervene in the Dakota Conflict and the patently unjust trials and executions that followed it. The struggle to voice dissent resulted in Wakefield's self-consciousness about the limitations of conventional modes of expression and perception. In *Six Weeks in the Sioux Tepees,* she registers the ways the platforms available for conveying her story—trial testimonies, letters, popular histories, and the captivity narrative itself—failed to accommodate her protest. Feminist theories of rape rhetoric clarify how a dominant cultural narrative allows officials and cultural gatekeepers to usurp the authority of eyewitnesses like Wakefield. I demonstrate how Wakefield works to reclaim narrative authority in the second edition of her narrative by calling attention to the ways female political agency is encumbered by the influence of dominant discursive and interpretive practices. Wakefield's determination to tell an unauthorized story is compelling, but her entanglement in a dialectic between individual and collective testimony ultimately silences her. Still, her narrative stages a parallel protest of the limits of discourse that suggests how women begin to constitute their own political agency through critiques of established modes of expression.

Sigourney entered debates over U.S. Indian policy more intentionally than did Wakefield, as a supporter of the Cherokee people and the cofounder of an unprecedented campaign by eastern white women to protest the Removal Act of 1830. Her poems on Native subjects reflect an activist impulse that has been overlooked by most critics, but they also register the ways conventions of both political and literary discourse can inhibit the possibilities of political reform. With my second chapter I move back in time to the era of removal but forward in terms of women writer-activists' capacity to remake literary conventions to articulate dissent. I examine Sigourney's lyric depiction of scenes of Native grief and loss in the context of popular-literary and popular-political sentimental discourse on Native exile and extinction. Perhaps because of her status as a professional writer, Sigourney critiqued and adapted the literary genre she used more deliberately than Wakefield did. In her poetry she reveals an awareness of the operations of convention as she works to reinvent the Indian lament poem. Descriptions of Indian grief in poems such as "The Cherokee Mother" (1831), "Remonstrance of the Creek Indians, against Being Removed from Their Own Territory" (1827), and "Pocahontas" (1841) expose the national crimes covered over in other Indian laments. At the same time, such poems register Sigourney's frustration with a reformist political discourse so mired in conventions of sentiment as to be counterproductive. The emphasis in women's anti-removal rhetoric on white female sympathy and indigenous melancholy crystallizes the very exclusions and oppressions—of both white women and Native Americans—that the campaign ostensibly contests. Drawing on Berlant's concept of the "countersentimental," I show how Sigourney recasts the Indian lament to condemn the specious sympathy of popular poetry and to problematize the use of sentimental conventions in women's anti-removal rhetoric.

Like Sigourney, Callahan confronted the limitations of sentimentality. My third chapter explores how the novelist redirected assimilationist protocols for reading and writing to protest U.S. nationalist and white supremacist projects. The didactic assimilationist novel, of which Marianna Burgess's *Stiya: A Carlisle Indian Girl at Home* (1891) is a prime example, was used to reinforce the values of assimilation in Indian boarding school students returning to reservation homes. A reading of *Stiya* demonstrates how sentimental literacy, a reading practice privileging white, middle-class values, functioned as a foundation for the national project to erase Native identity. The sentimental reading promoted in assimilationist reeducation is absorptive and self-negating; the assimilating student is trained to get lost in non-Native-authored texts and to lose her (Native) self in the process. Callahan's variation on the assimilation novel—written, evidence suggests, in direct response to Burgess's—explores an alternative sentimental reading practice. The engagement with mainstream texts in *Wynema* is self-authorized and informed. It makes room for critical reflection on policies like allotment, the subject of debate in Indian territories while Callahan was writing, and government actions such as the massacre at Wounded Knee, which took place just before her novel was published. And it affords a layering of emotional and critical engagement with the written word. Scenes of reading in the novel reveal the dangers of absorptive sentimental reading and encourage what I call "sentimental critique," reading that allows for an affective response that does not prohibit critical resistance. In this sense *Wynema* presents a metatextual analysis of the political implications of reading and writing. Recent work in critical affect theory suggests possibilities for rethinking the ways texts like *Stiya* and *Wynema* produce feeling and knowledge. Such theoretical interventions can help us reassess the sentimental-political writing of a Native author too often judged to be politically compromised by her adoption of non-Native literary protocols.

Late nineteenth- and early twentieth-century mass culture was a powerful instrument of U.S. national efforts to subjugate Native Americans, but indigenous editors and writers found ways to adapt and redirect mass cultural forms to construct a Native public sphere. In my fourth chapter I explore the possibilities for Native publicity in Eddleman's writing and editing. Aimed at both attracting a broad commercial audience and creating an arena for Native expression, *Twin Territories* emerges as a site of complex political and discursive negotiation. The magazine is accommodationist in its editorial support of allotment and assimilation. Yet the seriality and heterogeneity of the magazine form suit it to the public deliberations and contestations that helped to construct a Native counterpublic. I am particularly interested in the ways Eddleman's magazine mounts a challenge to dominant cultural and federal efforts to define Native and tribal identity. These efforts are evident in the mainstream press representations of Native people that Eddleman explicitly critiques in her magazine, as well as in the federal takeover of tribal enrollment that denied Eddleman and her family their Cherokee citizenship. In a feature that presents photographs of Native girls and women, the editor adapts the conventions of middle-class portraiture and souvenir Indian pictures to challenge reductive constructs of assimilated and traditionalist Native peoples. She remakes the correspondence column to discipline non-Native inquisitors and establish Native epistemological authority. Finally, in her own fictional contributions to the magazine, she reimagines racial indeterminacy and racial passing in order to assert a Native right of self-definition and economic independence. As it illuminates the ways Eddleman appraises and reinvents the commercial magazine, my analysis of *Twin Territories* ultimately argues for a fuller appreciation of the capacities of a mass cultural print form to perform indigenous resistance.

Unconventional Politics describes women writers' different struggles to articulate a politics of dissent through conventional literary forms in order to illuminate transformations and distinctions in women's and Native Americans' political expression over the course of the nineteenth century. I explore the implications of this argument in an epilogue that looks forward to the political and literary dynamics of the twenty-first century. Limiting my case studies to four, I make no claims of presenting a comprehensive picture of American women's protest against Indian policy here. Yet my assemblage of writer-activists suggests the development (if not along a strictly chronological trajectory) of American women's use of conventional print forms to register protest. At the same time, bringing together non-Native and Native writers allows me to uncover the surprising ways racial subject positions inform and informed political engagements with print conventions. For Wakefield, gendered and racialized conventions produced an epistemological and representational crisis, and she became constrained by mainstream modes of interpreting and describing racial conflicts. More self-consciously involved in both literary production and protest, Sigourney used her poetry to mark the limits of print and political conventions. But like Wakefield, she could not move beyond those limits, and she largely abandoned her activism and her poetry on Native issues. Callahan and Eddleman, on the other hand, more successfully reimagined the textual conventions they adopted, in transformations that amounted to an indigenization of mainstream print culture. In short, in tracing changes in women's control of print culture, I uncover the distinct possibilities for reshaping that culture—and reimagining protest—through Native perspectives. I use my collection of case studies to begin to theorize the advancement of Native women's creative political expression, and I test my theory by offering a contemporary instance of adaptation of a highly conventional, commercial print form in the comic book production of Kickapoo writer and artist Arigon Starr.

Lastly, a word on hope. I have suggested that Benjamin and Baldwin maintained at least an implicit confidence in the radical possibilities of creative literature, in its potential to illuminate injustice and reform society as well as in its capacity to reinvent forms and create new ways of seeing and knowing. This is a confidence, I am convinced, shared by all of us who do the hard work of literary history and criticism, notwithstanding the postmodern imperative for what Rita Felski labels a critical practice of "disenchantment."[48] My greatest ambition for this book is that it might help reanimate a progressive humanist sense of the promise of print culture to accommodate radically reparative impulses—that it might remind us of the ways literary and other print forms never truly lose their capacity to change and their power to make change. Despite their differences, the writer-activists gathered here joined in a representational project of using established modes of expression to construct female political agency and counter the injustices of racist national policies. It is only when we consider these writers in the context of both conventional print traditions and the unconventional politics they performed that we might fully appreciate the magnitude of their ideological and aesthetic interventions.

CHAPTER ONE

Nameless Outrages

The Dakota Conflict, Rape Rhetoric, and Sarah Wakefield's "Captivity" Narrative

In 1864, having lived through a spate of interracial violence on the plains of Minnesota, Sarah Wakefield found herself embroiled in a different kind of battle. The armed struggle between Dakota insurrectionists and the U.S. military that began on August 17, 1862, now known as the Dakota War or Dakota Conflict, had raged for six weeks, claiming the lives of military personnel and civilians; men, women, and children; Natives, non-Natives, and those of mixed race.[1] The white wife of a physician, Wakefield had been caught up in the violence as she traveled from her home at the Indian Agency at Yellow Medicine (also called Upper Agency) to Fort Ridgely, thought to be a safe haven. She and her two young children were sheltered in the family of a Mdewakanton Dakota man named We-Chank-Wash-to-don-pee, known to Wakefield as Chaska.[2] Escorted to Camp Release, the compound where hundreds of victims of the conflict were turned over to U.S. military authorities and where over one thousand Dakota people surrendered, Wakefield reported the kindness shown her by her Dakota friends. But she soon became involved in a fight for authority over her own story.

In the preface to the second edition of her memoir, *Six Weeks in the Sioux Tepees: A Narrative of Indian Captivity* (1864), Wakefield describes her efforts to articulate her experience even as she acknowledges how her story competes with a different narrative already in wide circulation:

> I wish to say a few words in preface to my Narrative; First, that when I wrote it, it was not intended for perusal by the public eye. I wrote it for the especial benefit of my children, as they were so young at the time they were in captivity, that, in case of my death, they would, by recourse to this, be enabled to recall to memory the particulars; and I trust all who may read it will bear in mind that I do not pretend to be a book-writer, and hence they will not expect to find much to please the mind's fancy. Second, I have written a *true* statement of my captivity: what I suffered, and what I was spared from suffering, by a Friendly or Christian Indian, (whether such from policy or other motives, time will determine.) Thirdly, I do not publish a little work like this in the expectation of making money by it, but to vindicate myself, as I have been grievously abused by many, who are ignorant of the particulars of my captivity and release by the Indians.
>
> I trust all errors will be overlooked, and that the world will not censure me for speaking kindly of those who saved me from death and dishonor, while my own people were so long—Oh, so long!—in coming to my rescue.[3]

Wakefield's preface pits her "*true* statement" against sensationalistic versions of her story that stray so far from the facts as to constitute character assassination. A casualty of war, she is now "grievously abused" by her own people. The repetition of the personal pronoun in her preface—"what *I* suffered, and what *I* was spared from suffering"—emphasizes the specificity of her firsthand narrative and sets it against stories produced by a nebulous and unknowing "many." Yet the presence of these other stories transforms her narrative. Originally intended as a private family document, the text becomes something more complicated: a self-authorized and self-vindicating corrective to the historical record, a defense of the Dakota people who protected her, a public critique of a government "so long" in coming to her aid, and a protest against the usurpation and manipulation of her own history. As I argue, the narrative is also an often painful confrontation with the constraints of literary genre and other forms of public discourse. Wakefield chafed against the limits of acceptable modes of expression for nineteenth-century white women. Notwithstanding its title, her narrative is in many ways a story about captivity not in Sioux tepees but in literary and cultural convention.

Wakefield's preface reflects the inevitable clash of personal experience and collective knowledge that occurs when national histories are under construction. Both during and in the aftermath of the conflict, a dominant narrative of white victimization at the hands of blood-thirsty Dakota insurrectionists was being inscribed in U.S. collective memory. It appeared in newspaper columns and letters to and from government officials, in dime novels and courtroom records, in popular histories and personal accounts. At the height of the uprising, white Minnesotans wrote government reports and editorials describing Native attacks on their communities. The hastily conducted war trials that followed the uprising produced testimonies from non-Natives who had suffered injuries, property loss, and the deaths of loved ones during the conflict, while the testimonies of Native defendants, when allowed, were essentially ignored in patently unjust proceedings. Within two years, three book-length histories and two dime novels had been published about the "Indian massacre," as the conflict is designated in many titles.[4] The rush to publish books on the event attests to the popular appetite for lurid descriptions of Indian violence, for "interesting incidents . . . of this cruel and barbarous conspiracy against human life" and tales "from which the heart recoils and the pen shrinks," as two of the most prominent histories advertised.[5] But it also indicates a collective desire to control the meaning of a controversial national action.

A secondary war, a "war in words," as Kathryn Zabelle Derounian-Stodola terms it, erupted in print as different constituencies tried to define the terms of the Dakota Conflict.[6] Reformers in the East blamed the U.S. government for the conditions leading to Native hostility, and they raised alarm at the heavy-handedness of the military response. An anonymous review of Isaac V. D. Heard's *History of the Sioux War and Massacres of 1862 and 1863* insists, "The more appropriate title for this book would have been simply, 'The Sioux Massacres,'—massacres perpetrated on the Sioux as well as by them."[7]

Westerners, meanwhile, feared the distraction of the Civil War was diverting attention from the crisis on the plains (in fact, a regiment of fifty men from the Upper and Lower Agencies had been called to the war in the South just before the eruption of violence). White Minnesotans often characterized their reports of the uprising as testimony that the court of public opinion refused to hear. "People cannot and will not believe it possible that any set of savages committed the outrages we say they did on the people of a civilized state," complained a white western lecturer.[8] An editorial in the *Saint Paul Pioneer* declared its writer "surprised, pained, even alarmed" at easterners' failure to comprehend the magnitude of violence on the borders.[9] Whereas eastern reformers aimed at mitigating further interracial violence, most white westerners offered accounts that rationalized U.S. aggression. Reports of Native barbarity supported a program of removal and extermination of indigenous peoples in areas of settlement. They produced a national history that would in turn justify and reinforce U.S. Indian policy.

Using firsthand accounts of her experiences, Wakefield worked relentlessly to counter the prevailing history coming from white westerners and to protest U.S. actions. She faced challenges at every turn. After delivering her story of finding protection among the Dakotas to military officials at Camp Release, she repeated it at Chaska's war trial. When her testimonies failed to save her benefactor from execution, she produced *Six Weeks in the Sioux Tepees,* revising and republishing the book a year later. Her persistence is an indication of the difficulty she had making her "*true* statement" of protest heard over the din of the dominant narrative. This chapter addresses that difficulty and the epistemological crisis it produced. Wakefield's trouble amplifying her story is partly due to the lopsidedness of the battle for narrative control: as she suggests in her preface, she writes in opposition to the *many* who spoke for (and over) her. But as I argue here, the difficulty also results from the limitations of the discursive forms and systems of knowing available to a nineteenth-century white woman to describe a personal experience of interracial cooperation in a time of war.

In testifying and writing her unauthorized story, Wakefield found herself ensnared in linguistic and interpretive modes that could not fully accommodate her experience. She wished to tell an unauthorized story of female autonomy and interracial cooperation, but the platforms available to her—the courtroom witness stand, dialogues with U.S. officials, and the captivity narrative genre—all worked within a dominant narrative frame that made her particular story illegible. The discursive forms Wakefield found herself channeled into invariably constrained her. More devastatingly, Wakefield's position in a racist and sexist cultural framework hampered her ability to decipher her own experience and use it to voice dissent.

To understand this captivity in form and interpretative framework, I read Wakefield's narrative within several overlapping discursive paradigms: the emphasis on white women's sexual vulnerability in captivity narratives, the official story of mass rape during the Dakota Conflict, and broader cultural narratives of interracial rape circulating in the South. Each of these paradigms racializes and genders experiences in racial conflicts in ways that encroach on Wakefield's efforts to register protest. These are important contexts for understanding *Six Weeks in the Sioux Tepees,* not just because they reveal its competition with dominant narratives but also because the specific structural and epistemological effects of rape rhetoric impinged on Wakefield's capacities for expression. Nineteenth-century accounts of rape transfer easily from the control of the female victim to the authority of men. Rape is at once unspeakable—a "nameless outrage," in the parlance of the day—and an important rhetorical tool for controlling white women and men and women of color. The authority of the eyewitness erodes in the face of a commanding, politically motivated discursive system that reinforces racial and gender hierarchies by universalizing interracial rape and silencing women.

The meaning Wakefield wished to convey exists in dramatic tension with the literary convention she engaged and the historical, judicial, and political discourses she entered. Her incipient awareness of that tension presents an opportunity to theorize more deeply American women writers' political and aesthetic interventions in conventional genres. In the swirl of accounts that followed the Dakota Conflict, Wakefield was overwhelmed by a pressing dominant narrative and by her position within a patriarchal, white supremacist interpretive system. These forces worked together to produce a culturally specific version of truth that was, in the end, quite different from the truth of her experience. Reading Wakefield's narrative in the context of the generic and cultural modes she was obliged to engage calls attention to a crisis of representation in nineteenth-century women's expressions of protest.

Wakefield faced an epistemological crisis as well. If she wrote and spoke from within discursive contexts that silenced her, she also interpreted the experiences that she wrote about from within cultural frameworks that blinded her. As evidenced in changes made to the second edition of the narrative, she was increasingly troubled by the difficulties of interpreting her experience, and her dilemma results in "oscillation between conformity and incomprehensibility" in the revised text (to borrow from Priscilla Wald).[10] Wakefield wavered between refutation of other narratives circulating in the culture and the recognition that she remained trapped within a dominant cultural interpretive field that made it impossible for her to understand her own experiences. While Wald finds the movement between conformity and incomprehensibility productive for writers from Frederick Douglass to Gertrude Stein, it was not so for Wakefield. Instead, it paralyzed. In calling into question conventions that define race relations, she had also to interrogate her own interpretive stance and recognize the extent to which her testimony was shaped by white cultural imperatives.

The disruptions and questions in Wakefield's narrative reflect entrenched discursive systems that ultimately limited her ability to protest—or even, in the end, to know her own unconventional truth. She found herself caught in the impasse of the witness whose testimony is nameless, the activist who cannot fully articulate her dissent, and, worst of all, the subject who cannot fully process her experience. At key moments, as she tried to describe her experiences, she evinced a consciousness of this epistemological and representational crisis. As a result, her attempts to tell an alternative story of the Dakota Conflict and to protest her government's actions were also confrontations with conventional ways of knowing and expressing. Read with attention to Wakefield's sometimes self-conscious encounters with the boundaries of representation in political and popular convention, *Six Weeks in the Sioux Tepees* can be seen as not just a halting and broken protest but also an inchoate, proto-feminist, anti-racist literary critique.

Taking a/the Stand

The struggle for narrative authority over the history of the Dakota Conflict sheds light on the status of the eyewitness in the production of national history. Dominant cultural accounts of the conflict erode boundaries between public and private testimony: the individual's experience gets taken up and manipulated by the many as part of a collective interpretation in service to national interests. Wakefield also blurred lines between individual and collective experience and between personal history and protest tract. In her preface, she declares a primary motive for writing is her desire to vindicate herself against rumors that she had taken a Dakota lover; at the same time, she seeks posthumous justice for Chaska, who was wrongly executed. She wants to intervene, additionally, in larger public debates over the treatment of Indians, to "speak kindly" for a group of people defined as enemies of the United States and to register criticism of her own people for their destructive policies. Her narrative publicly condemns a U.S. government that had broken its promises and abandoned both Native and non-Native inhabitants of western territories at the start of the Civil War. Yet as Wakefield took a stand against U.S. Indian policy, she contended with those who wanted to take the witness stand away from her.

I return later to Wakefield's self-interested desire to clear her reputation, but for the moment I want to emphasize how her personal narrative serves as an expression of political protest. Wakefield was well aware that an expansionist national agenda created the conditions that led to the initial outbreak. When Congress declared Minnesota a U.S. territory in 1848 and a state ten years later, a rapid influx of white settlers and a series of questionable treaties diminished Dakota landholdings and made tribal subsistence unsustainable. By the summer of 1862, the Dakota had been waiting for several months for overdue annuities, monies granted the Dakota by treaty but held in bureaucratic limbo by the uncertainties of the

Civil War. Without the payment, U.S. officials would not release the stores of food held in agency warehouses, and as several thousand Dakota waited, starvation was widespread. The catastrophe was intensified because harvest among "farmer Indians," those largely assimilated Dakota who had adopted European American agricultural practices, had been poor, and "blanket Indians," those who upheld traditional Dakota practices, had delayed their annual buffalo hunt to wait for payments. As the Dakota starved, unscrupulous traders increased tensions by charging hugely inflated prices, and agents refused to distribute the provisions that filled agency warehouses on credit. In the racial conflicts of the frontier, Wakefield insists, "our own people, not the Indians, were to blame. Had [the Dakota] not, for years, been suffering? Had they not been cheated unmercifully, and now their money had been delayed; no troops were left to protect the frontier, and their Agent, their 'Father,' had left them without money, or food or clothing, and gone off to the war" (100).

When violence broke out, the government's response was sluggish and plagued by missteps, and Wakefield censures military leadership throughout her narrative. Concluding that the Dakotas most responsible for the uprising were likely long gone by the time U.S. soldiers arrived, she remarks with caustic irony, "I suppose the troops were fatigued, if they marched all the way from St. Paul as fast as they did from Yellow Medicine—taking over fifty hours to travel twenty-five miles" (115). The grossly biased military trials after the uprising capped the government's offences. Wakefield expresses outrage at a military commission she recognizes as "not acting according to justice, but by favor" (116).

Wakefield's criticisms of the U.S. government were pointed, but they were either ignored or drowned out by the official narrative of the conflict. Nowhere is this more evident than in the aftermath of her court testimony in Chaska's defense. Wakefield was one of only four white women who remained in the area to testify during the war trial of hundreds of Dakota men (three others testified against the two defendants accused of rape).[11] She defended Chaska against charges that he had murdered George Gleason, the white storekeeper who drove the wagon carrying Wakefield and her children.

As the wagon approached Fort Ridgely, Chaska and another Dakota man, Hapa (who is sometimes identified as Chaska's brother-in-law), stopped it, and Gleason was shot.[12] Wakefield testified that Chaska only "snapped his gun" after Hapa had already shot Gleason, either misfiring, firing over the white man, or firing "to put him out of his misery." She insisted that Chaska "expressed great feeling for whites," and that he had saved the lives of her and her children more than once.[13] Although another witness corroborated her statement, asserting Chaska was "a very good Indian," and though no other evidence was introduced, Chaska was convicted of murder and hanged, along with thirty-seven other Dakota men, on December 26, 1862, in Mankato, Minnesota.[14]

While Wakefield elaborated on her testimony in *Six Weeks in the Sioux Tepees* after the execution, she could not dislodge the dominant characterization of Chaska as a bloodthirsty savage. Six years later, a scrolling, backlit panorama depicting the conflict was presented before paying audiences. It featured a portrait of Chaska. As the image rolled by in front of spectators, the narrator intoned, "Shaska, one of the prominent actors in this fearful drama, was the murderer of George Gleason and the capturer of the Wakefield family."[15] This version of events persisted well into the twentieth century, when historian Louis H. Roddis reports that Chaska "killed [Gleason] with a shot in the breast" and "was convicted by the testimony of Mrs. Wakefield who was an eyewitness of the dreadful scene."[16] By referencing the eyewitness account without granting it a hearing, Roddis demonstrates the endurance of a collective narrative that continued to silence Wakefield's testimony nearly a century after she delivered it.

In fact, the collective narrative circulating in the aftermath of the conflict called into question the legitimacy of eyewitness testimony in general. The controversy over the results of the war trials following the hostilities reflects a contest for the authority to tell the story of the Dakota Conflict. More than three hundred Dakota men had been sentenced to death in the trials. The hastiness and patent injustice of the proceedings—nearly four hundred cases were heard in six weeks, defendants were deprived of counsel and translators, and the judicial commission was made up of military officers of the

Minnesota regiments that had recently battled the Dakota—alarmed many reformers and politicians.[17] Federal statute required that the president approve all executions, and a list of the condemned was sent to Washington. Apparently troubled, Abraham Lincoln asked for the full record of the trial. After reviewing it he reduced the death sentences to thirty-nine, writing out the names of the condemned by hand.[18] White westerners argued vehemently against clemency. Before the final execution order was issued, three Minnesota lawmakers—Senator Morton S. Wilkinson, Representative Cyrus Aldrich, and Representative William Windom—wrote to the president urging him to approve the sentences of all the condemned. The letter was published in newspapers, entered into the Senate record, and preserved in trial documents, a testament to the ways it articulated the views of a majority of white westerners.[19]

Like Wakefield, the lawmakers claim exclusive authority to convey the truth of what happened. "Mr. President, let us relate to you some facts with which we fear you have not heretofore been made acquainted," they begin. They go on to describe a scenario of mass rape in which the accused "seized and carried into captivity more than one hundred women and girls, and in nearly every instance treated them with the most fiendish brutality." Strikingly, where Lincoln turned to the trial transcripts to make his decisions, the lawmakers implicitly dismiss the transcripts, and the judicial process itself, as inadequate representations of the "facts" of the conflict. Such facts could not be conveyed in the trial, their letter suggests, because social codes prohibit specifying the occurrence of sexual assault. The "facts" that evidence mass rape "are well known to our people," the lawmakers claim, but they cannot be set in print or described with specificity, as "delicacy forbids that we should mention the names of the parties to whom we refer." The record of mass rape does not appear in the trial transcript because rape victims—the primary eyewitnesses to the crime of rape—could not speak of or even be associated with the crimes committed against them. These discursive constraints make it possible for the Minnesota lawmakers to replace eyewitness accounts of the conflict with a narrative of pervasive Native male sexual predation. While the letter also describes nonsexual acts of aggression by Dakota men during the conflict, it places rape at the center of all white female captives' experiences. The congressmen describe the gang rapes of two girls before concluding, "without being more specific, . . . that nearly all the women who were captured were violated in this way."[20]

The struggle for narrative authority evident in the congressmen's letter and Wakefield's narrative—the struggle for command over "facts" and the assertion that only some people could make a "*true* statement" of what had happened—has implications for our understanding of the vexed relationship between testimony and history, between individual and collective memory, and between politics and public expression. At the heart of that relationship is a contest for the position of the eyewitness. U.S. officials from the West believed that people far removed from the scenes of violence could not possibly understand the magnitude of the crisis. In a telegraph to Lincoln, for instance, Minnesota's governor insists, "no one not here can conceive the panic in the state."[21] In claiming the authority to testify based on their physical proximity, however, officials themselves appropriated the voices of eyewitnesses, particularly those of white females caught in the actual conflict. They implied that eyewitnesses like Wakefield could not tell their own truth. The Minnesota congressmen usurped the witness stand, substituting a more generalized and nationalistic narrative of events for first-person reports. Stepping into the role of eyewitness to the Dakota Conflict, they silenced testimonies of individual experience.

As the letter suggests, the discourse surrounding claims of rape is emblematic of this appropriation of the role of eyewitness because of the ways rape resisted direct representation by its victims. Nineteenth-century norms of feminine propriety prohibited the victim of rape from describing her assault; the only first-person testament to the rape of a white woman was, paradoxically, silence. At the same time, in representations of interracial violence, sexual assault performed a metonymic shift from individual incidence to mass trauma, from a literal attack on one person to a figurative threat to white racial integrity and the United States itself. The inexpressibility of actual rape made it a convenient figure for a dominant discourse that purported to function within the allegedly disinterested processes of trial and history but actually used sensationalism to promote a distinct political agenda. The congressmen's universalizing of rape—"nearly all the women who were captured were violated"—upholds the notion that indigenous people would continue to imperil the lives and futures of white settlers until they were eliminated from contested areas. Part of an official narrative emphasizing Native sexual violence, the congressmen's letter supports the state's program of displacing and exterminating indigenous people. While they evoke official judicial processes, such versions of the conflict move away from the particularity of eyewitness testimony and toward a formless, ubiquitous terror created by the existence of savage others. These acts of narrative appropriation offer an important context for understanding the impediments to Wakefield's protest.

Wakefield found her experience "nameless," inexpressible in conventional terms, and she became increasingly absorbed with the underlying question of how to be heard in discursive contexts that did not accommodate her alternative version of events. The result is a text in which anxieties of representation threaten to overwhelm the author and raise questions about the possibilities for woman's protest in the nineteenth century. According to Shoshana Felman, testimony mediates "a crisis of truth" when "historical accuracy is in doubt and when both the truth and its supporting elements of evidence are called into question."[22] Such a crisis is revealed in the conflict between the congressmen's descriptions of universal rape of captives and Wakefield's description of universally respectful treatment. Clearly, both accounts cannot be true, and in fact, neither is. The congressmen claimed rape of captives was nearly universal, but only two of the Dakota prisoners were convicted of rape.[23] Wakefield makes the general claim that she was treated like "a lady" during her ordeal, but she also reports being threatened by Dakota men other than Chaska (86). My intention is not to enter into the historical debate over the extent to which rape was part of the military or social practice of western tribes.[24] I focus here less on questions of truth than on a crisis of expression, one that emerges when the circulation of a gendered, racialized, and nationalistic official narrative silences testimony of eyewitnesses like Wakefield.

"This I Witnessed": Wakefield's Testimonies

To be sure, the dismissals of Wakefield's multiple testimonies do not approach the magnitude of the injustice done to her Native protector, and indeed to all Dakota defendants, whose testimonies were made utterly meaningless. The silencing of these Native voices is part of a national tragedy of cataclysmic proportions, the largest mass execution in U.S. history. Chaska's ability to "speak some English, and read and spell very little" (69) would have been an advantage at a trial conducted with wholly inadequate translation, had it not been that the judicial decisions were all but predetermined. As one official glibly admitted, merely "the fact that they were *Indians*" implicated all accused.[25] Not surprisingly, Chaska was found guilty of murder despite eyewitness testimony to his innocence. President Lincoln removed Chaska's name from the final execution order, but he was nonetheless put to death, purportedly as the result of a procedural mix-up.

Certainly the chaos that characterized the trial proceedings and the rush to fulfill white settlers' demands for retribution set the stage for tragic procedural errors. At least three other condemned were also called Chaska or a variant of that name. Reverend Stephen R. Riggs, a Dakota-speaking white clergyman who ministered to the condemned, was friendly with one of them, Robert Hopkins, also called Chaske or Chaskaydon.[26] Riggs's request for clemency for Hopkins was granted. Lincoln's secretary's warning "to guard against the possibility of [Hopkins] being executed by mistake" registers the sense that errors were likely.[27] Each prisoner was given a number during trial, and Lincoln's directive used these designations. Yet because court records had been sent to Washington, officials at Mankato had no access to the original register connecting names to numbers.[28] Riggs explained to Wakefield that officials had forgotten that Chaska was tried under his full Dakota name, We-chan-hpe-wash-tay-do-pe (as Riggs renders it). "We knew he was called Chaska in the prison," he writes to her; "We never thought of the third [Chaska]; so when the name Chaska was called in the prison that fatal morning, your protector answered it and walked out. I do not think anyone was really to blame."[29]

All of these factors suggest the wrongful execution was not deliberate.[30] But the gross injustice of the trial itself—and, more broadly, the amplified rhetoric condemning all Native men and demanding retribution—put Chaska in harm's way in the first place. In focusing here on the discounting of Wakefield's testimonies, it is important not to understate the travesty of justice that denied indigenous prisoners like Chaska the right to defend themselves in a fair trial. Yet a focus on the dismissal of a *white woman's* testimony both in and out of the courtroom reveals the breadth of forces aligned against Chaska and others. It shows how social and political discursive protocols contributed to such national tragedies as the mass hanging at Mankato.

Even before the trial, Wakefield advocated on Chaska's behalf, ever in search of an audience willing to accept her version of events. When she met with white officials at Camp Release, several, including Riggs and Colonel Henry Sibley, commander of the white militia, asked her to point out Chaska among the surrendering Dakota. The white officials "shook hands with him, and made quite a hero of him for a short time" (111). Soon after, Wakefield described her experiences to other authorities (113). She argued with fellow white refugees, none of them eyewitnesses to Gleason's death, who called Chaska a murderer (115). Later, outraged at Chaska's execution, she demanded a meeting with Riggs, ultimately eliciting the letter of apology (121). Not satisfied, she wrote to Lincoln urging him to punish those responsible for the procedural error she and her husband considered "intentional." "Where the fault lies I know not, but it would be extremely gratifying to me to have these heedless persons brought to justice," she tells Lincoln. "Now [Chaska's] poor old Mother is left destitute, and broken hearted, for she has feeling if she is an Indian, surely we are Brothers all made by one God?"[31]

Each time Wakefield repeated her story, she revealed a painful awareness that her account clashed with an official story being circulated. When she initially described her experience to officials, she was made to understand how her testimony of interracial cooperation conflicted with a prevailing account of universal rape. "I related to them briefly what I have here written," she reports, "after which, Col. [William] Marshall said, 'If you have anything more of a private nature to relate, you can communicate it to Mr. Riggs.' I did not understand until he explained himself more fully. I told them it was just as I related, it was all. They thought it very strange I had no complaints to make, but did not appear to believe me" (113–14). Wakefield describes a similar response to her testimony during Chaska's trial: "I told them all I could say would be in his favor. They thought it very strange I could speak in favor of an Indian" (115). The repetition here is telling: in both unofficial and official attempts to testify, strangeness marks the contrast between her story and the extra-judicial one she was urged to repeat.

Because of her resistance to telling the right kind of story, officials were quick to appropriate Wakefield's role as witness. Colonel Marshall first claims the position of the testifier, "explain[ing] . . . fully" as he presses Wakefield to tell a more authorized story, presumably an account of her sexual abuse at the hands Dakota captors. When she refuses, her testimony is dismissed. "I was angry, for it seemed to me as if they considered my testimony of no account," she writes, "for if they had believed what I said, he would have been acquitted" (116). In her letter to Lincoln, Wakefield pleads for help in making her "strange" story heard: "I beg pardon for troubling you but there is much said in reference to his Execution. The world says he was not convicted of Murder then why was he Hanged? Then they draw their own conclusions: if this could be explained to the world a great stain would be lifted from my name."[32] Implicit here is the notion that the hanging itself reinforced a predominating narrative that contradicted her experience.

Wakefield's self-interest in clearing Chaska's name in order to lift the stain from her own undermines the assertion elsewhere that she sought justice on behalf of Chaska's "poor old Mother." But her comments also point to the heavily sexualized nature of the dominant interpretation of the conflict. If Chaska was executed despite Wakefield's assertions of his innocence and Lincoln's reduction of his sentence, "the world" infers it was because of illicit sexual contact between the Dakota man and white woman. Just as she refuses to articulate the scenario Colonel Marshall describes, Wakefield declines to be more explicit in the letter to Lincoln about the world's "conclusions." Such refusals demonstrate an unwillingness to be a mouthpiece for a racialized and sexualized dominant narrative. Yet Wakefield is surely deliberate in her irony when she follows the description of the ways others interpreted Chaska's execution by hinting at an even more scandalous conclusion. She conveys her husband's suspicions that the man responsible for the mix-up resulting in Chaska's death was "a certain 'Officer' at Mankato, who has many children in the Sioux tribe."[33] The insinuation turns the dominant narrative on its head, countering rumors about Wakefield's relationship with Chaska with one about the illicit sexual practices of a white military man, his status as a leader and a gentleman called into question in ironic quotation marks. Still, Wakefield remains aware of the difficulty of making any such alternative story heard; her appeal to Lincoln suggests that only the highest political authority in the land could legitimate her version.

Wakefield's accounts resist the story of interracial sexual contact so forcefully that they cannot be absorbed into the dominant-cultural histories being inscribed. Sensitive to the power of official idiom, she invokes the language of testimony in her captivity narrative; as she describes the starvation among the Dakota living near the Upper Agency in the weeks before the uprising, she declares, "this I witnessed. It is no idle story" (64). But like the authorities at Camp Release and the jury at Chaska's trial, nineteenth-century historians of the conflict deemed Wakefield's testimony "of no account." Histories such as *Dakota War Whoop; or, Indian Massacres and War in Minnesota, of 1862–3* by Harriet E. Bishop McConkey and *A History of the Great Massacre* by Charles S. Bryant and Abel B. Murch reproduce accounts of many individual white victims but omit Wakefield's. The omission occurs even though some experiences of interracial cooperation were being celebrated in the dominant culture. Accounts of "friendlies," assimilated Christian Dakotas who protected white captives from violence, were well received in the weeks and months following the conflict.[34] Some Dakota who participated in battles were pardoned because of their assistance to non-Native captives, and in one case, a Dakota prisoner was saved from execution because his brother had led a group of white settlers, including Wakefield's husband, to safety.[35] The Dakota woman Snana was widely celebrated for her kindness to white captive Mary Schwandt.

As discussed later, reports of Schwandt's rape in captivity became sensationalistic fodder for historians, and we might speculate that accounts of Snana's benevolence gained traction because Schwandt's experience as a victim of rape so neatly fit the dominant narrative. By contrast, Chaska was excluded from catalogues of "friendlies" even though he was known as one of the more assimilated Dakota (a trait Wakefield emphasizes in her trial testimony, when she asserts, "He had on leggings at the time Gleason was shot," and in her narrative, when she reminds readers, "Chaska had lived in a house previous to the outbreak, and was a good farmer, and worked hard" [96]).[36] Where Wakefield's experience is mentioned in the popular histories, it is only in the barest of terms. "Mrs. Wakefield and children were held as prisoners, and were reclaimed with the other captives at Camp Release," write Bryant and Murch; "Mrs. Wakefield and her children were carried into captivity, there to remain until the time of the great release had come," summarizes McConkey.[37] As prosecutor in the case against Chaska, Isaac V. D. Heard, later a state senator, questioned Wakefield at Camp Release and heard her trial testimony firsthand, recording it himself in the official record. His popular *History of the Sioux War and Massacres of 1862 and 1863,* however, makes no mention of her.

Given Wakefield's repeated efforts to communicate her version of events and in light of her notoriety, the exclusion of her story from popular history can only be deliberate. Wakefield's criticism of the U.S. military and judiciary and her eagerness to call attention to the injustice of Chaska's execution no doubt rankled authorities. More importantly, Wakefield's story of cross-racial and cross-cultural cooperation disrupted the dominant narrative in unacceptable ways. June Namias rightly attributes the exclusion of Wakefield's story to the depth of nineteenth-century biases that made voluntary sympathetic relationships across both racial and gender lines difficult to imagine.[38] We must further recognize how Wakefield's account could not be accommodated within a politically motivated history that foregrounds sexual violence by Native men. The histories being written resisted the displacement of that master narrative by negating Wakefield's experience altogether. Thus, unlike other released captives, Wakefield apparently had to print and promote her book herself: an advertisement in the back of the second edition calls for booksellers to direct inquiries to the author.[39]

Wakefield refused to alter her testimony to fit the dominant narrative. More than this, she purposefully reversed the terms of that narrative. Countering assumptions of universal rape of captives, she insists: "I do not know of but two females that were abused by the Indians. I often asked the prisoners when we met, for we were hearing all kinds of reports, but they all said they were well treated, that I saw" (117). Her estimate corroborates the results of the war trial, in which only two prisoners were found guilty of rape, as Lincoln noted in his final execution order.[40] Wakefield also defends her own honor, sullied by rumors that she had been Chaska's lover, by repeatedly defining her relationship with her captor as platonic. Her vindication had to not only establish the purity of her relationship with Chaska; it also had to overturn the racist stereotypes broadcast by white westerners: "My father could not have done differently, or acted more respectful or honorable; and if there was ever an honest, upright man, Chaska was one. . . . Very few Indians, or *even white men,* would have treated me in the manner he did" (84). The comparison of Chaska with her father defines the relationship as chaste; the further assertion that Chaska was more chivalrous than most white men speaks directly to the racialized narrative being produced in letters, newspaper articles, and histories at the time of her writing.

Going still further, Wakefield characterizes her treatment by U.S. soldiers after her release as bordering on abuse:

> When I got to the camp I found the soldiers in a state of great excitement, and all were eager to catch a glimpse of us. I was conducted to a large tent and soon it was surrounded with soldiers. We nearly suffocated for want of air. . . . I was a vast deal more comfortable with the Indians in every respect than I was during my stay in that soldiers camp, and was treated more respectfully by those savages than I was by those in that camp. . . . I have many times been forced to go to some officer and request a guard around us, so we could cook without molestation. (111–12)

Although the term "molestation" would not acquire its connotation of sexual assault until the twentieth century, Wakefield's description reverses a dominant narrative that defined white men as the chivalrous opposites of sexually aggressive Native men. Predominating accounts represented the scene at Camp Release as a moment in which grateful women were rescued from sexual slavery; Sibley, for instance, describes the relief of victims released from the "loathsome bondage" in which they had suffered "nameless outrages at the hands of their brutal captors."[41] Wakefield, on the other hand, had to ask military officers for protection from their own men, whose attentions suffocate the refugees. The language of constriction she uses calls into question orthodox definitions of "captivity" and "release," to say nothing of assumptions about "civilized" and "savage" male behavior. By insisting that aggression and exploitation in its various forms are not racially determined, Wakefield upends the official story.

Narrative Captivity

If Wakefield challenged the dominant narrative, she also underlined it throughout *Six Weeks in the Sioux Tepees,* in large part because the literary convention through which she testified forced her to do so. She likely defined her account as a captivity narrative in order to attract readers. The cultural shorthand of "captivity" promised scenes of white female vulnerability and Native savagery, which could create a larger audience for her particular story. What she delivered was certainly very different from what her readers must have expected. But the generic imperatives of the captivity narrative impeded her ability to convey her unorthodox story.

Scholars have described the ways the Indian captivity narrative underwrote U.S. expansionist and genocidal projects and the subjugation of women, especially as the genre shifted its emphasis from the spiritual concerns of the seventeenth century to the racial and territorial conflicts of the nineteenth. Beginning in the 1830s, "the genre's allegiance to U.S. imperial gain prevails," with sensationalistic scenes of Native violence serving as nationalist propaganda that helped to justify policies of removal and extermination.[42]

Because most white captives were women, real and fictional captivity narratives also reinforced gender norms. Namias argues that unlike earlier variations of the genre, nineteenth-century captivity narratives (both nonfictional and fictional) feature "Frail Flowers," white women who accord with stereotypes of "True Womanhood" in their lack of agency and their vulnerability.[43] Such representations encouraged a correlation of captivity and sexual victimization. As Christopher Castiglia points out, women writers of captivity narratives have always been obliged to refute assumptions that they had been raped by captors.[44] The clash between readers' expectations of captivity narratives and the truth captives attempt to record can produce a representational crisis.[45] Convention influences Wakefield's story from the outset, as most of her readers would come to her book with predetermined ideas about the sexual traumas of the woman captive. The genre Wakefield took up was already compromised as a stage from which to testify or protest.

Castiglia's larger argument suggests the ways captivity narratives may be transgressive despite such conventionally racialized and gendered preconditions, as productive sites of female agency and disruptive, cross-cultural subjectivities.[46] Without displacing this important revaluation, I would argue that it does not exhaust the complexities of women writers' relationships to the captivity narrative form. What does it mean that writers of captivity narratives are situated within literary forms that are so very predetermined in the popular imagination? In Wakefield's case, assumptions about the rape of the white female author of a captivity narrative operated in conjunction with broader beliefs, systematically reinforced in official and popular discourse, that Dakota men committed mass rape in Minnesota. The captivity narrative genre, with its foundations in the figure of the white female victim of sexual violence, impinged on Wakefield's ability to testify in print. More significantly, the convention *shaped* her literary testimony. Even the term "captivity" operated on Wakefield's story, transforming it from an account of protection to one of forced detention. The title converts beneficence to sexual violence, inhibiting her telling of an alternative story and stifling her protest.

The captivity narrative form connoted sexual violence in ways that made it difficult for women caught in interracial conflicts on the frontier to tell their stories. But the particular ways white Americans thought about and talked about incidents of interracial rape also affected women's testimonies. To appreciate how literary convention and official narratives impeded Wakefield's ability to tell an unconventional story, we must attend to broader structures of rape rhetoric in the nineteenth century.

Rape Rhetoric and the Appropriation of Testimony

Many other white westerners joined Congressmen Wilkinson, Aldrich, and Windom in broadcasting a story of universal sexual aggression by Dakota men. A petition signed by three hundred Minnesotans claimed that insurrectionists "spared neither age nor sex, only reserving, for the gratification of their brutal lust, the few white women whom the rifle, the tomahawk, and the scalping knife spared."[47] General John Pope responded to Lincoln's request for the trial transcripts by assuring him that "the only distinction between the culprits is as to which of them murdered most people or violated most young girls. All of them are guilty of these things in more or less degree."[48] One of the few white men held captive during the conflict avowed that, "with very few exceptions," female captives were routinely gang raped.[49] On seeing the released captives, Sibley wrote to his wife, "there is one young lady, very respectable and of fine personal appearance, a Miss Williams, who has been very much abused; indeed I think all the young ones have been."[50] Such assertions universalize the characterization of Native men as rapists ("all of them are guilty") and white women as victims ("all the young ones" were raped); like the letter from the congressmen, they make claims "without being more specific." Wakefield registers her recognition of the fraudulence of such generalizations. "The Indians were as respectful towards me as any white man would be towards a lady," she writes, "and now, when I hear *all* the Indians abused, it aggravates me, for I know *some* are as manly, honest, and noble, as our own race" (86, emphasis added). The distance between "all" castigated in the dominant narrative and "some" personally known to Wakefield marks precisely where the official and personal accounts diverge: one totalizes, the other particularizes.

Wakefield's specificity speaks to generalizing tendencies in dominant discourse that usurp the eyewitness's authority to testify about rape. Critics have attributed the deployment of rape rhetoric in nineteenth-century accounts of captivity to the propagandistic value of "outraged virginity" and to the influence of sentimental fiction—that is, to the intersecting social forces of politics and popular literature.[51] Certainly, the descriptions of mass rape in accounts of the Dakota Conflict were designed to elicit affective responses that would convince Americans of the justice of U.S. government actions, to bring readers to tears in order to win support for a national cause. But interpretations of rape rhetoric in captivity literature have not clarified the relationship between captives' testimonies and the dominant discourses in which their experiences became inscribed, nor do they account for the particular discursive effects of that rhetoric. As Sabine Sielke has it, "rape narratives relate to real rape incidents in highly mediated ways only."[52] Within the context of the struggle for narrative authority over the Dakota uprising, dominant discourse worked to displace and silence individual witnesses by generalizing the crime of rape. Claims of universal rape not only sensationalized; they also shifted control of the story of racial conflict from eyewitnesses to outside authorities. Rape rhetoric enabled nineteenth-century European American historians, politicians, and journalists to commandeer the story of the Dakota Conflict, displacing actual witnesses, like Wakefield, whose testimonies might not have been contained easily within the official story.

To understand how rape rhetoric functioned in official narratives of the Dakota Conflict, we might look to its operation in what has been called the southern "rape complex," in which ideas about African American male sexual aggression and European American female vulnerability were used to legitimate lynching.[53] Whereas readings of captivity narratives have explained the emphasis on rape in terms of its propagandistic value for western expansion, analyses of rape terror in the postbellum South uncover its function within the patriarchal and white supremacist system aimed at maintaining racial hierarchies after slavery. Rape rhetoric controlled white and black women, as well as black men, in part because it gave white men the power of testimony. Scholars characterize southern rape rhetoric as marked by refiguration, displacement, and silence. Sandra Gunning, for instance, finds women's texts about rape in the South to be preoccupied with "the problem of establishing female subjectivity within a public debate whose terms are universally established by men."[54] Likewise, Sielke identifies a "metonymic drift of the paradigm of rape and lynching" in which "the 'objects' of such violations are left behind in the debris of displacement." Discourses surrounding claims of rape confirm and maintain unequal social structures. For Sielke, "the rhetoric of rape is one of many discourses in which [differences of race and gender] are being ascribed, victims and violators othered, set off, while the subject who assigns difference remains unmarked and unlimited in his or her possibilities."[55] Such a reading is in keeping with theories of rape and representation that focus on the ways sexual assault is framed by a dominant perspective predicated on masculinist fantasies of power. As Lynn A. Higgins and Brenda R. Silver have written of rape rhetoric, "unmasking the privilege accorded masculine points of view reveals how patriarchal perspectives have prevented courts as well as texts, authors, and critics from asking who is speaking, who is hearing, and in what circumstances."[56]

The questions of who is speaking and who is hearing are particularly pressing in the context of the struggle for narrative authority over the events of the Dakota Conflict, for as the account of mass rape unfolded, eyewitness testimony was repeatedly displaced to accommodate a master narrative grounded in politically motivated stereotypes. "Transposed into discourse, rape turns into a rhetorical device," a figure of speech in a story in which the racial other poses an immense, amorphous threat to national and racial integrity.[57] Just as that device could be deployed in service of white supremacy in the South, it could support the eradication of Native people in the West. As in the South, accounts of sexual violence in the West were appropriated, generalized, and redirected by the dominant culture to produce a narrative that reinforced white male authority. If we acknowledge the central apparatus of nineteenth-century rape rhetoric in prevailing descriptions of the Dakota Conflict, we must also recognize the government's execution of thirty-eight Dakota men as a mass lynching.

That rape is figured as "nameless" in the dominant discourse of the nineteenth century suggests its usefulness in the production of a master narrative about Native sexual violence. Nineteenth-century moral codes departicularized representations of rape. Whereas journalists, politicians, and historians reported on most of the violence of the Dakota uprising in what can only be described as excruciating detail, narrating scenes of torture, for instance, in which a fetus is carved out of its mother's belly and nailed to a tree, they demurred when it came to accounts of rape, as, in the words of one historian, "it is improper to detail publicly all the cruelties to which [white women] were subjected."[58] Acts of rape are referenced euphemistically, as "heartless indignities," "fates worse than death," and "nameless outrages." Rape could be neither named nor located with any specificity: in many cases, reports of "outrages" during the conflict identify the victim only by her age or marital status. The lack of identifying detail made rape on the frontier seem insidious and ubiquitous, its victims faceless white women everywhere.

The dominant culture staked its claim to the story of the Dakota Conflict in the shift from specificity to generalization in descriptions of rape. Colonel Sibley in his letter moves from an individual victim of sexual abuse, "a Miss Williams," to the generalization that "all of the young ones have been" raped. In a parallel shift, the description by Wilkinson, Aldrich, and Windom of the rapes of a "beautiful little daughter" and a "refined and beautiful girl" shade into a generalization that all white women captives suffered the same fate.[59] And the congressmen's letter as a whole, which moves from the specificity of the trial transcripts to "some facts" not represented in the court proceedings, replicates the shift from specific evidence or testimony to generalization. Because the court record does not corroborate the story of universal rape, the letter from the congressmen reveals a tension between the particularities of legal testimony and the generalities of politically expedient narratives. Attempting to draw Lincoln's attention away from the trial transcripts, the congressmen write,

> These savages, to whom you purpose to extend your executive clemency, . . . indiscriminately murdered all the men, boys, and

> little children they came to; and although they sometimes spared the lives of the mothers and daughters, they did so only to take them into a captivity which was *infinitely worse than death.* . . .
>
> These Indians whom (as we understand) you propose to pardon and set free, have . . . ravaged our frontier for a distance of more than a hundred and fifty miles north and south.[60]

The terms of this passage themselves perform a rhetorical move from the specific to the general: the prisoners Lincoln's order protects from execution become "these savages" and "these Indians," generic indigenes responsible for all the violence of the conflict, which was delivered "indiscriminately." Further, "mothers and daughters" of Minnesota become nothing less than "our frontier," which has been "ravaged" like a woman captive. The coded language used to describe rape easily lends itself to the rhetorical shifts from real to metaphorical assault and from individual crimes to an explosion of wholesale savagery targeting the nation. The rhetorical effect helped to justify not just legal execution but martial annihilation.

The move away from individual testimony reassigned narrative control of the conflict from those testifying about personal experiences to those writing the authorized history of the U.S. borderlands. But if the shift empowered some westerners in their particular telling of the story, it left them in the curious position of denouncing other official narratives as inadequate representations of the truth. The politicians attempting to sway Lincoln, for instance, disavow conventional judicial processes even as they urge the president to follow through with sentences imposed by the court. Although their letter closes with the plea, "*let the law be excuted* [*sic*]—*let justice be done our people,*" it proceeds from the assumption that the judicial processes that produced the legal judgment would be inadequate because they fail to reveal fully the crucial "facts" that would have insured the harshest possible punishment for the majority of defendants—the "facts" of universal rape.[61] The court successfully implemented the totalizing tendencies of the dominant narrative in convicting most Dakota men; however, it did not produce a record that sufficiently articulated the generality of Dakota crimes, leaving a loophole through which some prisoners might escape death. The congressmen's success in convincing Lincoln to authorize the wholesale execution of captured Dakota men depended on their demonstrating the court's failure to tell the story of universal rape. Court proceedings, it seems, are simply too specific. Accordingly, the letter proceeds to render judicial practices moot by warning that, should all prisoners not go to the gallows, "the outraged people of Minnesota will dispose of the wretches without law."[62]

Just as the congressmen displaced trial testimony in their letter to Lincoln, the authors of dominant histories displaced the testimonies of captives as they worked to control the narrative of events, as is evidenced in Wakefield's excision from their accounts. The popular histories incorporate the written statements of a large number of women captives, but despite the claims of widespread rape, very few of these narratives include firsthand accounts of sexual abuse. Moral codes discouraging rape victims from identifying as such might explain the absence of eyewitness accounts. Victims' stories do not disappear entirely, however. Rather, they are taken up and mediated by authorities who fit them into a general narrative of widespread "outrage." Historians were quick to substitute sensationalistic rhetoric for the actual words of eyewitnesses. McConkey, a white Minnesotan who interviewed former captives to write *Dakota War Whoop,* describes the forty-day captivity of the same "Miss Williams" alluded to by Sibley. Her retelling transmits Mattie Williams's account of her capture while referring to sexual abuse only obliquely, as "the cruel, brutal treatment which may not be penned."[63] Bryant and Murch apply a similar strategy in delivering the first-person account of Mary Schwandt. Appended to *A History of the Great Massacre by the Sioux Indians,* Schwandt's narrative is, despite its deployment of conventional euphemisms, surprisingly direct: "They then took me out by force, to an unoccupied tepee, near the house, and perpetrated the most horrible and nameless outrages upon my person," she reports. "These outrages were repeated, at different times during my captivity." Yet here her story is interrupted for a bracketed editorial note: "The details of this poor girl's awful treatment, in our possession, are too revolting for publication.—EDITORS."[64]

Each of these editorial intrusions was ostensibly made to protect victims, but the suppression of Williams's and Schwandt's own voices, and the substitution of the sensationalistic unnamed, demonstrate the ways editors and other non-eyewitnesses controlled the historical narrative. That Schwandt's story is characterized as the "possession" of editors is telling. Thus Higgins and Silver insist that understanding rape rhetoric means paying attention to who controls narrative and who is silenced. "The process of unraveling the cultural texts that have obsessively made rape both so pervasive and so invisible a theme—made it 'unreadable'—is multilayered," they write. "It involves listening not only to who speaks and in what circumstances, but who does *not* speak and why."[65]

Dissent and the "Diseased Imagination"

When court testimony proves inadequate to the task of telling a particular kind of story, historians and politicians appropriate the status of eyewitness and generalize testimony. Paradoxically, the courtroom was an inadequate platform for Wakefield's particular story as well—or, rather, the witness stand failed to amplify that story. Ignored in court but refusing to be silenced, Wakefield attempted to tell her story as a narrative of "captivity." As we have seen, she resisted the convention of equating captivity with sexual attack in her reiterated assertions of Chaska's gentlemanliness. Yet the pressures to tell a different story impinged on Wakefield's text, and as a result, her narrative, especially in its second edition, diverges from other nineteenth-century captivity narratives most strikingly in the ways it registers her struggle for narrative control and interpretive authority. *Six Weeks in the Sioux Tepees* stands out in its tendency not just to speak to and against other narratives already in circulation but also to disclose its own representational limitations. If predominating assumptions about Native sexual violence and the constraints of the captivity genre impeded Wakefield's telling of her story, they also complicated her own understanding of what happened during and after the conflict. Wakefield's efforts to understand and communicate her experience remained entangled within an intransigent cultural imaginary that made it difficult to know and tell her own truth.

From the outset of her second edition of the narrative, Wakefield voices a desire to reclaim control over her own story. Her preface bemoans "omissions and misprints" caused by "malice and gross carelessness of the printer" in the first edition, some of which she hoped to correct (53). Wakefield also added dozens of pages of material. Namias sees these additions as introducing several new themes: maternity, Dakota life, the dangers of life in captivity, and her growing sense of guilt over Chaska's death.[66] More than simply adding depth and detail to the story, however, the additions reveal Wakefield's increased preoccupation with the telling itself. Her revised text alternately invokes the authority of the eyewitness and calls attention to the ways cultural modes impede her ability to know and speak the truth. This rhetorical dilemma results in a fixation with questions of perception and an underlying sense that Wakefield's history is, in the end, inexpressible in conventional forms.

Beginning with its prefatory claims to tell a truth not represented by those "ignorant of the particulars of my captivity and release," *Six Weeks in the Sioux Tepees* addresses other accounts of the conflict in circulation. Wakefield writes in response to authors and speakers who "think I prefer Indian to civilized life" (75), as well as "many persons [who] told entirely different stories respecting their treatment, after Sibley came, than they did before" (124).[67] References to published captivity narratives increase in the second edition, which adds passages calling into question the lauding of those "friendlies" celebrated in mainstream accounts. The narrative describes Snana, the Dakota woman who saved the life of Mary Schwandt, as cruelly indifferent to Wakefield's own suffering (93). Wakefield notes that Paul, a Wahpeton "friendly" praised for aiding whites in the Spirit Lake massacre of 1856, "troubled [her] very much," continually pressuring her to become his wife (96). These additions, undoubtedly designed to put Chaska in a better light by contrast, attest to Wakefield's desire to revise the public record established by mainstream versions of events.

Several paragraphs added to the opening of the second edition describe Wakefield's arrival on the prairie in 1861 and her interactions with Dakotas before the outbreak of violence. In addition to providing a context for her subsequent peaceful interactions with Dakota friends during the conflict, these paragraphs illuminate by example the problems of perception that plagued Wakefield's efforts to make her testimony and protest heard. She describes her initial reactions to the Minnesota prairie and its Native occupants as the European American tourist's one-dimensional perspective. One vista reminds her of "a beautiful panorama" (55); her traveling party enjoys another scene "as much as pleasure-seekers did their visits to the old castles and scenery on the Rhine" (56). In these early encounters, her views of Native peoples are, also like a tourist's, by turns xenophobic and romantic. On first seeing Native people, she recalls, "I could not help exclaiming, 'Is this where I am to live?' for all I saw was one log hut and about six hundred filthy, nasty, greasy Indians" (55). Soon after, she writes, she found a Dakota village "a pretty and a novel sight. . . . The Indians, playing their flutes, made music quite pleasant to our ears" (56). Such objectifying views of the region's Natives as exotic others belie Wakefield's later humanistic defense of Dakota who became trusted friends, and the disjunction reverberates throughout the narrative.

In fact, Wakefield makes clear the limits of her initial view in a description of her first night at her Agency home, which introduces a theme of the dangers of misperception. On that first night, Wakefield and her fellow travelers, "ignorant of Indian customs," hear the Dakotas at their councils and fear an attack. When they perceive "the noise of a hundred horsemen," she and her housemates are terrified—until they realize the noise is from the hoof-beats of their own horses escaping a swarm of mosquitoes (57). The inclusion of this minor incident points to the ways fear of the racial other contributes to what Wakefield later refers to as a "diseased imagination" (77–78). She presents the scene as a fable for those reading her account and absorbing dominant stories about the conflict: "This gives, in the beginning, an idea of many Indian scares. Many times we were needlessly frightened, but at last came one that was real, as our friends and our country know to their sorrow" (57). The distinction between real and imagined "Indian scares" alerts her readers to the dangers of a predominating cultural imaginary.

Critics have identified ambivalence toward captors and Native people in general as characteristic of the captivity narrative tradition.[68] The uniqueness of *Six Weeks in the Sioux Tepees,* however, lies in its conscious and unconscious probing of its own ambivalence, its willing exploration of the complex processes of perception and interpretation. The additions of Wakefield's myopic initial views of indigenous people and the episode of mistaken terror reflect a particular aim of her project, for as the work pokes fun at her own ignorance as a fresh emigrant, it also exemplifies the ways conventions influence our understanding of what is real. With such introductory materials ("in the beginning"), the author asks nineteenth-century readers to approach her text with attention to the ways cultural obstructions might inhibit their *own* understanding of the Dakota Conflict.

Yet Wakefield was not always conscious of the ways her cultural context clouded her own vision, and her oscillation between biased and more objective perception threatens to destabilize her position as an eyewitness. The next paragraph reveals the incoherence created when she moves from the dominant cultural perspective to an alternative eyewitness point of view. The paragraph swings back and forth between a totalizing and individualizing view, between what Michel de Certeau terms the fiction of the "voyeur-god" and the knowledge of "everyday life."[69] It first describes Wakefield's experience among Dakota she sees as warm and hardworking people mistreated by mission teachers and others. Next it describes the view from a favorite elevation near Wakefield's home, from which she sees Dakota women and children who "looked like babes, the distance was so great" (58). Moving from the ground view that individualizes and encourages sympathy for the Dakota to the hilltop view that literally belittles them, this sudden shift replicates the official narrative's movement from specific experience to racialized generalization. But the paragraph quickly returns to its ground-level outlook:

> I often wondered what an Eastern person would think, to ride through those woods, as we did, unprotected. I usually, after the first few weeks, went with my little boy, alone, to Hazelwood, often returning long after the sun was down, and very often passing

> through the Indian camp, which about the time of payment consisted of about five thousand Indians. I never knew one to be cross, but on the contrary [they] were very kind and pleasant. I often was stopped and asked to take a puff from their pipes. (58)

This second shift returns the reader to the perspective of the "everyday," and does so by privileging the writer's position as eyewitness. Differentiating herself from the eastern tourist, Wakefield suggests that her particular perspective as one who lives among and admires the Dakota allows her insight into their true nature. By extension, the moment grants Wakefield the authority to write a "*true* statement" of events. And yet in its curious spatial shifts, this description demonstrates an uneasy negotiation of interpretive positions. Just as she notes the "strangeness" of her court testimony on behalf of Chaska in the context of the unfolding official narrative of universal rape of captives, Wakefield registers the disjunction of her eyewitness viewpoint with the racist perspective of the larger culture, of another emigrant from the East who could be walking in her shoes. That she herself had relocated from her native Rhode Island only a few years before further complicates her position. In effect, the interpretive perspective of "an Eastern person" hovers over Wakefield's narrative, invisibly shaping her textual production.

Consequently, tropes of shifting perspectives and the patterns of perception, misperception, and re-vision pervade the second edition of the narrative. Wakefield often places herself in the role of a reader misled by false information. As a victim of the conflict, she must read the world critically, sifting through rumors and false reports from both Dakotas and whites. Hostile tribe members frequently tell Wakefield her husband is dead and she and her children will be killed; fellow white captives spread rumors that she is in love with Chaska. More than rumors and lies, however, Wakefield combats terrors produced by her own imagination. In a description added to the second edition, she recalls a night when winds overturned tepees and exposed the occupants around their fires:

> It looked like some picture I had seen where witches were holding their revels; for, crooning over the fires, were the old women of the families, who seldom ever sleep in the night, but sit smoking

> their Kinnikinnick until day begins to dawn; then, with a prayer to the sun, they retire. I have often in the night sat and watched these old creatures as they smoked, talked and cooked, until I really thought their magic spells were really at work upon me; for they would take the form of very devils, in the midnight hour, over their fires, singing and moaning in their half-stupid state. I don't know as this is always so. It might be they were fearful of losing their prisoners. Such nights as these I have described helped my already diseased imagination, until at times I was nearly frantic, for with all this was the continual firing of guns, and I really thought every one sent some poor creature into eternity, and expected every minute my turn would come. (77–78)

This addition to the narrative contains a multivalent ethnography. Wakefield follows conventions of captivity narratives by reporting on the unfamiliar habits of her captors, their singing, praying, and pipe-smoking rituals. But she also offers an ethnographic detail of European American culture in her references to fantastic images of witches working spells. The fancied scene of witches over their cauldron, disseminated by artists from the Grimm brothers to Shakespeare, colors Wakefield's reaction. That her "diseased imagination" is fed by "some picture I had seen" as much as by the behavior of the Native women suggests the ways prevalent iconography affects perceptions of experience.

Given contradictions and inconsistencies in her statements and actions, some contemporary scholars have concluded that Wakefield was so unhinged, either by nature or as a result her traumatic experience, that she was incapable of objectivity. One historian warns that a "penchant for exaggeration and rash judgments" undermines the reliability of her testimonies, and even Derounian-Stodola, who otherwise champions Wakefield's advocacy on behalf of the Dakota people, describes *Six Weeks in the Sioux Tepees* as "schizophrenic" and its author as unstable.[70] Wakefield did speak and act rashly. In her narrative she expresses regret for saying things she should not have at Camp Release because her "mind was in a dreadful state" and she was "not capable of acting rationally" (116). At one point she threatened to shoot anyone who tried to execute Chaska, behavior she attributes to her inherently "violent impulsive disposition" (114). Most striking in her description of the Native women around their fires on a stormy night, however, is her consciousness that her perception has been shaped as much by the cultural imaginary she carries into the conflict as by the trauma of her wartime experience.

Indeed, the loss of objectivity is precisely the point of the passage. Here is an eyewitness keenly, even agonizingly aware that her cultural orientation constrains her capacity to understand and testify to what happens in interracial conflict. She cannot discern whether the Native women are praying, performing black magic, or simply giving voice to their sorrow and anxiety in wartime. It is not only the terror of being caught in the crossfire that contaminates Wakefield's imagination but also the entrenched conventions of her own culture. Thus she quickly undermines her own overtly racist description of the women "singing and moaning in their half-stupid state" by questioning her ability, even as an eyewitness, to comprehend Dakota folkways: "I don't know as this is always so."

"I don't know": the phrase itself destabilizes the authority of the eyewitness. If what the witness sees or hears is shaped by her participation in hegemonic cultural structures, to what truth can she testify? The passage underlines the ways imaginations are diseased by cultural convention even as it brings to light the limits of Wakefield's narrative authority in the judicial, social, historical, political, and literary contexts she enters. Like other authors of captivity narratives, Wakefield bemoans her inability to put words to her experience, admitting, "Now, as I write it . . . I can scarcely hold my pen" (68). In the second edition, the conjunction of her inability to understand and express and her audience's unwillingness to attend to her story constitutes a deeply felt crisis. "Can anyone imagine how I suffered?" she asks. "No! they can not. I now do not realize my agony" (73). The failure of imagination carries over from audience to author, making her testimony something that the witness cannot know as well as something others will not hear. As she engages in the struggle for narrative authority, taking on multiple discourses that make up to the dominant narrative, Wakefield's frustration mounts: "I felt the change from civilized to savage life as much as any one, but it would do no good to keep drawing comparisons; I was there, and it was no use to borrow trouble, but try to be as contented as I could under the circumstances, but every word and action has been remembered, and turned against me to my disadvantage" (95). Aware that she is caught in a whirlpool of circulating stories that impinge on her own, Wakefield ultimately seems to agree with the military commission that her testimony must be "of no account." "I was there" might suggest the authority of the eyewitness, if it were not for the prevalence of competing narratives that turn her own words against her. The influence of the dominant culture narrows her perceptions, encumbers her testimony, and stifles her protest.

The Useless Witness

The incommensurability of eyewitness testimony with the authorized narrative of the Dakota Conflict might be crudely summed up in the words of an unnamed correspondent writing in the *Saint Paul Pioneer* at the time of the Dakota trials. The writer responds with impatience to easterners' alarm that the courts failed to call many witnesses for the defense: "Perhaps this may seem, to those who were not on the ground, an unjustifiably summary mode of proceeding; but it was as lengthy an examination [as] necessity would permit, and 'whatever necessity requires, it justifies.' Besides, no individual injustice is probably done, as ninety-nine hundredths of these devils are guilty, and witnesses in their favor would be about as useless as teats on a boar."[71] We see a characteristic shift from the specific to the universal in this rationalization, from the unlikelihood of "individual injustice" to the generalization that "ninety-nine hundredths of these devils are guilty." More strikingly, the gendered analogy confirms that, as Martha Hodes has it, "the history of racial categories is often a history of sexuality as well."[72] The idea that testimony would be "useless as teats on a boar" hints that the writer had a specific witness in mind, for it speaks to the ways Wakefield acted out of gender bounds in her refusal to identify as a victim of sexual assault and in her attempts to wrest narrative authority away from white men. While Wakefield may have been masculinized in her continued insistence on bearing witness, the way she was silenced by authorities who would speak for her—and, of course, the account of sexual victimization they would impose, itself a metaphoric rape—recode her as female.

With the end of the second edition, Wakefield seems to sense futility in her efforts to speak out. The first edition ends with a description of Wakefield's friendship with the Dakota before the outbreak and the ways her kindnesses were repaid when she was taken under protection by Chaska and his family: "Their actions have proved the bible true to me, for it says 'Cast your bread upon the water, and after many days it shall return to you' " (125). By the time she revised the narrative, Wakefield had learned enough about the clout of dominant discourse to be more pessimistic about interracial relations in the United States. Three paragraphs were added to the narrative that shift the focus of the story away from Wakefield's personal experience: one that tells the story of her husband's escape from Yellow Medicine, one that criticizes the military campaign and the brutal policy of removing remaining tribes to infertile land west of the Missouri River, and one that bemoans the plight of so many of her former Dakota friends and neighbors. The emphasis on political statements in the last two paragraphs represents Wakefield's final attempts to inscribe an alternative history of the Dakota Conflict and to register her protest. Still, just after this appeal the second edition ends abruptly, with the words, "And now I will bid this subject farewell forever" (127). The silence at the close of the book punctuates efforts by authorities to erase Wakefield's testimony. True to her word, Wakefield apparently made no more attempts to make her story heard; instead she rejoined her husband and lived out the rest of her life in Saint Paul. When she died in 1899, her obituary memorialized her not as a witness, author, or political protester but as "a Prisoner of the Sioux," a designation that solidified her status as a conventional captive and presumed victim of sexual assault.[73] In the end, her testimony that she was something else entirely was "useless," "no good," "of no account," and utterly dispensable.

Dispensable, that is, in her time. In ours, Wakefield's text speaks volumes about the capacities of conventional print forms to perform unconventional politics. It registers the intense competition for authority over the record of U.S. race relations, the power of dominant narratives, and the voicelessness of witnesses and those accused. *Six Weeks in the Sioux Tepees* becomes caught in the dialectic between individual and collective testimony. Wakefield's difficulty negotiating that conflict may explain why present-day literary critics of captivity narratives have not analyzed her work in much detail.[74] The oscillation of perspectives in the text and Wakefield's preoccupation with problems of interpretation (her own as well as her readers') creates a minefield of ambiguity that must be negotiated with care. Reading Wakefield, it is easy to become disoriented: as resistant as she is to the dominant narrative and to the political constraints of the captivity narrative, she nonetheless occasionally echoes the racist rhetoric of her age. Indeed, even as Wakefield's book rejects the prevailing history of the conflict, her position as witness requires that she tell a story that is comprehensible in the context of the dominant understanding of race relations in the West. Whether she was speaking from the witness stand or composing her captivity narrative, she had to attend to the authorized story despite the fact that her experience departed from it. She found ultimately that her experience was in many respects unknowable, as well as inexpressible.

Still, Wakefield's efforts to testify and the competition of narratives in general reveal fissures in the national historical narrative. Such fissures can always be expected, and must always be attended to, in cultural crises where the representation of violence becomes a political apparatus. Calling our attention to dissent from dominant narratives, the discursive forces unleashed against it, and the difficulty of bearing witness in violent national crises from within conventional modes of discourse, *Six Weeks in the Sioux Tepees,* in that sense, overcomes its own silence.

We might attribute Wakefield's collapse under the pressures of dominant cultural discursive modes to her general inexperience with textual production. As she avers in the prefatory comments with which this chapter opens, she did not claim to be "a book-writer." But could a successful professional author have better negotiated the conflicts between protest and conventional literary production? In the next chapter I turn to poetry on Native subjects by

Lydia Sigourney, arguably the most prominent female "book-writer" of her generation and an activist for Native rights. The assumption that Sigourney was deeply mired in generic convention has made it difficult to recognize both her activism and her deliberate aesthetic interventions. I explore these overlapping aspects of her poetry. Like Wakefield, Sigourney confronted the limitations of the discursive constructs she occupied in an effort to protest U.S. Indian policy. The result is an interrogation of the very modalities that define those constructs, an immanent critique of the sentimental that exposes its considerable political concessions.

CHAPTER TWO

"She Wept Alone"

The Politics and Poetics of Lydia Sigourney's Indian Laments

The March 12, 1831, issue of the *Cherokee Phoenix, and Indians' Advocate* features Lydia Sigourney's "The Cherokee Mother," one of a handful of published poems that expressly protest the Indian Removal Act of 1830.[1] The poem imagines a Cherokee woman on the threshold of exile who confronts the whites who have forced her and her family from their home:

> Ye bid us hence.—These vales are dear,
> To infant hope, to patriot pride.—
> These streamlets tuneful to our ear,
> Where our light shallops peaceful glide.
>
> Beneath yon consecrated mounds
> Our fathers' treasur'd ashes rest,
> Our hands have till'd these corn-clad grounds,—
> Our children's birth these homes have blest,
>
> *Here,* on our souls a Saviour's love
> First beam'd with renovating ray,
> Why should we from these haunts remove?
> But still you warn us hence away.—
>
> *Child, ask not where!*—I cannot tell,

Save where wide wastes incultur'd spread,
Where unknown waters fiercely roll,
And savage monsters howling tread;

Where no blest Church with hallow'd train,
Nor hymns of praise, nor voice of prayer,
Like angels sooth [*sic*] the wanderer's pain;
Ask me no more.—I know not where.

Go seek thy Sire.—The anguish charm
That shades his brow like frowning wrath,
Divide the burden from his arm,
And gird him for his pilgrim-path.

Come, moaning babe! Thy mother's arms
Shall bear thee on our weary course,
Shall be thy shield from midnight harms,
And baleful dews, and tempests hoarse.

But thou, Oh Father! old and blind,
Who shall *thy* failing footsteps stay?
Who prop thy sorrow-stricken mind
Driven from thy native earth away?

An exile in thy hoary hairs,
And hopeless when life's toils are o'er
To mix thy mouldering dust with theirs,
Those blessed sires, who weep no more.

Ye call us brethren. When ye mark
The grass upon our thresholds grown,
Our hearth-stone cold,—our casements dark,
Our fated race like shadows flown,

Amid your mirth, your festive songs
Will no remourseful image lower
No memory of the Indian's wrongs
Rise darkly o'er your musing hour?

Will a crush'd nations deep despair,
Your broken faith,—our tear-wet sod,

The babe's appeal,—the chieftain's prayer,
Find no memorial with our God?[2]

In its representation of a scene of Native mourning, the poem both resembles and departs from a common poetic form, the Indian lament. Popularized by such well-known figures as William Cullen Bryant and John Greenleaf Whittier and proliferating in the era of removal, Indian laments typically dramatize the sorrow of the last living member of a Native tribe. Like the elegy, the form for which Sigourney is famous, the Indian lament memorializes, but it does so in service to a national project rather than as a means of private consolation. By presenting Native loss and disappearance as unfortunate but inevitable, Indian lament poems exorcize white guilt for crimes against the continent's original inhabitants. Their compensatory scenes of mourning, as Max Cavitch puts it, "naturalize and anteriorize the fatal consequences of political and military protocols of removal."[3]

Yet "The Cherokee Mother" is activist, not apologist. If it borrows from the funeral scene of the traditional elegy, it also points to the ways Cherokees were denied the right to mourn their dead: the "tear-wet sod" the speaker and her family must vacate includes "consecrated mounds" beneath which their ancestors lie. The poem also refuses the Indian lament's fantasy of Native peoples' acquiescence to their own disappearance. Far from resigned, the speaker asserts that though her tribe may be "fated" to disperse like shadows, there is nothing natural in its vanishing. The speaker's blunt opening words, "Ye bid us hence," indict her white audience for the unfolding tragedy, with the caesura underlining her anger. The confrontational opening is matched by a closing question mark that punctuates the immorality of Indian removal. The grieving Cherokee mother censures and resists. There is no palliation of white guilt here.

"The Cherokee Mother" emerged from an unprecedented campaign by American women, one that deployed conventions of feminine sentiment to influence federal policy.[4] As Paula Bernat Bennett notes, the word "memorial" in Sigourney's final line calls attention to the many petitions (commonly called memorials) against Indian removal that white, middle-class women presented to Congress between 1829 and 1831.[5] In fact, the poem is preceded in the *Cherokee Phoenix* by its own memorial, a letter from an "Association of Ladies" pleading with U.S. legislators to halt removal. The letter acknowledges the novelty of women's involvement in discussions of national policy but argues that good motives justify the protesters' transgression. In the letter, sentiment is the unique instrument of women's political action. "It will probably be alleged that we have viewed this subject solely through the medium of *feeling*," it predicts, adding, "this was our intention."[6] If women's entrance into political debates was unusual, so, too, was their affective approach to mediating political conflict. The letter makes feminine feeling, the stock-in-trade of sentimental print culture, a resource for political action.

And yet just as "The Cherokee Mother" departs from the sentimental conventions of the Indian lament by refusing its bogus consolations, it also rejects faith in the political expediency of "the medium of *feeling*" championed by the white women's anti-removal effort. To be sure, in both the poem and letter, female feeling gives women a platform for expression they would be denied otherwise. These texts reflect an emerging language of women's civic involvement, shedding light on the role of gendered cultural discourse in the deliberate constitution of women's political subjectivity in the early nineteenth century. But in significant respects the politicizing feeling in the poem diverges from that in the letter. Like the rhetoric of women's anti-removal petitions, which I analyze later in this chapter, the letter in the *Cherokee Phoenix* figures both white women protesters and the Native people for whom they advocate as passive objects of white male machinations. It thereby crystallizes the very exclusions and oppressions anti-removalists ostensibly contested. More than this, it describes the intense emotion experienced by both women and Natives as fundamentally othering and disempowering, an oppression in itself. Sigourney's poem, in contrast, deploys the Cherokee mother's enraged grief to indict the nation for its broken promises, its false friendship, and its indifference to suffering. It reimagines the possibilities for a doubly marginalized figure's oppositional agency, and it mobilizes sentiment to register a more powerful political protest.[7]

In brief, the letter begs the nation's pity; the poem demands its shame. It is tempting to ascribe the difference between them to the stereotypes of race, gender, and class that narrowly circumscribed emotional expression in the nineteenth century. According to this reasoning, middle-class white women might register their sadness and anxiety about removal, but they were obliged to leave less "civilized" reactions to removal, like anger and defiance, to an imagined indigenous proxy like Sigourney's speaker.[8] Yet because "The Cherokee Mother" also transforms the conventions of the Indian lament, we must recognize the poem as both an entrance into and a critique of popular-political rhetoric that constrains female political protest.

In the women's anti-removal rhetoric and Indian lament poetry, conventional sentiment depletes the political force of the scene of indigenous loss. Although it situated femininity on a public stage, the women's anti-removal movement asserted a female political agency that was stuck in the subjugating protocols of white feminine feeling. Feeling both justified women's intervention and neutralized their political authority. For its part, the Indian lament idealizes indigenous feelings in ways that cover over national acts of theft and genocide, assign the grieving subject to the irretrievable past, and confirm structures of white patriarchal power. Indian lament poems pathologize indigenous grief as a symptom of Native peoples' failure to progress. Sigourney's poem, on the other hand, re-politicizes feminine feeling. It at once exposes the shallowness of white sympathy for Native people and registers an emotional response that is distinctly oppositional—enraged grief rather than resigned melancholy. Such writing reflects the poet's attempts to escape the depoliticizing effects of racialized and gendered conventions of sentiment in politics and literature, to make literary affect perform a more honest political resistance.

In this chapter, I argue that Sigourney critiques and manipulates literary convention and political discourse in lyric protests against Indian removal. Aesthetic and social reform intersect in Sigourney's poetry on Native themes, as the poet expands the boundaries of convention to accommodate expressions of female and Native political agency that were otherwise prohibited. In the poems I examine, Sigourney recasts the sentimental Indian lament to condemn the specious sympathy dominating European American representations of suffering Natives. At the same time, she responds to the contradictions of women's anti-removal rhetoric by challenging its facile deployment of sentiment. In effect, her writing opposes formal as well as political oppression. Considered in relation to the political and literary expressions of its moment, Sigourney's poetry on Native loss reveals both the possibilities of print conventions and the pressure that must be applied to them in order to register protest.

Sentimentality, Countersentimentality, and Critique

"The Cherokee Mother" suggests the need to reconsider the relationship between Sigourney's poetry and her political activism. Until recently, critics have dismissed Sigourney's poetry as market-driven and overly formulaic, far too bound up in the strictures of elegiac sentimentality to be politically provocative. Countering such dismissals, Bennett, Nina Baym, Sandra A. Zagarell, Karen L. Kilcup, and Tricia Lootens emphasize how Sigourney's writing addresses political issues, especially the plight of North America's indigenous people in the face of colonization and westward expansion.[9] But the poet's advocacy for Native people was not limited to her poetry. It began when she organized her female students to contribute to mission efforts in the early decades of the nineteenth century, and it extended into the 1840s, when she wrote to a congressman urging him to grant citizenship to those displaced by removal.[10] Her poetry on Native American subjects reflects activist intentions that critics have yet to appreciate fully. The epic poem *Traits of the Aborigines of America,* all but ignored by scholars, details Native people's suffering under European colonization, while the original version of the widely anthologized "Indian Names" includes a pointed condemnation of the removal policy that is likewise often overlooked.[11]

If scholars have missed Sigourney's activism, they have also underestimated her aesthetic inventiveness. Most critics take for granted the poet's determined adherence to standard literary protocols; even those working to recuperate her reputation tend to see her use of literary convention as strategic, not transformative. For Eliza Richards, the poet's formal consistency in the deployment of elegiac sentimentality is "arguably a great accomplishment" that serves as "the building block of Sigourney's republican project."[12] Mary Louise Kete argues that Sigourney used "the characteristic diction of the sentimental mode" and "the characteristic rhetorical figures of sentimentality" to promote a resolution to national strife.[13] As Bryan Sinche points out, however, when critics "take her sentimental outlook and aesthetic as more or less a given," they may overlook the possibility of the poet's "reconsideration of sentiment as a remediative force."[14] Like Sinche, Bennett argues that Sigourney was capable of thinking critically about literary forms. Bennett reads the 1854 poem "The Lost Lily" as calling into question the traditional structures of Christianity, patriarchy, and sympathy that lie at the heart of sentimentality.[15] Such readings ask us to consider, as we test the capacities of literary sentimentalism to do political work, how the poet appraised the literary conventions she took up.

"The Cherokee Mother" challenges our assumptions about literary convention and political expression. So, too, do poems about Native loss and grief that are less directly concerned with removal, such as "Indian Girl's Burial" (1838) and "Pocahontas" (1840). These poems offer meta-literary critiques by questioning the efficacy and integrity of conventional sentiment. Sigourney's writings on Native themes transform women's protest in ways that condemn hollow sympathy, expose the deceit of its advertisement of affiliation, and assert its objects' political subjectivity against a predominating narrative that would subordinate them. It performs what Lauren Berlant identifies as the "countersentimental," a form of textual resistance that refuses to sacrifice political will to the satisfying fantasies of consolation and redemption that ultimately fortify normative political structures.

For Berlant, liberal sentiment deployed by the culturally privileged at once builds alliances around suffering and confirms the hegemonic valuation of subjects in the United States. Conventional sentimentality depoliticizes through its substitutions: "The ethical imperative toward social transformation is replaced by a passive and vaguely civic-minded ideal of empathy," and "the political as a place of acts oriented toward publicness becomes replaced by a world of private thoughts, leanings, and gestures."[16] Sentimentality retreats from political action into a dream of unconflicted togetherness. Countersentimentality addresses the problem of liberal sentiment by rejecting this dream and reinvesting representations of feeling with political import. I do not mean to suggest that Sigourney's poetry is "counter" in the sense of being exempt from the consolidating seductions of the sentimental; indeed, Berlant stresses that countersentimentality is "lacerated by ambivalence" about the promise of collective belonging embedded in convention, and I explore that ambivalence later in this chapter by tracing the poet's evolving understanding of the politics of sentimentality.[17] Rather, I contend that Sigourney's most politically resistant poetry challenges sentimentality's structural association of emotion with consent.

Berlant's concept is useful both because it suggests the possibility of a meaningful political resistance based in feeling and because it points to the ways conventional texts might function as critiques of convention. The countersentimental mode "challenges the place literature and storytelling have come to stand for in the normalization of gestures of emotional humanism," revealing the contradictions and compulsions of popular form.[18] Berlant locates such critical resistance in James Baldwin's "Everybody's Protest Novel" and Toni Morrison's *Beloved,* but she also finds it in a less likely place: Robert Waller's *The Bridges of Madison County,* a contemporary American novel widely seen as oversaturated with conventional sentiment. That such a text resists the compromised politics of sentimentalism suggests the ways writers might critique and revise literary protocols and forms *from within.* For Berlant, Waller's mobilization of affect suggests possibilities for politico-aesthetic revolution, for producing "a story worth telling," a "story of sentimental radicalism" told against the contradictory and fraudulent claims of national consent found in popular culture.[19] Similarly, Sigourney's poetry on Native themes challenges and transforms from within the conventional sentimentalism of the Indian lament and women's antiremoval rhetoric. My most ambitious claim in this chapter is that in moments of political crisis, the deployment of literary convention can engender a self-conscious interrogation of the possibilities and limitations of popular expression itself. Sigourney's attempt to use convention to effect political change results in a reassessment of both literary and non-literary uses of sentiment, and the process opens possibilities for reinvention of literary modes.

Works like "The Cherokee Mother" deploy the countersentimental in response to the sentimentality of two forms of discourse, one popular-cultural, the other popular-political. The Indian lament uses sentiment to bury the nation's indigenes, in the twinned sense of memorializing their passing and laying to rest their living protests and claims. The rhetoric found in white women's anti-removal essays and petitions, in contrast, exploits the language and value of sentiment to speak out on behalf of oppressed Native people. And yet these two modes of expression are alike in their tendency to absolve the nation of responsibility and simultaneously reinforce dominant structures of power. They both use feeling—the grief of the imagined last tribe member, the anxious sympathy of middle-class white women for the oppressed—in ways that reflect the national effort to process guilt for acts of colonialist violence, as well as to manage marginalized constituencies' claims to political subjectivity through dishonest narratives of consent. As such, they represent generic variations in a cultural discourse that obfuscates white male culpability and denies female and Native agency. To understand Sigourney's political and aesthetic work, we must first consider the ways these popular discourses deploy sentiment, and to what effect.

Indian Removal and the Indian Lament

The tears of indigenous people flowed freely in nineteenth-century American popular representations, and they irrigated a nostalgic nationalism. When Czech composer Antonín Dvořák set out to create a distinctly American music in 1893, for example, he found inspiration in a widely disseminated representation of indigenous loss and grief, Minnehaha's funeral scene in Henry Wadsworth Longfellow's *Hiawatha*. The result was the "nostalgic, dark, and melancholy, or even elegiac" second movement of his "New World" symphony.[20] His similarly funereal composition written in the same year, *Sonatina for Violin and Piano,* would become known popularly as "The Indian Lament." A nineteenth-century reviewer took note of the Czech composer's preoccupation with Native sadness occasioned by settler colonialism: "When the star of empire took its way over those mighty western plains blood and sweat and agony and bleaching human bones marked its course. Something of this awful buried sorrow of the prairie must have forced itself upon Dr. Dvorak's mind when he saw the plains after reading 'The Famine' [chapter 20 of *Hiawatha*]."[21] Actually, defining America by evoking the "awful buried sorrow" of Native loss did not require a trip to the plains. Having read Longfellow in Czech translation, Dvořák composed his symphony in New York, before his first trip west.[22] Indeed, by the time of his arrival in the United States, the crying indigene was an established American icon, having reached a peak in the second and third decades of the nineteenth century—specifically, in the age of Indian removal.

The removal era was a "time of Indian mourning," to use Dana Luciano's multilayered phrase. Luciano refers to the appealing asynchronicity non-Natives imagined in Native sorrow, as well as the historical moment when representations of grieving Native Americans proliferated, just as real Native people were being cleared from their home territories.[23] President Andrew Jackson had made relocating eastern tribes a priority of his administration, and in 1830, he pushed through legislation authorizing him to negotiate treaties to remove tribes living east of the Mississippi River (primarily the so-called Five Civilized Tribes) to territories in the West. Tribes fought Indian removal in two highly publicized Supreme Court cases, *Cherokee Nation v. Georgia* (1831) and *Worcester v. Georgia* (1832), which elicited decisions that seemingly upheld tribal autonomy, if in decidedly limited iterations. However, Georgia disregarded these decisions, and Jackson refused to enforce them. Soon after, the illegitimate Treaty of New Echota, signed by a minority faction of Cherokees, set in motion the forcible removal of more than sixteen thousand tribe members remaining in Georgia. Between two and six thousand Native people died in the ethnic cleansing. A Choctaw chief speaking with a journalist reportedly described the forced march of exiles out of eastern lands as a "trail of tears and death."[24] That "Trail of Tears" became embedded in the popular lexicon confirms the association of Native people with loss and sadness.

The imagined scene of the Indian lament was useful for spinning a story that validated federal policy and eased fears of political resistance.[25] Both official justifications for removal and popular representations of Native grief figured Native disappearance as inevitable. In his State of the Union address of 1830, Jackson characterized the Indian Removal Act as essentially easing Native people into extinction. "Humanity has often wept over the fate of the aborigines of this country, and Philanthropy has been long busily employed in devising means to avert it, but its progress has never for a moment been arrested, and one by one have many powerful tribes disappeared from the earth," he said. "The present policy of the Government is but a continuation of the same progressive change by a milder process."[26] Representations of Native mourning extended this fantasy. Dvořák's late-century musical interpretations of Native sorrow had several predecessors in popular song, including an 1846 number, "The Indian's Lament," with the lyrics "I stand alone as the last of my race, / Upon this earth I feel I no more have a place."[27] The most famous tale of Native disappearance, James Fenimore Cooper's *The Last of the Mohicans,* ends with a funeral scene in which Chingachgook's elegy for his son shades into a lament: "my race has gone."[28]

As scholars of the "Vanishing American" topos have pointed out, romantic depictions of the last member of a tribe grieving the loss of his or her people serve a collective fantasy in which potential resistance gives way to an aesthetically pleasing melancholic resignation.[29] Dvořák's nineteenth-century reviewer unknowingly hints at the cultural work this kind of representation does: the record of systematized violence against indigenous peoples that was once marked by "blood and sweat and agony and bleaching human bones" has been effectively "buried" in the composer's interpretations. Sorrow—that of "humanity" for "the fate of aborigines," and that of the imagined last member of a tribe for the loss of his or her "race"—covers over the systematized violence responsible for Native suffering.

The work of burying a history of imperialist violence involves positioning the lingering Native mourner as at once *in* and *out of* natural place and time. Scholars have described the ways recurrent motifs of ecological or meteorological decay in Vanishing American representations—those comparing indigenous people to falling leaves, melting snow, or the decline of day, for instance—naturalize Native erasure as part of ongoing organic processes.[30] In Cooper's novel, Chief Tamenund's closing words associate Native disappearance with diurnal cycles: "The pale-faces are masters of the earth, and the time of the red-man has not yet come again. My day has been too long. In the morning I saw the sons of Unâmis happy and strong; and yet, before the night has come, have I lived to see the last warrior of the wise race of the Mohicans!"[31] The metaphors here obscure a history of colonial and expansionist violence in romantic references to natural processes. Yet something else happens here as well. As the Vanishing American rhetoric naturalizes disappearance, it makes the Native mourner a deviant hanger-on whose presence delays the forward movement of the nation. Tamenund defines the persistence of Native people on the continent as irregular and isolating. His own exit into the past is overdue; having lasted "too long" already, his sorrow comes from surviving as an aberrantly alive relic and witness to the end of a noble people. Countering his own hope that natural cycles will bring back "the time of the red-man," the chief figures himself as a pathologically remnant figure standing still in the stream of time. The scene dramatizes the Native person's failure to properly memorialize the dead by letting go and moving on.[32]

More than just defining Native death and disappearance as natural and therefore inevitable, the conventional scene of the melancholic last-of-the-tribe uses sentiment to characterize indigenous people as enervated, static, and disconnected in a dynamic, forward-moving, affiliative world. Native mourners in such representations lack both individual agency and political community. In this respect, representations of Indian mourning stand in contradistinction to the mainstream American elegy as described in recent analyses, which emphasize the form's consolidating strategies. Looking at the circulation of middle-class elegies in nineteenth-century

America, Kete argues that "sentiment . . . structures a collaboration through which individuals can join together and solve the seemingly local problem of grief in the face of death."[33] For Cavitch, elegies "establish hierarchies and communities of abjection within and against which alliances and identities are worked out."[34] Extending the idea of elegiac consolidation into the post-9/11 moment, Judith Butler contends that the public expression of loss "furnishes a sense of political community of a complex order."[35] In frontier fiction, too, mourning may bring people together across divides of race, class, or culture, if momentarily. Just prior to Tamenund's speech, Natty Bumppo and Chingachgook grasp hands "in the warmth of feeling . . . and in that attitude of friendship . . . while scalding tears fell to their feet, watering the grave of Uncas, like drops of falling rain."[36] Yet by figuring the Native mourners like Tamenund as out of time in two senses—that is, both on the brink of extinction and off the beat of human progress—scenes of Indian grief typically set the subject apart from the emotional, structural, and political communities that other expressions of mourning organize.

As they naturalize indigenous disappearance, conventional scenes of Indian mourning construct political boundaries via racialized representations of affect. They prohibit the social bonding that expressions of sentiment presumably create to address tragedy and injustice. They illustrate, then, Berlant's sense of the fundamental contradiction of conventional sentimentality. The production of emotion shared between an imagined suffering subject and a sympathetic audience, which we might think would encourage civic-minded progressive action, actually privatizes pain and reinforces its structural causes.

Cooper anticipates his concluding scene of Native mourning in an early chapter that cites a famous Indian lament poem. As chapter 3 opens, Chingachgook and Natty Bumppo debate the morality of whites' role in the decline of the Mohican tribe. The white scout justifies European American incursions into tribal territory as fair conquest: "Your fathers came from the setting sun, crossed the big river, fought the people of the country, and took the land; and mine came from the red sky of the morning, over the salt lake, and did their work much after the fashion that had been set them by yours;

then let God judge the matter between us, and friends spare their words!" His companion counters that whites' use of firearms and their introduction of alcohol in tribal communities unjustly decimated his ancestors, so that "foot by foot, they were driven back from the shores, until I, that am a chief and a Sagamore, have never seen the sun shine but through the trees, and have never visited the graves of my fathers."[37] Chingachgook's history calls momentary attention to European Americans' culpability in the disappearance of his tribe, and his complaint that he has been denied the right to grieve over the graves of his ancestors refuses the idealized closure proffered by the conventional depiction of the resigned Native mourner. And yet the conversation that precedes this complaint—a discussion of river currents and ocean tides—aligns Native disappearances with natural processes of movement and change. More significantly, the epigraph Cooper chooses for the chapter connects the disputes of the French and Indian War of the novel's setting to the racial conflicts of Cooper's own historical moment, as it presents the politically consolidating gestures of Indian lament. The epigraph, from William Cullen Bryant's 1824 poem "An Indian at the Burial-Place of His Fathers" stands out as one of only two by Cooper's American contemporaries.[38] The choice of these particular lines to open the chapter underlines the ways Native mourning could be used to support U.S. expansionist enterprises.

In Bryant's poem, a Native speaker visits the site of sacred burial grounds now covered over by farmlands. The tribe's warriors are buried and forgotten, their weapons "scattered in the furrows," their bones thrown up by the white man's plow. The process emblematizes the disempowerment of a people the speaker now remembers as "ashamed and weak," a "wasted race" that has withdrawn from the field of battle. As the language of disempowerment and decay denies Native people agency, it also conceals white responsibility for Native disappearance. The poem flirts with assigning blame when the speaker insists it is "the pale race, who waste us now," but it quickly retreats from this idea with figurative language that naturalizes and anteriorizes Native erasure: "like April snow / In the warm noon, we shrink away."[39] The farmer's plow has not caused Native people's extinction; it only unearths their remains long after they are gone. In fact, an emphasis on natural processes in the poem, on which Cooper capitalizes in selecting his epigraph, suggests the inevitability of Native disappearance. The penultimate stanza Cooper extracts from Bryant's poem presents "the standard topos of fluidity" that characterizes both elegiac expression and Vanishing American representations.[40] In it the speaker describes a time "Before these fields were shorn and tilled," when

> Full to the brim our rivers flowed;
> The melody of waters filled
> The fresh and boundless wood;
> And torrents dashed and rivulets played,
> And fountains spouted in the shade.

The final stanza of the poem, not reproduced in Cooper's novel, uses this memory of watery abundance to sound a warning note: the waterways, like the Native people who once congregated on their banks, eventually may retreat from the land now under tillage. The mournful speaker predicts that "The realm our tribes are crushed to get / May be a barren dessert yet." Still, what resonates most in the poem for Cooper, as, presumably, for white readers of the Indian lament, is not the hint of repressed guilt in the conspicuously passive construction in a poem written as the nation debated removal ("the realm our tribes are crushed to get"), but the correlation between Native disappearance and natural fluctuations in the environment. Like Cooper's chapter, the poem buries indictment of violence in images of organic transformation. A race of people disappears, snows melt, springs dry up—all are part of the cycles of biological and geological existence. If, as the Native speaker speculates, one day the white race "may vanish hence, like mine," it will be a natural process, not a moral reckoning.[41]

Where Bryant and Cooper naturalize Native disappearance, Sigourney reminds readers that the tragedy of the Vanishing American is manmade. I have already noted how the active register of the opening words of "The Cherokee Mother"—"Ye bid us hence"—indicts whites. The poem also challenges conventions that figure Native people as passive components of the environment that succumb to the forces of nature like falling leaves. The Cherokees, Sigourney's speaker reminds us, are an agricultural people: "Our hands have till'd these corn-clad grounds." They have built the homes (and schools, churches, and businesses) they are being forced to abandon. In stark contrast to Bryant's long-gone indigenes, whose bones have become part of a natural realm being transformed by the white farmer's plow, Sigourney's Cherokees are actively present, shaping the landscape themselves. Here, fluidity suggests not natural processes of change but the violence of removal. The displaced Cherokee will be forced into wastelands "where unknown waters fiercely roll." In stark contrast to Bryant, that is, Sigourney denaturalizes the iconic scene of Native loss.

Where Bryant voiced support for removal, a fellow author of the Indian lament, John Greenleaf Whittier, strongly opposed it.[42] In an 1830 editorial, Whittier, an activist-poet best known for his abolitionism, rails against "the arm of arbitrary power" poised to outrage "the eternal principles of justice, and the sacred claims of humanity" by forcibly removing Cherokees and others from their rightful homes. Yet when he evokes the familiar image of a tribal burial place, Whittier reflects a deep-seated assumption about the anteriority and inevitability of Native disappearance. "The march of civilization has been over the grave of the Indian," he writes. "Every advancing footstep has trodden him down, like an armed heel planted upon a human and beating heart."[43] The mixed metaphors here are striking: on the one hand, the government's actions are brutalities against the living, the "human and beating heart"; on the other, the disappearance of Native people is a *fait accompli* registered in the grave already being trampled by the march of civilization. Like the unearthed bones in Bryant's poem, the burial place in Whittier's protest represents Native extinction as inevitable. If it condemns unrestrained westward expansion, it also makes the disappearance of indigenous people from the continent a foregone conclusion.

Whittier's well-known antislavery poems testify to his deployment of literature as a weapon in the activist's arsenal. Still, in the rare moments when he turned to Native subjects in his poetry, he practiced a conciliatory politics. In Whittier's representations, Natives are already removed from the scene, "flitting, passing, seen and gone," as he describes them in the pointedly titled poem "The Vanishers."[44] The scene of the Indian lament naturalizes this disappearance while denying Natives the agency to fight for survival. "The Indian Girl's Lament" (1831) is presented in the voice of Shawnadithit, the celebrated last member of the Beothuk tribe of Newfoundland, who died of tuberculosis shortly before Whittier wrote his poem. Whittier follows convention in connecting Native erasure to meteorological and biological transformations. The descriptions of the sun moving across the sky, the waxing and waning of the autumn moon, "the changes of the changeful leaves," make the Beothuks' extinction seem as inevitable as the passage of time. As in Bryant's poem, the gravesite metonymically signals Native disempowerment: "The bow of strength is buried," "the spent arrow slumbereth," and "the song of war has died away." Left to mourn is a wasted symbol of tribal deterioration,

> A solitary one
> Whose life is waning into death, like yonder sinking sun!
> A broken weed, a blighted flower, that lingereth still behind,
> To mourn its faded sisterhood, and wrestle with the wind.[45]

Instead of using the Native girl's story to address the colonization that destroyed her people or to speak out against U.S. government actions, like removal, threatening tribes closer to home, Whittier depicts her mourning as a pathological hanging-on, a sign of disempowerment and alienation. Like Tamenund, she "lingereth," her "broken" and "blighted" grief almost morbid in its stagnation. So weakened is she that resistance would be as meaningless as fighting the wind. Here, again, the production of emotion privatizes public calamity, turning it into a depoliticized commodity for readers' consumption. Any condemnation of injustice gets washed away in a passive exchange of feeling, as white readers sympathize with people they cannot possibly help given the inevitability of indigenous decline.

Whittier's scene capitalizes on a cultural privileging of *feminine* affect in particular. It is not unique in this respect, as many Indian laments featured women and girls. (Bryant published his own "Indian Girl's Lament" in 1825, for example.) In such poems, grief is bound up with ideas about feminine passivity and weakness to emphasize Native peoples' incapacity for halting their slide into oblivion. In stark contrast, the sorrow displayed by Sigourney's "Cherokee Mother" signals the Native woman's defiance. Through her tears the Cherokee mother demands, "Why should we from these haunts remove?" The distance between Whittier's poetic representation of Native resignation and decline and the outrage in his anti-removal writing suggests that literary conventions of female sentiment could overwhelm even the most deeply felt political intentions. And yet Sigourney found ways to redirect feminine tears so as to accommodate expressions of political resistance.

Another Sigourney poem, "Indian Girl's Burial" revises Indian lament conventions in ways that more explicitly challenge its idealizations. The poem describes a Sac mother mourning beside the grave of her daughter as an unfeeling white crowd looks on:

> A voice upon the prairies
>   A cry of woman's woe,
> That mingleth with the autumn blast
>   All fitfully and low;
> It is a mother's wailing;
>   Hath Earth another tone
> Like that with which a mother mourns
>   Her lost her only one?
>
> Pale faces gather round her,
>   They mark'd the storm swell high
> That rends and wrecks the tossing soul,
>   But their cold, blue eyes are dry.
> Pale faces gaze upon her,
>   As the wild winds caught her moan,
> But she was an Indian mother,
>   So she wept alone.[46]

Initially, the mother's sorrow defines an essential femininity that could be radically equalizing. "A mother's wailing" is a universal tone that transcends boundaries of race and nation. But the possibility of radical unity disintegrates quickly, as "a mother" becomes "an Indian mother," the object of racialized spectacle. Rather than mark the universality of maternal love, the Native mother's feelings set her apart as something for "pale faces" to "gaze upon."

This scene revises the standard Indian lament by widening the frame on the scene of Native mourning. In the conventional Indian lament, the grieving subject is isolated and the witness unnamed; the reader consuming her suffering remains an offstage, privileged observer. Here, Sigourney zooms out to focus on whites watching the mother as she mourns. The unfeeling gazes of those gathered near the grave put the lie to the idea that reform-minded whites shared in Natives' suffering under colonization and expansion. Racism prohibits real sympathy: the dying girl suffered the ravages of consumption, "But she was an Indian maiden, / So none deplor'd her pain." Indigenous sorrow becomes ethnographic display, and not just for those white observers at the burial. Although Sigourney was inspired by the newspaper report of a scene in Wisconsin Territory, the descriptions in the poem of the mother's and daughter's deserted cabin, couch, and seat, "lone and empty all," and their fields of corn left to "ripen on the plain," recall the cold hearthstone and the "corn-clad grounds" left behind in "The Cherokee Mother."[47] "Indian Girl's Burial" thus obliquely links its subject's misery to that of the thousands of southeastern Native people suffering removal. If the Native girl's burial is a spectacle for white consumption, so too is the suffering of Native people on the "Trail of Tears."

In this sense, the poem performs both political protest and metaliterary critique and revision. In staging white spectators' cold response to the mother's grief, "Indian Girl's Burial" condemns non-Native consumption of Native suffering and the disingenuousness of expressions of white sympathy. Here Sigourney dramatizes the practice of reading conventional Indian lament poetry: like the whites at the graveside, the readers of popular poetry passively consume scenes of Native sorrow. Meanwhile, Sigourney's revision of the Indian lament recuperates that sorrow as a potential agent of resistance. Despite her alienation, there is neither resignation nor debility in the mother's outpouring of grief. Meteorological metaphors point not to the naturalness of Native disappearance but to the force of the mourning figure's emotional response, an internal storm that rivals the "autumn blast" and "wild winds." In sum, Sigourney's poem makes interventions both political and poetic. It reveals the hollowness of white sympathy for the Vanishing American, it breaks down the division between private loss and public policy, and it redeploys Native female feeling as an instrument of empowered resistance.

Whittier's "Indian Girl's Lament" suggests how the culture of femininity redrew a line between sentiment and political action at the very moment when women were entering into public debates about Native rights. Sigourney's "Indian Girl's Burial" reclaims the political force of feminine sentiment. The rhetoric of the women's anti-removal effort, to which I now turn, ostensibly bridged the gap between female feeling and public action. Women anti-removalists presented feminine sympathy as justification for their activism; theoretically, they made women's tears instruments for changing the world. But conflicts and contradictions emerged in their deployment of generic sentimentality. Against the retracted female political power posited in women's anti-removal rhetoric, Sigourney exposes the emptiness of sympathy and redeploys indigenous and womanly feelings for a more meaningful protest.

Protest in the Empire of Affection

The white women's anti-removal effort was spurred by the 1830 publication of "Circular Addressed to the Benevolent Ladies of the U. States" by Sigourney's friend Catharine Beecher. Like Whittier, Beecher expressed anxiety about the national sin of removal, a "wicked project" that she believed would turn the United States into a "guilty land." Given the threat of such a moral failing, she asks, "Have not then the females of this country some duties devolving upon them in relation to this helpless race?" Her "Circular" sets out a powerful argument for white women's involvement in debates over removal. For Beecher, woman's higher moral character and deeper sensitivity obliged her to intervene, as "to woman it is given to administer the sweet charities of life, and to *sway the empire of affection*." But the essay's closing statement raises questions about how far such protest should go. "Let every woman who peruses [the "Circular"], exert that influence in society which falls within her lawful province," Beecher writes, "and endeavour by every suitable expedient to interest the feelings of her friends, relatives, and acquaintances, in behalf of this people, that are ready to perish."[48] Woman should influence public debate only from her "lawful province," the private sphere. "Suitable" female political activity involved stimulating the feelings of those (presumably male) friends, relatives, and acquaintances authorized to shape policy; it did not include testing the boundaries of acceptable gender behavior.

As Alisse Portnoy points out, the women's anti-removal movement was "novel, but not radical."[49] In responding to Beecher's call, women petitioners against removal asserted their authority as citizens, claiming, in the words of the first of their appeals to Congress, "a right to speak on the subject."[50] But they simultaneously defined themselves and the Native people for whom they spoke as disconnected from the operations of politics and power. The contradictions in women's anti-removal letters and petitions—the assertion of female political authority that was simultaneously a disavowal of agency—resulted in self-limiting protest. Drawing on gendered conventions of sentiment that positioned white women and Natives as the objects of white male activity, these expressions subsumed radical impulses under that consolidating realm of feeling, the "*empire of affection.*"

Beecher's phrase is fascinating in its implication of a connection between sentimentalism and imperialism. Amy Kaplan identifies that connection in Beecher's writings on housekeeping, where "domestic discourse both redresses and reenacts the contradictions of empire through its own double movement to expand female influence beyond the home and the nation while simultaneously contracting woman's sphere to police domestic boundaries against the threat of foreignness both within and without."[51] We can interrogate Beecher's use of sentimental discourse in her anti-removal essay in similar fashion. How does an emphasis on feminine feeling in the "Circular" relate to processes of expansion? What are the political costs of voicing protests through conventional representations of white, female, and Native American feelings? In distinguishing a feminine realm organized around "the sweet charities of life" from a presumably unfeeling masculine public arena, Beecher meant to disrupt the removal process. She proposed a radically democratic bond that could challenge assumptions about racial hierarchies, with white female sympathy for oppressed Native people, who are also set apart in a realm of affect as melancholic subjects, creating a cross-racial association that would counter the divisive strategies of U.S. Indian policy. White women involved in the anti-removal movement ostensibly felt for and *with* oppressed Native people. But the use of sentimental conventions in women's anti-removal rhetoric amounted to a contraction of the capacity to resist U.S. national agendas and establish cross-racial bonds.

The specter of a federal removal policy prompted a contentious public exchange—Martin Van Buren, vice president under Jackson at the time, later wrote that "a more persevering opposition to a public measure had scarcely ever been made"—and the moral terms of the debate made possible women's involvement on an unprecedented scale.[52] The best-known male anti-removalists were spiritual leaders. On the Senate floor, Theodore Frelinghuysen of New Jersey, whom William Lloyd Garrison dubbed the "Christian statesman," led the opposition.[53] Eleazar Lord, a businessman who presided over the New York Sunday School Union and served in the American Home Mission Society, was an anti-removal organizer, as were religious reformer Reverend George Cheever and Beecher's father, Reverend Lyman Beecher. The architect of the petition movement was evangelist Jeremiah Evarts, author of the widely read "William Penn" essays protesting removal.[54] For Evarts, a Yale-trained lawyer turned missionary, at stake was nothing less than "the soul of America."[55] Henry Clay, Jackson's opponent in the 1832 presidential race, recognized a natural affiliation between Evarts's moral arguments and middle-class white women's piety, and in 1830 he advised Evarts to recruit women to the anti-removal cause.[56] Evarts was already a step ahead. While visiting with his friend Lyman Beecher in 1829, he told the minister's eldest daughter, "American women might save these poor, oppressed natives."[57] Inspired, Catharine Beecher wrote the "Circular" and distributed it to members of women's benevolent societies in several cities. In addition to

Sigourney, women drawn to the anti-removal effort included literary luminary Lydia Maria Child and abolitionist Angelina Grimké.

In petitioning Congress to halt removal, American women laid claim to political power more forcefully than they ever had before, and they gendered their politics female. While individual women had long used petitioning as a means of asserting the rights of the disenfranchised, the anti-removal movement was the first collective effort by women to lobby federal representatives. The cooperative and wide-reaching action of women's anti-removal petitioning reflected a decided advance in women's political power, Susan Zaeske notes, for "by sending their petitions directly to Congress, women who opposed Cherokee removal advanced a step beyond benevolent ladies who limited their petitioning to local bodies and often employed a male intermediary."[58] Amy Dunham Strand argues that because petitioning in itself asserted women's rights to be heard by their government, the women's anti-removal movement can be seen as a precursor to demands for enfranchisement.[59] The transgressive nature of this assertion of female agency did not go unnoticed; men on both sides of the debate expressed anxiety about women's intervention in policy debates. Garrison initially viewed women's petitioning on behalf of the Cherokee with alarm. In his antislavery newspaper *Genius of Universal Emancipation,* he called a petition signed by seven hundred Pittsburgh women an "uncalled for interference" in public proceedings, and he worried that if women's petitions were accepted, "there would then be no question agitated in Congress, without eliciting the informal and contrariant [*sic*] opinions of the softer sex."[60] The pro-removal chairman of the Congressional Committee on Indian Affairs, Thomas Hart Benton, was blunter: "I would recommend it to these ladies, not to douse their bonnets, and tuck up their coats, for such a race, but to sit down on the way side, and wait for the coming of the conquerors."[61]

Although Benton suggested female petitioners enacted a kind of cross-dressing performance of male authority, taking off their bonnets and shortening their coats to enter a male arena, women anti-removalists saw their intervention as essentially female. Beecher's essay draws a careful distinction between women's and men's political practices: women "may *feel* for the distressed" in ways men do not.[62] Similarly, many petition writers who answered Beecher's call defined their activity as uniquely grounded in feminine sentiment. Women anti-removal petitioners in Steubenville, Ohio, describe their intervention as an expression of "the small voice of *female* sympathy."[63] A Huntsburgh, Ohio, petition signed by fifty-four women uses the same language as a petition signed by Huntsburgh men in the town, except that it adds an introductory statement describing the petitioners as acting "with modesty & reverence becoming our Sex & with all the ardour of female tenderness."[64] Such qualifications make space for feminine sympathy in the political realm and present an explicitly gendered protest.

Repositioning feminine sympathy in the public sphere, women's anti-removal rhetoric disrupts the partisan structures and social hierarchies that constituted U.S. political deliberation. "Sentimentalists strive to save the political from politics," asserts Berlant; they tend to vilify conventional political activity as ethically compromised and in conflict with ideals of national unity.[65] Women anti-removalists thus describe themselves as transcending the competitive world of public debate, positing a female political activism that is distinctly, and paradoxically, apolitical. Their lack of party affinity becomes another justification for their intervention.[66] In her "Circular," Beecher argues that women are "protected from the binding influence of party spirit, and the asperities of political violence." Unlike men, she insists, they "have nothing to do with any struggle for power, nor any right to dictate the decisions of those that rule over them."[67] Women petitioners from Lewis, New York, likewise "disclaim any intention or ever wish to interfere with the political ritations [*sic*] of the general government."[68] Steubenville petitioners begin with a similar disavowal and add a veiled condemnation of "ordinary" partisan politics: "Your memorialists would sincerely deprecate any presumptuous interference on the part of their own sex, with the ordinary political affairs of the country, as wholly unbecoming the character of American Females."[69] Monson, Massachusetts, anti-removal women imaginatively position themselves far from the halls of Congress, in a female realm where only "the melting cries of the oppressed have broken in on the stillness of our retirement."[70] Likewise, the letter in the *Cherokee Phoenix* preceding Sigourney's "The Cherokee Mother" posits a female transcendence of normative politics: "Disclaiming in truth, every political motive, every party prejudice, we simply ask your pity for our Indian brethren in the name of our common Redeemer."[71] Their outsider status authorizes women anti-removalists; as Strand argues, "it is precisely women's extra-political position that grants them the right to intervene on behalf of others."[72]

At the same time, the reference in the *Cherokee Phoenix* letter to "our common Redeemer" exemplifies the ways women's anti-removal rhetoric sought to form radically democratic bonds through an appeal to Christian humanism. The Steubenville women petitioners ask for "*all* who can feel the woes of humanity" to halt removal; Monson petitioners appeal "in behalf of suffering humanity."[73] Beecher makes women's intervention in the crisis the product of a timeless and universal tradition of womanly mediation when she compares it to the Old Testament story of Esther. As Portnoy points out, Beecher's use of the Biblical tale allows her to "put God's word above the United States' conventions regarding women's participation in this federal debate."[74] Such rhetorical maneuvering radically recasts relations between Natives and non-Natives, positioning them as affiliates in the fight against injustice.

Woman's special status places her above the law, Beecher suggests in the "Circular": "It may be, that female petitioners can lawfully be heard, even by the highest rulers of our land. . . . It may be this will be *forbidden;* yet still we remember the Jewish princess who, being sent to supplicate for a nation's life, was thus reproved for hesitating even when *death* stared her in the way."[75] The repeated hypotheticals here signal the uncertainty of women's relationship to the U.S. government: "it may be" lawful for a woman to speak out, but such unprecedented interference "may be" forbidden. The petitioner's legal status hardly matters, however; because woman is obligated to God and humanity first, she must act even when her intervention is unprecedented or disallowed. Like the Jewish petitioner Esther, women of the anti-removal effort are governed by a higher law.

In this formulation, the white anti-removalist woman's transcendence of man's law links her to the Native person for whom she advocates. Beecher objects to the enforcement of state laws aimed at subjugating southeastern tribes, such as Georgia statutes nullifying Cherokee legislation or forbidding Creek or Cherokee witnesses from testifying in court. While she warns of the devastating effects such laws will have on Georgia tribes, she also suggests that Native people, like women, transcend them. "The Indians have never been subject to any man," Beecher writes. "They consist of different, free-born, independent tribes. They are attached to their native soil, and have again and again refused to relinquish it. They know they have a perfect *natural* right to it."[76] Like women's moral authority, Native people's "*natural* right" supersedes the laws the state or nation would impose. At least provisionally, the "Circular" posits female and Native subjectivities that contest established authority and structure unprecedented political coalitions.

Apolitical, supranational, radically inclusive, and extralegal, women anti-removal activists would seem to be extraordinarily unruly subjects. Yet Beecher's condoning of "*forbidden*" female political action is contradicted by her concluding warning that woman must operate within her "lawful province." To make the leap from potentially forbidden intervention to that which is strictly lawful, Beecher fits the activist woman into a cultural convention that mitigates the political agency she has just invoked. Just after she authorizes women's political intervention, Beecher invokes a classical model of white male activity and female passivity: "In the days of chivalry, at the female voice, thousands of lances would have been laid in rest to protect the helpless and oppressed."[77] It is worth pausing on the curious involution here, which grants "the female voice" the authority to arrest male action even as it draws on a tradition predicated on women's powerlessness. A class of chivalric American men, Beecher suggests, will emerge from a cultured masculine elite sensitive to the "female voice" of intervention: "The liberal and refined, those who are delighted with the charms of eloquence and poetry; those who love the legends of romance, and the records of antiquity; those who celebrate and admire the stern virtues of Roman warriors and patriots; will these permit a race to be swept from the earth?"[78] This appeal constructs, by implication, a new political geometry. The conflict described is between "liberal and refined," chivalric (northern) white men who might be swayed by her appeal and the presumably unrefined (southern) white men supporting removal, rather than between white men and Native people or between white male legislators and white female protesters. As agency shifts away from victims and advocates, "the female voice" becomes a catalyst for white patriarchal power.

In Beecher's modern American chivalry, both the Native people subject to removal and the white women supporting their cause come under white male authority. The Cherokees previously described as "independent nations and distinct communities" become "oppressed and threatened" groups who need "protection and help." Beecher quotes a chief who describes his tribe as entirely powerless: "Our hands are not strong. We are a small people; we do not know much. The king of Mississippi has strong arms, many warriors, and much knowledge. He is about to lay his laws upon us; we are distressed."[79] The language here suggests a particularly gendered vulnerability, with the governor's intention to "lay his laws upon" the distressed Cherokees evoking the specter of sexual assault. Further, such laws included provisions that no Creek or Cherokee individual could serve as witness in a court of law, a circumstance that Beecher suggests left indigenous women and children doubly vulnerable: "Even their wives and children could be murdered before their eyes, and no Indian might approach a court of justice to testify of wrongs received."[80] Beecher's reference to such statutes calls attention to the parallel legal situation of white women and Native people, both denied a voice in the nation's political and judicial processes. And yet the picture of murdered wives and children reinforces this exclusion by transforming Native agency into victimhood.

In a similar way, Beecher makes white women themselves vulnerable under the threat of removal, for forced removal of tribes would be a national crime that would incur the wrath of God. She asks readers to "ponder with dread and awe these fearful words of Him, who thus forbids the violence, and records the malediction of those, who either as individuals, or as nations, shall oppress the needy and helpless. . . . '*If thou afflict them, and they cry at all unto me, I will surely hear their cry: and my wrath shall wax hot, and I will kill you with the sword, and your wives shall be widows, and your children fatherless.*' "[81] Strikingly, in this concluding gesture Native victims of removal disappear to be replaced by (presumably) non-Native women and children, the collateral damage of God's anger at the injustice of removal, the modern version of the widows and fatherless children of Exodus 22. In Beecher's shifting formulation, transcendent female sympathy grants women agency only momentarily.

Like Beecher, other white women anti-removalists situated themselves firmly within the conventional structures of race and gender that authorized white men. Steubenville women petitioners address legislators as "the constitutional protectors of the Indians within our territory" who must act to "save this remnant of a much injured people from annihilation" and "shelter the American character from lasting dishonor."[82] A petition by women of Hadley, Massachusetts, asks members of Congress to "interpose your lawful authority and rescue this defenceless [*sic*] people from injustice" and "spread over them the shield of . . . protection." Similarly, a petition by Abington, Massachusetts, women begs Congress to "extend to [Native people] your powerfull [*sic*] protection. . . . Shield them from the horrors of the threatening storm."[83] Newburyport, Massachusetts, women petitioners appeal to legislators to "save our country from the imputation of fraud & tyranny" that would result from implementing the Treaty of New Echota.[84] In asking white men to fulfill their roles as the protectors of vulnerable Natives and white women, these texts reinforce conventional gender and race hierarchies that deny agency to the marginalized.

Some petitions inspired by the "Circular" similarly apply conventions of chivalry to the removal issue. The Steubenville, Ohio, women's petition includes a celebration of white American men, whose respect for and deference to women, "an honorable and distinguishing trait," has "often excited the admiration of intelligent foreigners." The petition goes on, "When, therefore, injury and oppression threaten to crush a hapless people within our borders, we, the feeblest of the feeble, appeal with confidence to those who should be the representatives of national virtue as they are the depositories of national powers, and implore them to succor the weak & unfortunate."[85] The appeal asks the men of Congress to live up to their reputation for chivalry by attending to women's concerns and protecting both white women and Native people. It expressly links women anti-removalists, "the feeblest of the feeble," to the Native subjects of removal, "a hapless people," making both groups the passive objects of white male violence or protection. In this articulation, women's intervention reinforces rather than dismantles social hierarchies. The feminine feelings that ostensibly authorized the American mothers' and daughters' political activity now endorse established "depositories of national powers."

The letter in the *Cherokee Phoenix* similarly links white women anti-removalists and the Cherokees for whom they advocate, not as political subjects but as objects of white male action. "Anxiety for the fate of that portion of our aborigines who are in danger of dismission from their native territory, has painfully oppressed our minds," the writer declares. "Nor will it be deemed unnatural that the cause of the helpless should excite commiseration in a sex whom nature has taught both the *need* and the *value* of protection." Here, shared feeling does not condition women's and Native people's inclusion in the civic body; rather, it confirms their marginality as the "oppressed." The letter suggests feminine sympathy authorizes women's intervention only to galvanize white males: "After having manifested that feeling which it would have been painful to suppress, we count it a privilege to submit its guidance to a wisdom which we do not possess, and a power to which we have neither the right, nor the ambition to aspire. We have also confidence to believe that a delegation from the *State of Connecticut* will not disregard an appeal for justice and mercy, however humble its source."[86] Feminine politics sustained by "manifested . . . feeling" only goes so far. Conventional gender ideology requires ceding the political ground the letter initially claims.

These shifts reflect the tendency toward autoerasure that Berlant identifies in sentimental politics, which "works on behalf of its own eradication."[87] Women's anti-removal rhetoric reflexively converts the threat of disruption it introduces into an expression of continuity. That conversion is most evident in Beecher's "Circular" in the gap between her biblical allusions: the courageous and independent Esther is a far cry from the defenseless women of Exodus 22, those vulnerable widows who would suffer should their husbands provoke God's wrath. Esther acts; the widows suffer the consequence of men's actions. Beecher entered into removal debates inspired by Jeremiah Evarts's suggestion that women could help Native people find justice, but she closes her "Circular" with a focus on masculine intervention. In attempting to constitute an acceptable, "lawful" form of female mediation, the rhetoric of women anti-removalists withdraws the political agency it nominally grants.

Given this impasse, it is little wonder that Beecher found herself retreating from the position, voiced at the opening of the "Circular," that women are duty bound to intervene politically in the nation's conflicts over race. When, within a few years of the publication of her "Circular," Beecher addressed the suitability of women's petitions to Congress to protest slavery, she deemed them "IN ALL CASES, to fall entirely without the sphere of female duty."[88] "Twenty years before Harriet Beecher Stowe showcased feeling in *Uncle Tom's Cabin* as the spark for ethical behavior," Kilcup argues, "Sigourney and her activist colleagues established a feminine rhetorical authority that effectively combined accommodation and subversion."[89] Yet the "Circular" and Beecher's eventual conclusions cancel out the possibility of subverting established structures of power.

Kilcup's comment raises another question: to what degree did Sigourney participate in the compromised sentimental politics of the women's anti-removal movement, and to what extent did she resist such politics? Sigourney convened the Hartford women's anti-removal group and helped distribute Beecher's essay; there was popular speculation that Sigourney authored the "Circular."[90] She likely wrote the letter published in the *Cherokee Phoenix* on behalf of "an Association of Ladies," as she served as the group's secretary.[91] I have been arguing here, however, that Sigourney's poetry on Native issues rejects the rhetorical strategies of the women's anti-removal movement. Whatever her involvement in writing the prose pieces, she exploited the expressive latitude of poetry to protest removal in a way that did not compromise the possibilities of female and Native political agency. Her poems specifically protesting removal focus a more critical eye on the contradictions of sentimental politics. These works are frankly admonitory in their address and countersentimental in their critical capacities. They exert pressure on the central assumption that white female sympathy will compensate for

Native suffering. The difference between the poetry and prose suggests that Sigourney found leverage for pushing against the constraints of convention in imaginative literature.

The poems about removal directly challenge the integrity of white sympathy and at the same time privilege Native feeling as a powerful force for change. In "The Cherokee Mother," expressions of white sentiment that should halt removal are revealed as disingenuous, variations on the "*broken faith*" that has long characterized white intentions toward the continent's indigenous peoples. White bystanders celebrate as Natives suffer; Cherokee expressions of "deep despair" reverberate against white bystanders' "festive songs." The assertion "*Ye call us brethren*" registers irony not just because of its syntactical relation to the opening phrase ("Ye bid us hence"), but also because the context of forced exile reveals its deceit. The counterfeit nature of white sympathy haunts the scene of removal.

Another poem, "Remonstrance of the Creek Indians against Being Removed from Their Own Territory" (1827) similarly registers the absence of real sympathy for suffering Native people. The speaker asks readers to look at the land from which the Creeks are being driven as something other than property to be appropriated:

> See ye those mounds so green and fair,
> Where rest the dews, where smiles the sky?
> There sleeps our father's dust and there
> Our own shall lie.
>
> See ye these vales? Our children rose
> Like plants within their peaceful glade,
> And where our lifeless forms repose
> Shall theirs be laid.

The mounds and vales of Creek territory are the forging grounds of sentiment, sustaining human attachments that transcend boundaries between living and dead. The Creeks ask only for the right to remain in the place where they can continue to feel for their loved ones, to visit the graves of their forebears and "dejected sigh o'er buried years, / And sooth [*sic*] their frowning heroes' shade / With bitter tears." Sentimental literature ostensibly encourages readers to shed tears alongside the victims of injustice, but the poet insists in the closing stanza that the Creeks' outpouring of feeling has been met with "hatred."[92] Despite the speaker's plea to white readers to "see" Creek suffering differently, no sympathetic identification or compassion emerges. The concluding emphasis on hatred rejects conventional fantasies in which political conflicts find resolution in shared sentiment.

In the absence of white sympathy, Sigourney recasts Native feeling as a political force in its own right. The poem's title suggests a political, not poetic, articulation: like a memorial or a petition, a remonstrance is an official document directed at a governing body. In marrying the language of official political appeal to sentimental discourse, the poet constructs a new kind of politics, one that mobilizes feeling without abdicating marginalized figures' authority to enter into public deliberation. As in "The Cherokee Mother," lament shades into confrontation. The last two stanzas transform Native mourning into an emblem of resistance, with italics emphasizing a spirit of defiance:

> Though hatred arm oppressive foes,
> And war invade their sad retreat,
> Still, where their *earliest* breath arose,
> *Their last shall fleet.*[93]

Like "The Cherokee Mother," and "Indian Girl's Burial," "Remonstrance of the Creek Indians" performs an immanent critique of the sentimental by mobilizing the scene of Native mourning. Sigourney deploys sentimental convention through the Creeks' tears, but she refutes the operating fiction of the Indian lament, the assumption that Native mourning signals resignation.

Indian lament poetry and women's anti-removal rhetoric reverberated against one another in the obfuscation or idealization of white male agency and the sublimation of resistance. These forms give voice to the marginalized, to the Native figure bemoaning the disappearance of his or her tribe and the disenfranchised middle-class white woman suffering anxiety over the fate of the dispossessed. They do so, however, only to confine the speakers to scripts that reinforce the very structures of authority that have occasioned Native and white female distress in the first place. Although the Indian lament covers over the violence of U.S. Indian policy while women's anti-removal rhetoric putatively protests against it, they perform the same consolidating function of enlisting the oppressed in national projects that subjugate them. I have been arguing that when read in the context of Indian lament poetry and women's anti-removal rhetoric, Sigourney's poems on Native subjects reveal a complex engagement with both political and literary modes of expression. In the remainder of this chapter, I consider the evolution of this engagement in Sigourney's historical poetry on Native Americans. Sigourney struggled over the course of the removal era to reimagine the conventions that gave support to structures of power. Differences between her epic *Traits of the Aborigines of America* (1822) and long poem "Pocahontas" (1841) reveal her increasing unease with the inherent contradictions of politico-sentimental discourse and her growing pessimism about the reparative capacities of popular literature.

Epic Protest: *Traits of the Aborigines of America*

Sigourney's first published work on Native Americans was also the longest and most ambitious poem of her entire career. Yet *Traits of the Aborigines of America,* the poet would later reflect, "was singularly unpopular, there existing in the community no reciprocity with the subject."[94] Sigourney's comment understates the dissent voiced in the text, which over the course of five cantos and more than four thousand heavily footnoted lines condemns the violent course of European colonization and European American expansion. The poem's repeated, historically specific censure of colonization sets it apart from other white-authored epics that uncritically rehearse the Vanishing American myth, such as Sarah Wentworth Morton's *Ouabi* (1790) and James Eastburn's and Robert Sand's *Yamoyden* (1820).[95] Sigourney's history begins with Columbus and his crew, whose "secret aim / Was theft and cruelty," and it describes the typical colonizer as "snatch[ing] / His trophies from the savage, with a hand / More savage still."[96] Rather than burying European invasion in the past, the poem places it in a historical trajectory, delineating its specific and ongoing effects. The poem's blank verse construction and its heavy use of enjambment link it to the rhetorical arguments on Native rights circulating in the poet's day, some of which Sigourney references in her detailed footnotes.[97] As Tiya Miles argues, the poem reflects the influence of Sigourney's correspondence with a Cherokee woman, Peggy Scott Vann Crutchfield, who was active in Cherokee women's anti-removal efforts.[98]

One way Sigourney voices protest in the epic is by repurposing the conventional scene of the Indian lament. Canto III, the structural center of the poem, opens with a classic description of a Native chief mourning a tribe "banish'd and lost, of whom not one remains, / To pour their tears for him" (89, III:18–19).[99] It then meanders through topics drawn from ethnographies and popular histories, with long passages devoted to the sophistication of Native healing arts, the retelling of a romantic Sioux legend, and an admonitory speech by the Seneca chief Corn-Planter. But at the core of the canto is a question posed to a group of Native delegates on a visit to New York that returns readers to the opening scene of mourning. Viewing the domes and spires of Manhattan, the delegates become despondent. Their "unmov'd" white hosts inquire, "Why are ye sad?" (110, III:482, 484). The host's question is one the Indian lament refuses to ask. By presenting Native suffering as the result of natural decline and disappearance, conventional Indian laments suggest that whites need only acknowledge Native sorrow to bring closure to the process of Native erasure. Sigourney's scene, in contrast, requires readers to reflect on the systematized European American violence that occasions that sorrow.

The delegates answer their hosts with a catalogue of injuries dealt their people by Europeans and European Americans. This leads the speaker to contemplate the deep history of Western crimes against humanity across the globe and then to turn to more local and recent crimes. The canto closes with a series of descriptions of U.S. military assaults on southeastern tribes that extend to the moment of Sigourney's writing: the 1783 massacre of Christian Delaware Indians on the Muskingum River; the 1788 murder of Cherokee Chief Malaanthe (Old Tassel) under a flag of truce; the 1813 killing of Creek women and children in a brutal attack on Tallushatchee village during the Creek War; and the 1818 attack by Georgia militia on Creek men, women, and children at Chehaw village during the First Seminole War (126–28; III:841–905).[100] The index of violence forces recognition of the connections between past colonization and present depredations. It also subverts romanticized conventions of the Indian lament by associating the delegates' tears with the U.S. government's most recent depredations.

The finale of this canto fully politicizes both the opening scene of a chief mourning the eradication of his tribe and the central scene in which sorrowful delegates read a history of European American brutality and theft in the architecture of the city. The recital of recent outrages against Native people anticipates Sigourney's anti-removal activism: the 1813 and 1818 military attacks on non-hostile Creeks in Tennessee and Georgia, for which Andrew Jackson was a commanding officer, inflamed sentiments against Jackson and his Indian policy as the government moved toward removal.[101] Sigourney presses on readers a sensational, present-tense description of the 1818 massacre in which

> Angry bands
> Urge wide the work of death. Tir'd day declines
> Yet still their hands unshrinking clench the sword
> Reeking in gore. (127, III:877–80)

In doing so, she remakes the Indian lament into an instrument for holding the nation accountable for its sins. "Who are these, / Red from the bloody wine-press, with its stains / dark'ning their raiment?" her speaker demands of white readers, before offering an answer that reverses racist convention: these savage "redskins" are none other than "Thy Countrymen!" (129, III:905–7, 910).

The root cause of military brutality toward indigenous people is captured in the New York host's lack of sympathy. Like the consumers of the Indian lament, he is an unmoved spectator. But *Traits of the Aborigines of America* does not refuse the possibility of politically transformative emotion; rather, it defines white affect as a not-yet-actualized vehicle for change. Building on the revolutionary potential of feeling, Sigourney's epic suggests, requires establishing its relationship to specific political acts, both destructive and redemptive. Unlike the writers of conventional Indian laments, Sigourney binds sympathy to accountability and reparation: rather than remaining unmoved, whites "ought to weep / O'er [the Indians'] deep woes, and send a cordial balm / To heal the wounds, made by our fathers' swords" (117, III:637–39). In the speaker's view, white sentiment can begin to redress the profound injustices of the frontier, but only if whites honestly acknowledge the pain they have inflicted.

Nonetheless, the poem does not fully rise above the social politics of its moment. The imperative to feel for and with the oppressed should affirm the equality of human subjects, but the final sections of the poem reinforce subjugating structures of race and gender. As Baym points out, Sigourney's heavy promotion of Christian evangelism and assimilation efforts in the last two cantos reflects an assumption of the superiority of European American cultural traditions.[102] If *Traits of the Aborigines of America* admonishes whites to take responsibility for Native suffering, it also advocates a white Christian paternalism that defers reparations to the afterlife. "Their heritage / On earth ye cancel," the speaker intones, "oh! provide a home / In future worlds" (132, IV:46–48). At the same time, the poem defines white women's duty to intervene on behalf of the subjugated in ambivalent terms that anticipate Beecher's backpedaling on female political agency. The speaker asks white middle-class women, "who reign in the mild sphere / Of sweet domestic pleasure," to

> think of your humbled sex,
> 'Mid those degraded tribes the lowest still,
> Bearers of burdens, tillers of the earth,
> Cut off from every joy reciprocal
> That sweetens life, and so opprest with woe
> As in despairing horror to destroy
> Their female offspring, lest they too should share
> Their servitude and misery—oh think,
> Think! of these sisters. Think of that blest word,
> That pure religion, which has raised your lot
> To what it is, and if warm Pity move
> The tear, the wish to rescue from despair

But one sad suffering slave, if Love inspire
To follow Him, who *went to seek* the lost,
Oh speak, and it is done. (173, V:437–51)

This sensationalistic passage at once calls for sympathetic bonds and draws dividing lines between Native and non-Native "sisters." It rehearses a racist ethnography that defines women in traditional Native communities as unimaginably degraded, and it uses affect to extend the distinctions between white and indigenous women. Sympathy and pity flourish in the privileged "mild sphere" of white, middle-class domesticity, while Native women are so broken by their degraded state as to be driven to infanticide.

The passage also minimizes the possibilities for white women's political intervention by decoupling feminine sympathy from civic action. It confines white women's protest to private contemplation ("Think!"). The correlative charge to "speak" anticipates women anti-removal activists' insistence on their "right to speak" about U.S. Indian policy, yet the simplistic relationship between speech and social change, as well as the pointed failure to define what change must happen—"Oh speak, and it is done"—suggests the limitations of the agency constructed here. Feeling privatizes experience, resistance dissolves into a fantasy of magical Christian redemption, and female political agency becomes little more than an abstract gesture. In this appeal, the imperative for women's sentimental activism collapses under the weight of its own contradictions. Sympathy presumably crosses boundaries of race, but to be moved by the suffering of others is not necessarily to act on others' behalf in meaningful ways.

"Useless Things": "Pocahontas" and the Limits of Sentimental Politics

Sigourney would later reveal a more complex understanding of the relationship between feminine feeling and political realities. In the middle of her long poem on the life of Pocahontas, the poet contemplates the results of her heroine's famous display of sympathy for John Smith. Summarizing Pocahontas's rescue of the Englishman, an act that saved the embryonic American nation, Sigourney's speaker asks, "Know'st thou what thou hast done, thou dark-hair'd child? / What great events on thy compassion hung?"[103] The speaker then compares Pocahontas's act to Pharaoh's daughter's rescue of Moses in the Old Testament. As Christopher N. Phillips indicates, the comparison points to the tremendous costs of womanly sympathy, since, in the Pocahontas tale, as in the Exodus story, a heroine's rescue of an enemy leads to the downfall of her own people.[104]

In the context of the removal debate, Sigourney's question about Pocahontas's action raises a parallel question about the power of women's sympathy. By the time Sigourney composed "Pocahontas," Congress had enacted a series of gag rules that tabled women's petitions. Gag rules were intended to silence abolitionists, but they specifically targeted the only platform for middle-class American women's participation in national politics—a platform created by the women's anti-removal movement.[105] The suppression of women's political voices shadowed Sigourney's composition of "Pocahontas," but so, too, did the failure of the anti-removal effort, which could not stop the expulsion of thousands of Native people from eastern territories. Resituating "Pocahontas" in the context of the conclusion of the women's anti-removal movement reveals a felt pessimism rooted in the profound and paralyzing contradictions of the politics of feminine affect.

In offering her version of Pocahontas's life, Sigourney joined a popular trend. Countless fictional, nonfictional, dramatic, and visual representations of Pocahontas circulated in the antebellum period.[106] The history of the Pamunkey woman was so familiar that one writer could claim in his own 1837 version that "the story of my heroine is in every heart."[107] Not surprisingly, the story seeped into debates over U.S. Indian policy. It provided a literal backdrop for the legislative discussions and processes of removal: entering the Capitol's west door, congressmen on their way to debate would have passed under Antonio Capellano's 1825 sandstone relief *Preservation of Captain Smith by Pocahontas,* while John Gadsby Chapman's large mural *The Baptism of Pocahontas* was being sketched in the Capitol Rotunda as removal was implemented. (The mural would be finished the same year "Pocahontas" was published.) Those on both sides of the removal debate made use of the story's emotional power. In a speech advocating removal, Superintendent of Indian Affairs Thomas Loraine McKenney invoked Pocahontas and Massasoit, the Wampanoag sachem who saved Plymouth colonists from starvation, to suggest that their heroism amounted to a bequest of the continent to English colonizers: "Who can doubt that those generous savages gave us this country; or that, with other dispositions than those which animated them, we might not have possessed it for centuries to come, if ever?"[108] Arguing the other side of the issue in the *Cherokee Phoenix,* "Ruricola" described reading William Wirt's 1803 essay on Pocahontas in the context of the passage of the Indian Removal Act. The writer recalled enjoying the essay as a boy, "but . . . never, until after the cold hearted policy, of this administration towards the Indians, had been fully developed . . . never until then! did the sentiments expressed in that story come home to [his] heart."[109]

Sigourney capitalized on both the popularity and the political currency of the Pocahontas story. Aesthetically ambitious, "Pocahontas" borrows its unusual, modified Spenserian stanza form from English poet Felicia Hemans's epic *The Forest Sanctuary* (1825). Yet it might be said to reverse Hemans's colonizing plot: whereas *The Forest Sanctuary* tells the story of a Spaniard's conversion to Protestantism and exile in North America, the poem by "the American Hemans," as Sigourney was sometimes called, describes an indigenous subject of colonization taken to Europe.[110] Sigourney's more critical and reflective stance on colonization is reflected in an opening description of the imposition of "the evil, and the sorrow, and the crime" of Europe on an idyllic "Clime of the West" (17, 19). As in *Traits of the Aborigines,* in "Pocahontas" the poet repudiates the unreflective celebration of European conquest by characterizing English colonists as driven by avarice. They are

> Dejected men, with disappointed frown
> Spoil'd youths, the parents' darling and their dread,
> From castles in the air hurl'd ruthless down,
> The sea-bronzed mariner, the warrior brave,
> The keen gold-gatherer, grasping as the grave. (110–14)

Readers in 1841 might have reflected on the endurance of this avarice, as speculation about gold on Cherokee lands was an underlying factor in the push for removal.

Similar to other variations of the tale, Sigourney's "Pocahontas" focuses much attention on events in her heroine's life that supported colonization: not only her rescue of Smith but also her conversion to Christianity and her marriage to another Englishman, John Rolfe. However, unlike most versions, Sigourney's extends the life history to detail the heroine's journey to England with her husband and young son and her death at Gravesend in 1617. In dramatizing Pocahontas's removal (albeit voluntary), her longing for home, and her lonely death in a foreign place, the poet shifts the emphasis from the optimistic possibility of unity symbolized in cross-racial love to the heartbreak of a home and culture lost to the processes of colonization. The historical tale becomes an opportunity to explore a failure of cross-racial sentiment that reverberates in the tragedy of removal.

But to capitalize on this opportunity, Sigourney first works through the possibility that womanly feeling can radically reorganize the world. Initially, "Pocahontas" fantasizes a feminine sentiment that at once transcends politics and grants women the agency to remake relations between races. Like the rhetoric of the women's anti-removal movement and the opening stanzas of "Indian Girl's Burial," the poem attributes to women a universal sensibility that rises above political and national distinctions. This, in the speaker's words, is "woman's world":

> It matters not
> Though in the trackless wilderness she dwell,
> Or on the cliff where hangs the Switzer's cot,
> Or in the subterranean Greenland cell:
> Her world is in the heart. (352–56)

Sigourney's heroine stands in stark contrast to both European and Native men in the poem, whom the poet describes in terms that bind them intractably to national, cultural, or tribal identities and interests. Pocahontas's father, Chief Powhatan, is characterized by the firmness of his allegiances and enmities: "Unchangeable his love, invincible his hate" (144). The English colonists display a similar single-mindedness, determined as they are to erase all signs of indigeneity to recreate Europe in the New World. In renaming the James River, they "leave unsung / The uncouth baptism of a barbarous tongue" (41–42). The renaming is also a silencing that forecloses the possibility of dialogue with the indigenous inhabitants of the New World.

In light of these figurations of male partisanship, Pocahontas's universal, timeless, and essential womanly sympathy stands out, at least momentarily, as the best possibility for resolving New World conflicts. Her famous rescue of Smith dramatizes the deployment of feminine feeling to transform enmity into cross-cultural understanding: springing forward "in tearful pity bold," she "subdue[s] [Powhatan's] gather'd ire" and wins a pardon for the Englishman (161, 168). The power of Pocahontas's transcendent feminine sympathy, however, is limited. Despite her intervention, "On sped the tardy seasons, and the hate / Of the pale strangers wrung the Indian breast" (199–200). The ambiguous preposition here—who hates, the Natives or the Europeans?—suggests the complexity and depth of the conflict. Pocahontas's compassion has not relieved her people of their fears that the colonists will erase them from their earth, and her love has not transformed the white men's aggression and greed into cooperation. Among the many creative representations of Pocahontas's life that emerged in the first half of the nineteenth century, Sigourney's is rare in including the heroine's abduction by Captain Samuel Argall, despite the fact that the episode was described in antebellum colonial histories.[111] In staying true to the historical record and including Pocahontas's kidnapping at the "rude hands" of colonists who hoped to manipulate her father, Sigourney reminds readers of the brutality of the processes of colonization (255). She also indicates that the cross-racial compassion demonstrated in her heroine's multiple acts of rescue could not arrest those processes.

The failure of a woman's sympathy to remake frontier relations is nowhere more evident in the poem than in the depiction of the heroine's death in a foreign land, which resonates with the suffering of Native people in Sigourney's own historical moment. In emphasizing Pocahontas's grief when she travels to Europe, Sigourney deliberately turns away from the idea that female sympathy transcends bonds of race or culture. It may be that "her world is in the heart," but after touring her husband's ancestral mansion in England, Pocahontas dreams of her father and her home:

> An aged father, in his cabin rude,
> Mix'd with her dreams a melancholy moan,
> Notching his simple calendar with pain,
> And straining his read eye to watch the misty main.
>
> Prayer, prayer for him! when the young dawn arose
> With its gray banner, or red day declined,
> Up went his name, forever blent with those
> Most close and strong around her soul entwined,
> Husband and child; and, as the time drew near
> To fold him to her heart with filial tear,
> For her first home her warm affections pined.
> That time—it came not! for a viewless hand
> Was stretch'd to bar her foot from her green childhood's land
> (384–96)

Despite the love that binds Pocahontas to her English husband and their son, the heroine grieves what she has lost. The descriptions of the suffering of a divided Native family echo representations of removal in "The Cherokee Mother" and "Indian Girl's Burial." As in "The Cherokee Mother" and "Remonstrance of the Creek Indians," displacement denies the indigene the right to mourn her dead (or in this case, attend to their dying). Given these associations, it is no surprise that the scene leads the speaker to consider victims of nineteenth-century removal, those whose "exiled murmurings deep and low" might be heard, two centuries after Pocahontas's demise, "from the far, far west" (476, 473). The speaker laments, "I would ye were not, from your fathers' soil, / Track'd like the dun wolf" (478–79).

These connections demonstrate how "Pocahontas" offers more than what Baym describes as "a weak, sentimental, acknowledgement of national crime."[112] Baym sees Sigourney as caught in the dilemma of celebrating American Christianity and republicanism while regretting its costs. Yet there is self-consciousness and irony in the ways Sigourney enshrines Pocahontas in cultural memory. These gestures suggest a more critical assessment of both mainstream American ideals and the politics of sentiment.

The last stanza calls attention to the hypocrisy of a dominant society that remembers Pocahontas as it seeks to forget its crimes against her people.

> The council-fires are quench'd, that erst so red
>   Their midnight volume mid the groves entwined;
> King, stately chief, and warrior-host are dead,
>   Nor remnant nor memorial left behind:
> But thou, O forest-princess, true of heart,
> When o'er our fathers waved destruction's dart,
>   Shalt in their children's loving hearts be shrined;
> Pure, lonely star, o'er dark oblivion's wave,
> It is not meet thy name should moulder in the grave. (496–504)

The stanza draws a contrast between the removal of eastern tribes, whose departures and deaths merit no monument, and the legacy of Pocahontas, whose myth is cherished. The use of the term "memorial" recalls as well the very recent end of the women's antiremoval effort, when social pressures and gag rules silenced petitions to Congress, leaving no remnant of American women's organized political resistance. At the same time, the altered Spencerian stanza form here allows for an extra rhyme in the seventh line that creates a link between the erasure of indigenous people from popular history and the sentimental memorialization of Pocahontas. No record of eastern tribes is left *behind;* only Pocahontas remains *shrined* in American history. The rhyme hints at causation: remembering the "forest-princess" serves a more general forgetting of the nation's violent past. Selective memory makes Pocahontas a national heroine, "the mother of us all" in the words of a modern historian, and the bright light of mythology blinds us to national crimes, to stories of injustice that do not get told.[113] Pocahontas is thus a lonely star shining over "oblivion."

"True of heart," Pocahontas saved the colonial fathers whose descendants would dispossess, remove, and exterminate Native

Americans in Sigourney's own moment. Far from resolving the conflict between Natives and non-Natives, the heroine's affective intervention—her love for John Smith, the colonists, and John Rolfe—helped make possible the erasure of her own people. Sigourney thus indirectly registers the inherent dangers of faith in a conventional female politics of affect. Conventional feminine sympathy might be deployed in an effort to radically reconfigure relations between races and genders and contest injustice, but in the end it suspends women's agency within the familiar structures of patriarchy and empire. In this sense, the poem interrogates the politics of sentimental literature. Sigourney's adoption of the Vanishing American trope at the end of the poem, making the disappearance of Native people a foregone conclusion, might suggest that the poet had given up on the idea of altering her nation's course of expansion and genocide. The poem is politically relevant, however, in its reassessment of the potential of conventionally conceived and represented female sentiment to resolve political conflict. In the Pocahontas story, as in the women's anti-removal effort, feminine "feeling" proves no match for the relentless advance of empire.

A letter Sigourney wrote midway between the passage of the Indian Removal Act and the publication of "Pocahontas" sheds light on this fundamental reconsideration of the politics of feminine affect. The 1836 letter, to a Dr. Sprague, apparently answers a request for some of Sigourney's personal papers. Sigourney writes,

> In searching, according to your suggestion, for manuscripts which might be of no other use, I put my hands upon some obsolete documents, prepared six or seven years since, when the contested removal of our poor Cherokees, was exciting public sympathy. The plan of the Ladies' Society, who had made me their Secretary, was to obtain the signatures of their sex, as generally as possible in New England, and to present a petition to Congress, in behalf of our Aborigines. This was eventually overruled, as too bold, too political, & the papers which had been drawn up, not being used, were thrown into a repository of useless things, from whence you will perhaps think it no compliment, that I should thus rescue them, for your service.[114]

The letter identifies the problem at the heart of the women's anti-removal movement, which claimed women's right to intervene in public matters by committing to ideologies that restricted women to a private sphere. Like Beecher and others in the movement, the women of the Connecticut anti-removal society Sigourney helped organize sought to do political work without being "too political," to engage in public advocacy without appearing unladylike or "bold." The documents, presumably petitions, were discarded. Sigourney's description of the papers as "useless" registers, perhaps, her frustration with a political movement that reflexively recoiled from confrontation in the interest of adherence to social norms. But the melancholy ending of "Pocahontas" reflects her sense that literature has its own political limitations. Sigourney recognized that, despite her activist intentions, her sentimental memorial participated in erasing the nation's sins and in assigning to "oblivion" the dispossessed. The poem critiques but does not escape its own generic requirements.

If women's sympathy remains mired in conventions that render it politically ineffectual, what good can it do? As Bennett argues, the interior contradictions of literary sentimentalism could produce instances of self-conscious struggle with the problematic limits of genre.[115] Sigourney's poetry suggests how even the most reform-minded sentimentality can work against itself. "Pocahontas" calls into question its own methods, indicting middle-class sentimentality as the accomplice of settler colonialism and ruthless expansion. In the end, when the heroine's act of compassion is memorialized as an iconic display of womanly feeling, the celebration of sentiment obscures the legacy of European colonization, a legacy painfully felt by the victims of Indian removal in the poet's own day.

I do not mean to imply that "Pocahontas" marked a radical turning point in Sigourney's literary aesthetics. If the American "high priestess of sentimentality" sometimes deconstructed popular sentimentality, she nonetheless produced a great deal of it during a long career.[116] What shifted was her faith in the powers of literary expression to perform political protest. She never returned with as much passion to what she named her nation's "injustice and hard-hearted policy with regard to the original owners of the soil."[117] In the context of the failure of the women's anti-removal effort, Sigourney's treatment of the Pocahontas myth reflects skepticism about the political power of conventional sentiment. Neither Pocahontas's compassion for the colonists nor the anti-removalists' sympathy for Native people could derail the machinery of empire. Sigourney registers her awareness that gendered structures of love and sympathy are necessarily and inextricably embedded in a system that disempowered women and racial others.

The conflict between political consciousness and art reflected in Sigourney's poems on Native issues suggests a more complex picture of the uses of and responses to sentimental convention than has been acknowledged. Near the end of the century, the Muscogee (Creek) novelist S. Alice Callahan would also test the political capacities of literary sentiment to accommodate political resistance. Like Sigourney, Callahan deployed sentiment in ways that critiqued generic conventions from within. But Callahan's focus on sentimental reading, as well as writing, opens new possibilities for generating political resistance through conventional texts. Her effort to reinvent the assimilationist romance as protest literature is the subject of the next chapter.

CHAPTER THREE

Reading Lessons

Sentimental Critique in S. Alice Callahan's *Wynema: A Child of the Forest*

Early in S. Alice Callahan's 1891 novel *Wynema: A Child of the Forest,* Genevieve Weir, a white mission teacher among the Muscogee (Creek) Indians, writes home boasting of her favorite student's progress on the path toward assimilation.

> She learns faster and retains more of what she learns, than any child of whatever hue it has been my fortune to know. She is a constant reader and greets a new book with the warmth of a friend. I have directed her course of reading, and I venture to say, there is not a child in Mobile or anywhere else who has read less spurious matter than she. It is amusing to see her curl up over Dickens or Scott, and grow animated over Shakespeare, whose plays she lives out; and it is interesting to watch the different emotions, in sympathy with the various characters, chase each other over her face.[1]

The student, Wynema Harjo, stands out not merely because of her literacy but also because of her conventionally affective response to books. While her reading material would not be described as sentimental (the selection probably reflects Callahan's own favorites), she experiences texts like the typical reader of nineteenth-century sentimental literature.[2] Her reading is absorptive, affiliative, and intimate; she "curl[s] up" with Dickens and Scott, sharing the emotions of the characters on the page. As Jaime Osterman Alves suggests, this reading is notably uncritical: "Easily taken by appearances and enthralled by sweet-talking characters, the guileless girl has no idea how to distinguish between the way things seem and the very different way they may truly be."[3]

Emotionally engaging with white characters in books is part of the assimilation process. As Wynema "lives out" textual experience, James H. Cox points out, "her reading, quite literally, helps remake her in the image of an Anglo."[4] Reading does not, however, grant Wynema the privileges of white personhood. Genevieve claims Wynema's advanced literacy makes her equal to children "of whatever hue," yet that literacy anchors an education in which racialized hierarchies are reaffirmed. "Directed" by the teacher's invisible hand, the student's reading at once solidifies her attachments to white culture and objectifies her in relation to her teacher. Fittingly, the object Wynema figuratively embodies is a text: Genevieve calls the well-read girl her "*vade mecum,*" a term that suggests both Wynema's progress along the road toward assimilation (the literal translation of the Latin is "go with me") and her position as an object (a portable reference book) that Genevieve can use in her mission on the reservation (*W,* 23). Sentimental, unreflective, and carefully controlled textual experiences attach the student to white society even as these events subjugate her in relation to that society. In this way, Native literacy training supports the U.S. national policies and social projects of assimilation.

If Wynema's reading is sentimental, so too is the novel itself. It is an apparently accommodationist romance that traffics in the plot and style conventions of nineteenth-century women's literature. Scenes of distress and compassion elicit readers' sympathies as a plucky, virtuous heroine encounters obstacles on her journey toward a happy ending of domestic comfort. The conventionality of the novel, the first published by a Native American woman, has troubled contemporary critics, many of whom see a clash between Callahan's adherence to the generic requirements of sentimental literature and her political situation as a mixed-race Native woman living in Indian Territory at a time of intense political crisis. Craig

S. Womack argues that Callahan's "rigidly formulaic" "bad writing" cannot accommodate a Creek political subjectivity.[5] Melissa Ryan sees sentimentalism in the novel as supporting not Native political resistance but white women's suffrage, an agenda that further marginalizes Native people.[6] Cari M. Carpenter usefully examines anger as an underappreciated component of Native women writers' sentimentalism, but in the end she reads *Wynema* as legitimating white female rage while largely denying Native people a political voice.[7] Such interpretations find an unresolvable conflict in the novel between popular aesthetics and activist politics—between a European American mode of expression and the possibilities for indigenous resistance.

Wynema's generic sentimentalism and Wynema's uncritical, assimilative reading would appear to foreclose any possibility for Native political opposition. And yet in later chapters that call attention to the travesty of allotment, the corruption of Indian agents, and the depredations of the massacre at Wounded Knee, the novel serves as a platform for protest against U.S. Indian policy. In this chapter I explore that complex intersection of literary sentimentalism and protest, arguing that *Wynema* is significant for the ways it takes up, critiques, and remakes conventional structures of textual production and consumption. Like Frances Ellen Watkins Harper, Sui Sin Far, and other women writers of color, Callahan worked to recuperate literary sentimentalism, late in its life, for the cause of racial equality. As Susan Bernardin explains, Callahan's writing reflects "the literary and rhetorical crossings between Anglo sentimental culture and the sentimentally inflected productions of writers marked as racially 'other.' "[8] Beth Piatote (Nez Perce) sees Callahan's novel as "something more [than] or different from sentimental fiction," an intertextual and hybrid work that reconstructs the debates of the Native public sphere.[9] Building on such appraisals of the novel as aesthetically innovative, I argue that by writing a new kind of sentimental literature, Callahan is also making a case for reading sentiment differently.

I start by describing the ways sentimental literature and sentimental reading supported the ultimately subjugating aims of assimilation. A novel circulated to students at mission schools in the same year *Wynema* appeared serves to illustrate the mechanisms of what Laura Wexler terms "sentimental reeducation"—and to suggest, by contrast, the ways Callahan deliberately reworked the conventions of assimilationist sentimental writing and reading.[10] Sentimental reeducation encouraged its Native subjects to read in ways that made them identify with members of the dominant society to the point of absorption and erasure; its goal was the loss of the (Native) self in books. The assimilating student's emotional reading was part of a process that foreclosed possibilities of critical reflection and left the Native reader in a liminal state somewhere between Native and white, middle-class identity. *Wynema* reveals this trap, emphasizing the ways conventionally sentimental reading contributed to the erasure of Native personhood and the loss of political autonomy. Representations of reading in *Wynema* dramatize the political implications of such normative engagements with texts. The novel stages a critique of reading practices that exposes the dangers of purely affective and absorptive reading.[11]

As an alternative, Callahan imagined a distinctive literacy that allowed subjects to maintain autonomy over their own reading by choosing from a range of sources, recognizing hidden motives, and reading between the lines—all without sacrificing the political energy generated by emotional responses to words on the page. She answered sentimental reading with what I name "sentimental critique," a process in which affective responses to texts coexist with analytical reflections on the cultural and political situations in which they are experienced. Recent work in book history examines "the way literary texts construct the reader's role through strategies necessitated and even produced by particular historical conditions."[12] Focusing on scenes of reading in *Wynema* reveals the development of a literacy that responds to the systematized subjugation of Native people in Indian Territories at the close of the nineteenth century, when assimilation worked to erase indigenous culture, allotment threatened the integrity of tribal communities, and the U.S. military exterminated hundreds of unarmed Lakota at Wounded Knee. Scenes of reading in *Wynema* suggest how emotional engagement and critical understanding can intersect to engender resistance to such oppressions.

In sentimental critique, readers scrutinize contexts and subtexts even as they feel for characters, applying judgment in ways that are politically empowering while maintaining the possibility of cross-cultural sympathy. The experiments in sentimental critique in the novel suggest reading and writing practices that encourage affiliative bonds without collapsing the distance needed for the critical interpretation that produces resistance. In this sense, *Wynema* is both an act of generic revision and a reading lesson. Although it has been dismissed as too sentimental to be radical, the novel actually calls attention to the fundamental tension between the sentimental literacy and expression promoted in assimilationist education and Native politic resistance. Callahan's writing registers the ways conventional sentimental literacy can abet dominant cultural strategies for maintaining racial hierarchies. She advocated for a more politicized literacy for white *and* Native readers.

"I . . . Lost Myself Reading": The Trap of Sentimental Literacy

In "The School Days of an Indian Girl" (1900), Yankton Sioux writer Zitkala-Ša recalls the "four strange summers" she spent on her reservation home when she was a student at an eastern "Indian school." Caught between childhood and adulthood in "the unsatisfactory 'teenth' in a girl's years," Zitkala-Ša finds herself, on her return home, equally caught between her birth culture and the one she has learned at the appropriately named White's Manual Labor Institute. Her literacy makes the pain of liminality particularly acute: "My mother had never gone inside of a schoolhouse," she laments, "and so she was not capable of comforting her daughter who could read and write." Her mother's offer of an "Indian Bible" only makes matters worse: "My enraged spirit felt more like burning the book, which afforded me no help, and was a perfect delusion to my mother. I did not read it, but laid it unopened on the floor."[13] Assimilation—a project aimed at separating Indians from their birth cultures in order to "kill the Indian . . . and save the man"—is marked here by the assimilating subject's ability to engage with the written (English or Dakota) word.[14] The daughter's literacy and the mother's experience of letters as "perfect delusion" define their separation. At the same time, Zitkala-Ša's violent rejection of the Bible indicates the profound crisis produced by learning to read printed texts. Reading makes her a stranger in her own home, but books provide no answering refuge.[15]

In the period that saw the publication of *Wynema,* making Native people more like whites was a national obsession, and literacy was a primary instrument of transformation. Schools within and outside of Indian Territory were deemed crucial to the project of "civilizing" Natives. The years between 1879 and 1894 saw the founding of twenty off-reservation government boarding schools, as well as many day schools in or near Native communities.[16] According to its advocates, "Indian Education" would integrate Native people into white culture. Commissioner of Indian Affairs Thomas Jefferson Morgan declared in 1889, "Education is to be the medium through which the rising generation of Indians are to be brought into fraternal and harmonious relationship with their white fellow-citizens, and with them enjoy the sweets of refined homes, the delight of social intercourse, the emoluments of commerce and trade, the advantages of travel, together with the pleasures that come from literature, science and philosophy, and the solace and stimulus afforded by a true religion."[17] Educators emphasized the power of the printed word in transforming students, bringing printing presses to boarding schools and creating school newspapers that supported the assimilationist curriculum.[18] Speaking to reformers at Lake Mohonk in 1895, the U.S. commissioner of education promised that learning to read and write in English would have transformative effects on Native children: "We will give them letters and make them acquainted with the printed page. . . . With these comes the great emancipation, and the school shall give you that."[19]

Of course, the project largely failed to deliver on the promise of "the great emancipation." English literacy would theoretically help protect Native people against exploitation by allowing them to decipher white-authored texts like treaties and contracts. But initiatives to educate for assimilation were designed to produce Native people who embraced the dominant culture while remaining subjugated within U.S. society. Most schools for Native children followed a curriculum aimed at preparing students for manual labor or domestic work in and around the homes of middle-class whites.[20] Female students, for instance, learned sewing, cooking, and laundering skills that prepared them not for possession of "refined homes" but for domestic servitude. Native students were encouraged to adopt merely an approximation of white identity; assimilation was to produce marginalized subjects who were, to borrow from (and reverse the implications of) Homi Bhabha's description of colonial mimicry, "almost the same, but not white."[21] Bhabha points to the ambivalence inherent in the mimicry demanded by colonial authority, which requires that assimilating subjects remain marginalized even as they approximate the dominant cultural identity. He argues that this contradiction destabilizes colonial authority. I use his phrase here to suggest how the privileges of the dominant culture are deferred for the assimilating/colonial subject, who is assigned a perpetual liminality as a subjugated facsimile who can only be "*almost* the same." Zitkala-Ša identifies this painful deferral as an effect of learning to read "the white man's papers."

Sentimental reeducation supported the processes of assimilation by teaching students not only how to read texts in English but how to *feel* about their reading. Even as sentimentalism faded from the literary scene in the last decades of the nineteenth century, Wexler argues, it dominated education movements aimed at acculturating African Americans, Native Americans, and immigrants in the United States and elsewhere. Sentimental literacy helped inculcate dominant cultural values in the racially and ethnically marginalized, cultivating emotional responses in line with the promotion of mainstream white society. Students at Haskell Institute, for example, were given Louisa May Alcott's *Little Women* (1868), a novel that could serve as a textbook on middle-class domesticity.[22] Conventional fiction was a primary way to make students admire and emulate a lifestyle very different from that of their birth culture. Sentimental reeducation operated like other kinds of sentimental culture, by directing subjects' feelings. In *Uncle Tom's Cabin* (1852), Harriet Beecher Stowe famously calls for her readers to "feel right," to be moved enough by her story to work to abolish slavery.[23] Proper feeling depends on the "right" kind of reading; as Elizabeth Fekete

Trubey notes, "by combining calls for reader-character identification with detailed metatextual instructions, Stowe schools her implied audience in the correct way to interpret the novel and to respond to its political exhortations."[24] Sentimental reeducation similarly pressures nonwhite readers to "feel right" by reading "right"—that is, to feel the sympathies and antipathies that support the aims of assimilation through affective responses to selected texts.

There is an important difference in the intended political effects of "right" reading for white, middle-class readers and Native students of assimilating institutions, of course. In the potential abolitionists Stowe targeted, appropriate reading, reading with feeling, ideally resulted in progressive political action. For the subjects of sentimental reeducation, on the other hand, "right" reading meant acquiescence to existing social structures. Learning to "read right" in order to "feel right" was a requirement of education for assimilation, but as Zitkala-Ša's rage illustrates, to "feel right" was not necessarily to feel good. The Native student transformed by white teachers was often left in limbo, unable to fit in at home but unwelcome as a fully realized, autonomous member of society. The bait and switch of sentimental reeducation taught Natives to love a middle-class lifestyle that would remain, for most, well out of reach. Sentimental literacy thus enacted a double alienation, wrenching subjects from their birth cultures without necessarily granting them entrance into the dominant culture. The "double-edged, double jeopardy nature" of sentimentalism aligned with other efforts to control marginalized people, imposing the ideologies of white, middle-class identity while withholding its privileges.[25]

Wexler most effectively links sentimental reeducation to literacy training in an analysis of two photographs displaying the "before and after" conditions of students at Hampton Institute, a boarding school for African American and Native students. In the first photograph, *On Arrival at Hampton, Va.*, three Native girls in tribal dress and blankets sit glumly against a wall; in the second, *Fourteen Months After*, the same girls, now in prim Victorian frocks, pose with props of white, middle-class domestic life—a game of checkers, a doll, and a book. It is the last item, Wexler argues, that is "the most crucial symbol of enforced acculturation in the photograph." The book in the Hampton photograph indicates the broken contract of literacy:

> In its most important aspect, that book is a promise to the girls themselves that what they have come so far for and suffered so much to get will, with hard work, be theirs. Yet here is where the photograph lies. Fourteen months is not long enough for an illiterate, unintended reader to even begin to read such a book, much less manipulate the many cultural codes it embodies. And chances were that a lifetime of reading would not have been long enough to transform the social chances of a Native American in white society in the late nineteenth century.[26]

The photograph is doubly deceiving: it counterfeits both the Native girls' ability to read *and* the European American middle-class lifestyle promised by even "a lifetime of reading."

The book in the Hampton Institute photograph may be more than a prop, however, even if the girls had not been schooled long enough to learn to read it. Some texts were specifically written for nonwhite readers as instruments of sentimental reeducation. A striking example of these assimilationist books emerged in the same year as *Wynema. Stiya: A Carlisle Indian Girl at Home* tells the fictional story of a Native student returning to her Pueblo reservation home after being educated for assimilation in an eastern boarding school. Written by Mariana Burgess, a white teacher at the Carlisle Indian Industrial School, the novel itself was "meant to be carried back to the reservation by returned students, and to be read and circulated locally and nationally as a . . . representation of the interior and exterior signs of evolution and 'right action' of 'good' Carlisle students."[27] In the novel, literacy proves instrumental to the assimilation project: reading school newspapers she carries home reinforces and extends the titular heroine's reeducation and sustains her efforts to make over her family according to white cultural ideals. Stiya is a poster child for the Carlisle program, both a sentimental reader and an ambassador for white culture. But in establishing Stiya's affective relationships to texts, Burgess unwittingly reveals the hidden costs of assimilationist literacy training.

Stiya arrives at the reservation fully acculturated and determined to transform her family home into the kind of middle-class domestic retreat she has learned to value. Repulsed by her parents' traditional clothes and adobe house, she at first longs to return to Carlisle. But she determines, "I can make this place better."[28] With an unswerving dedication to white domestic standards and plenty of elbow grease, she scrubs, launders, cooks, and decorates until her Pueblo home resembles a white one. Even faced with resistance from her community, she remains determined to prove wrong her mother's assertion that "they can't make you anything but Indian after all" (*S*, 64).

Burgess links the transformation of the domestic space to Stiya's education for assimilation by having two visiting Carlisle teachers evaluate her progress. Stiya proudly notes, "My teachers praised the Carlisle pictures and others which adorned the wall, and spoke well of the appearance of our best room, with its centre-table and rocking-chair and other furniture" (*S*, 114). The items singled out by the teachers as evidence of Stiya's accomplishments reflect the "double jeopardy" nature of her education. If Stiya's mother learns to clean and order her home in the white, middle-class style, Stiya must do the same chores outside her home, as the servant of a white trader, in order to buy the furniture that fills the family's "best room." Similarly, Stiya's father takes a job shoveling coal to earn enough money to buy a new house outside of the village, a purchase necessary to put distance between the family and "so many who want to go in the old Indian way" (*S*, 98). The family's servitude calls attention to the significant gap between the assimilated subject and white, middle-class personhood. Because Stiya and her parents must serve white society in order to afford the trappings of white, middle-class identity, their success is always dependent on their underwriting a standard of living they have little chance of enjoying fully.

The visiting teachers also admire the pictures of Carlisle Stiya has hung on the walls, and these have counterparts in the photographs reproduced in the novel. Like the photographs Wexler analyzes, the pictures in the house and the photographs in the text reflect the use of visual aids in the assimilation project. The "Carlisle pictures" keep Stiya connected to the process of assimilation, extending the reach of the school into the Pueblo domestic space. As representations of the educational institution, they indicate the assimilating subject's suspension between Native and white, middle-class subjectivity: even out of school, the heroine is reminded that she remains the object of reeducation rather than the author of her own personhood. In other words, Stiya's meticulously crafted domestic retreat signifies process rather than end; the work of assimilation must be ongoing in the Pueblo home.

As if to reiterate this point, the photographs reproduced in the pages of Burgess's novel juxtapose not "savage" and "civilized" reservation homes, as one might expect, but the "savage" lifestyle and the process represented by the primary instrument of assimilation, the boarding school. All but two of the photographs in the book show unassimilated Pueblo people and their environs. Children huddle together in the sun, a woman carries water in a jar, another woman washes clothes in a river, and dancers perform in a ceremony. These illustrations may have been included as ethnographic documentation or to emphasize the vast difference between the traditional Pueblo people and the products of boarding-school reeducation. For white reformers, they dramatized the magnitude of Carlisle's accomplishment even as they memorialized an everyday existence being erased by assimilation. It is likely, however, that the photographs also had a didactic purpose aimed at the assimilating Native reader. Photographs of traditional Pueblo practices represented the kinds of behaviors the assimilating student had to abandon. The contrast between these representations and descriptions of the conscientiously assimilating heroine and her remade home presents a variation on the before-and-after photographs produced by the boarding schools. It reminded returning students of the hard work they needed to continue to do to make the transition from "the old Indian way" to a "better" lifestyle.

Still, like the pictures on the wall of Stiya's house, the photographs in the book ultimately register how middle-class, autonomous personhood is unreachable for the assimilated subject. The first and last photographs in the book frame the narrative in such a way as to situate the assimilating student in a perpetual in-between.

The opening photograph presents a stand-in for the fictional heroine, a young Native woman wearing a starched dress and crucifix who poses behind a Victorian chair (fig. 1). The photograph advertises the transformations accomplished by the boarding school; at the same time, the caption, "Stiya, Carlisle Indian Girl," reminds readers that the subject of the photograph must be suspended in the processes of assimilation, as both an "Indian" and "Carlisle" girl. Despite her clear "progress," the assimilating subject remains in a liminal state under the authority of the white institution. Indeed, Lucy Tsisnah, the Chiricahua Apache girl Burgess chose to portray her Pueblo heroine, lived out the empty promise of education for assimilation. Like other female students (and like Stiya), Tsisnah was trained for domestic service. Her education included work assignments in white households through Carlisle's outing program.[29] Although there is little record of her life after Carlisle, it is unlikely she graduated to ownership of her own middle-class home. If the portrait at the beginning of the novel advertises Lucy's/Stiya's adoption of a middle-class American identity, its caption and the experience of its fictional and real subjects remind us that performing middle-class identity and joining middle-class society are two very different things.

The final photograph in the book, captioned "Indian School, Carlisle, Pa.," similarly suspends the assimilating subject even as it removes her entirely from the scene. The photograph shows several of the school's wood-frame buildings surrounding an empty courtyard (fig. 2). Oddly, given the hundreds of before-and-after images of Native children circulated in support of the assimilationist project, the photograph shows no students. Rather, the picture privileges the acculturating institution, Carlisle, over its human subjects. Like the pictures of the school that adorn the walls of Stiya's home, this image of boarding-school buildings and grounds reminds us that Native students never really exited the machinery of assimilation as fully realized, self-possessed individuals. Even the composition of the photograph suggests the assimilating subjects' terminal liminality: the expanse of manicured lawn at the center of the photograph represents a space inside the school boundaries but outside its buildings, suggesting a kind of suspension between belonging

FIGURE 1. "Stiya, Carlisle Indian Girl." In Embe [Marianna Burgess], *Stiya: A Carlisle Indian Girl at Home,* frontispiece. Courtesy Cumberland County Historical Society, Carlisle, Pa.

and not belonging. In this sense the photograph calls to mind Zitkala-Ša's feelings of being caught between "savage" and "civilized" existence.[30]

Stiya opens and closes with visual reminders that the privileges of white society remain deferred in assimilationist education. Subjects schooled for assimilation will always occupy a space outside of the mainstream. Native students may be made to approximate white, middle-class identity, as Stiya does, but they remain subjugated under the authority of the dominant class and its acculturating instruments. The novel's illustrations thus complicate the story told by the Hampton before-and-after photographs and others like them. Where the

FIGURE 2. "Indian School, Carlisle, Pa." In Embe [Marianna Burgess], *Stiya: A Carlisle Indian Girl at Home,* 114. Courtesy Cumberland County Historical Society, Carlisle, Pa.

images of traditional Pueblo activity reflect life before assimilation, the opening image of a Carlisle student and the final image of the school grounds represent what comes after assimilation—pointedly, not an "after" at all but a perpetual in-between. The first and last photographs reveal the unfulfilled promise of sentimental reeducation. Stiya's mother is right, suggest both the pictures on Stiya's wall and the photographs in the text: Carlisle does not make the girl anything but "Indian" (if an assimilating one), after all.

Visual aids in *Stiya* reinforce the lessons of Carlisle, but the propagandistic novel by definition relies most heavily on the power of written words to transform its Native readers. While the photographs of traditional Pueblo life suggest Burgess addressed a white audience in part, the novel was directed particularly at Native boarding-school students returning home. Leslie Marmon Silko, whose grandmother and aunt owned copies of the novel, reports that "all Carlisle Indian School graduates who returned to their home reservations received a copy of *Stiya* in an attempt to inoculate them against their 'uncivilized' families and communities."[31] The sentimental novel served as an extension of the assimilating institution represented in the pictures on Stiya's wall. Identifying with the properly assimilating heroine, reeducated Indian readers were to conform to Stiya's emotional responses and follow in her path toward assimilation. If reading *of* the novel supported the assimilation project, so, too, does reading *in* the novel. The heroine's reading practices provide lessons in sentimental literacy by demonstrating how reading "right" results in feeling "right" as assimilating subjects. Importantly, the affect evoked by literacy for assimilation is not limited to sympathy or affiliation but includes negative responses like revulsion and disdain. The novel coaches Native readers to be sympathetic and antipathetic, to feel both admiration for Stiya's assimilation and loathing for those who refuse to follow her lead.

In the imperial project, Wexler argues, sentimental literature establishes and reinforces boundaries, "encourag[ing] a large-scale, imaginative depersonalization of those outside its complex specifications."[32] What Stiya feels upon arrival at home is not just a nostalgic admiration for the white culture of Carlisle but a depersonalization of Native people, as articulated in her disgust for traditional Pueblo life. She attributes her antipathies to her sentimental reeducation at Carlisle:

> "I never in the world would have learned to be disgusted at this way of living, had I not been taken clear away from it, where I could not see it, nor hear anything about it for years. . . .
>
> "We *must* learn to feel disgust for these things. If we have no disgust for them we will never try to make them better.
>
> "We MUST be disgusted, I say, and I *am* thoroughly disgusted this moment at the way the Indians live, if *this* is the way they live." (*S*, 19–20)

In addition to teaching her how to sew and cook, Carlisle has taught Stiya how and what to feel: adoration for white, middle-class lifestyles; abhorrence for traditional indigenous ways. That she has "learned to be disgusted" indicates the affective focus of Stiya's reeducation. Affect separates the subject from her indigenous community (her parents become "the Indians") and binds her to whites as a soldier in the campaign for assimilation ("we . . . try to make them better"). As we have seen, the first-person plural pronoun is misleading, since Stiya, subjugated in relation to non-Native teachers and employers, will never be granted the authority of personhood that would make her part of mainstream middle-class society. Still, the scene neatly demonstrates how the novel might function as an arm of the assimilating institution, carrying its lessons on how to feel into the reservation. Reading about the fictional Stiya, Native students could also "learn to be disgusted" by their birth cultures.

In fact, Stiya models the kind of assimilative reading Burgess no doubt hoped her Native readers would practice when they returned to their families with the novel in hand. Stiya's trunk contains carefully preserved copies of the *Indian Helper*, the newspaper students in the Carlisle print shop produced under Burgess's supervision. Copies of the newspaper were sent west with returning students as part of the effort to "maintain a hold over these returnees, remind them of the standards and values taught by Carlisle, and counteract the influence of their families and communities."[33] The *Indian Helper* announced events, published letters from students and supporters, and reported on activities at the school, but its larger function was didactic and disciplinary. Moral lessons and public rebukes for misbehavior reinforced classroom instruction.[34] Like Burgess's novel, the newspaper carried the lessons of assimilation home.

The Carlisle newspapers Stiya brings with her from school function, significantly, as both material and emotional props of assimilation. They cover the table she purchases to keep her parents from sitting on the floor to eat, and they serve as a diversion and source of moral support when she becomes discouraged by the magnitude of her transformative project. When she refuses the tribal governor's commands that she attend ceremonial dances, bringing scorn on herself and her family, Stiya finds comfort reading these imported texts. "Talking to them as though they were a person," she remarks how happy she is to have them in her home. "I really believe I kissed the papers, I was so pleased to have them at that lonely hour of the night," she continues. "I sat down by the fire, and for an hour lost myself reading over what we had done at Carlisle in years gone by" (*S*, 108). The affection Stiya feels for the papers contrasts with her reactions to her family. Upon her return from school, she had found her parents so strange and unclean she was reluctant even to shake hands with them. She retreated instead into the arms of the white "*school*-mother" who accompanied her (*S*, 3). Once Stiya faces life on the reservation, copies of the *Indian Helper* substitute for the sanctuary her departed "*school*-mother" had supplied; just as she embraced the white woman, she kisses the newspapers. The newspapers become literal stand-ins for Stiya's teachers and the assimilating institution they represent.

The scene illustrates the kind of reading promoted by sentimental reeducation. Stiya reads in a way that at once separates her from her birth culture and fills her with "right" feeling. The emotion produced by the text is presented as diametrically opposed to an interpretive position that might yield insight about her political and cultural position. She turns to the papers because she cannot "allow [her]self to think another moment" about the rift her reeducation has created between her tribe and her family (*S*, 108). This unthinking experience of the text dislocates Stiya. Conventionally, sentimental reading can transport readers from the materiality of their own lives to a realm in which they feel affinity with characters whose lives are far removed from their own; Stowe's urging her white readers to put themselves in the place of a fictional slave mother desperate to save her son is a well-known example. As dramatized by Burgess, reading in sentimental reeducation takes this conveyance a step further. It not only imaginatively transports the assimilating Native reader; it also confirms her psychic detachment from her Native community. She turns to the papers because she is "lonely," and in reading them she becomes "lost." If the repugnance Stiya has learned to feel for traditional lifeways alienates her from her culture, her absorptive, emotional reading finalizes the separation. The school papers that transport her embody the processes of assimilation that deny indigenous identity even as they permanently forestall the American ideal of individual selfhood. Stiya gets lost in her reading in more ways than one.

Redirecting Reeducation

Stiya appeared in serial form in the *Indian Helper* in 1889. In addition to being sent home with Carlisle students, the *Indian Helper* was distributed to other schools for Indian children—including, it is quite likely, the two schools where Alice Callahan taught.[35] In fact, direct contrasts suggest Callahan not only read *Stiya* but wrote her own novel in response to it and perhaps others like it. In *Stiya,* white teachers visit the student's Pueblo home to monitor her progress in adopting white, middle-class practices. In *Wynema,* this dynamic is reversed: the white teacher lives with the student's family and must learn from her hosts about Native lifestyles. A central conflict of *Stiya* involves the main character's refusal to attend ceremonial dances she has come to consider barbaric. *Wynema* includes a chapter titled "The Dance" in which the Muscogee heroine joyfully describes the traditional Green Corn ceremony, or busk, and encourages her white teacher to join in the dancing. Stiya busies herself making "Carlisle biscuit" to take the place of the tortilla her mother prepares; Wynema introduces her teacher to the taste of traditionally prepared Muscogee blue dumplings.

As Callahan deliberately reverses the racist perspective of Burgess's novel, she also critiques the reeducation programs celebrated in assimilationist fiction in general. Like *Stiya, Wynema* is about assimilation, reading, and the transformative powers of sentimental reeducation. The subject was personal: Callahan left home to be educated at the Wesleyan Female Institute and returned to Indian Territory to teach at the Harrell International Institute, a school for Native and white children, and the Wealaka Mission School, where her father was superintendent. Her choice to settle in Okmulgee, Indian Territory, reflects a deep commitment to Muscogee life, despite a family history that might have taken her in a different direction. Callahan's mother, Sarah, was a white woman who fled the region at the start of the Civil War and could not be persuaded to return for twenty years. Her father, Samuel, of Creek descent, remained in Indian Territory and served as a leader in tribal government; a delegate during negotiations in Washington, D.C.; an editor; and a school superintendent. Callahan apparently spent her childhood in Texas with her mother, but on moving to Indian Territory as a teenager, she voiced both dedication to the education of Native people and support for Native political and cultural autonomy.[36]

Callahan's letters from this period record her enthusiasm for assimilationist learning and teaching as well as her sense that Native people should have control over their children's educations. She planned to finish her schooling and "build up a school of [her] own" in Indian Territory.[37] Her novel similarly promotes Native pedagogical authority. When Wynema asks her father to allow her to attend school at the mission sixteen miles away, he refuses but promises, "we can build you a school at home" (*W*, 3). The father's insistence on a local school counters the assimilationists' favored method of educating Native children in residential institutions. One agent's blunt remarks reflect the strategy behind Indian policy administrators' preference for distant boarding schools over local day schools: "It must be manifest to all practical minds that to place these wild children under a teacher's care but four or five hours a day, and permit them to spend the other nineteen in the filth and degradation of the village, makes the attempt to educate and civilize them a mere farce."[38] Wynema's assimilationist schooling commences, then, with a refutation of U.S. protocols and an assertion of the right of Native people to determine what kind of education is best for their children.

More specifically, the novel reconsiders the role of sentimental literacy in the processes of assimilationist education. Wynema's own absorption in English-language texts links her to Stiya, but her evolution toward critical reading marks her difference from the other heroine. "Reading right," as it emerges in this novel, is not the self-negating reading of Burgess's propagandistic text. In moving away from such reading models, *Wynema* produces a far more complex picture of the interactions between textual and sociopolitical contexts. Callahan works both within and against sentimentalism to interrogate the cultural work it purports to do. And she asks readers to come to a more progressive state of consciousness by reading differently.

Callahan begins by redirecting sentimental reeducation, making the white teacher, Genevieve, the subject whose feelings must be shaped and managed. As much as Genevieve asserts her Muscogee student's equality with whites, her initial reactions to Wynema's home and family reflect a fundamentally racist perspective that must be corrected. Stiya's learned disgust for Pueblo life finds a parallel in Genevieve's horrified responses to Muscogee "tough and tasteless" food; "weird" clothing; "strange, weird" rituals; and "barbaric" customs (*W*, 10, 13, 20, 21). The white teacher's overt racism exemplifies what Wexler describes as "the fierce devaluation of the extra-domestic life," "raw intolerance . . . packaged as education."[39] Genevieve's negative reactions give the lie to her assertions that sentimental literacy grants her student equal social standing with whites. Despite Wynema's emotional connection to white characters in the texts she reads, she remains, in Genevieve's eyes, part of an inferior culture.

Stiya and *Wynema* both address the assimilating Native's reading, but Callahan attends as well to the figurative and literal reading performed by whites—to Genevieve's interpretation of Native culture and to white readers' experiences of Genevieve's reactions. Like Wynema's literal reading of English texts, Genevieve's figurative reading of Muscogee culture produces emotional reactions in line with the dominant paradigms of white supremacism. At the outset, stereotyped descriptions of "happy, peaceable Indians" who "dream of the happy hunting-grounds" and live in "tepees" suggest an orientation toward readers whose perspectives would be closely aligned with the ethnocentric Genevieve (*W*, 1–2).[40] A description of ceremonial dances directly correlates Genevieve's horrified reaction and the emotions Callahan's white readers might experience when imaginatively transported to Indian Territory: "In the middle of the plain sat the medicine man, who seemed to be master of ceremonies, and all around him, in single file, danced first the men then the women. Danced? Well, not as you understand the word, my reader, but in a kind of hop, up and down—a motion not in the least graceful or rhythmic" (*W*, 20).

Such judgments, most prominent in the first several chapters, have led critics to charge Callahan with ambivalence toward her Muscogee heritage at best and capitulation to dominant cultural expectations at worst. Womack, for example, indicts Callahan's "intentional misrepresentation" of Muscogee life as a reflection of the author's deeply compromised politics.[41] But we might see stereotype and misrepresentation in the novel in the way Melissa Ryan does, as concessions calculated to draw in white readers in order to challenge the ways they interpret Native culture.[42] In fact, Genevieve functions as a stand-in for Callahan's white readers. In the words of Gerald Kiethly, the white missionary who supervises Genevieve, the teacher takes "the same view of the case that many others of our race have taken" (*W*, 28). As the novel represents the teacher's changing perspective, from blind prejudice to something closer to multicultural understanding, it encourages white readers to adjust their own lens. As Ryan points out, "what seems to be a story of Indian education is really about the (re)education of white women reformers."[43] In this way *Wynema* redirects its reading lessons toward white readers whose automatic, emotive response to indigenous life—feelings of disgust and superiority—support the subjugation of those others with whom they ostensibly sympathize.

The text indeed represents white racist perspectives, but it does so in order to challenge white readers' ways of knowing. In response to Genevieve's revulsion, Gerald argues against "depriv[ing] these people of all their customs and ceremonies" (*W*, 28). Wynema, too, works to broaden Genevieve's view, introducing her teacher to cherished Muscogee customs. With guidance, Genevieve recognizes her tendency to misread Muscogee culture: "It seems I can never see things as they are, in the true light," Genevieve concedes (*W*, 28). Interpreting with an eye to the truth requires unlearning disgust. In fact, Siobhan Senier makes the crucial point that *Wynema* presents subject positions of all kinds as candidates for revision.[44] Thus a scandal concerning misappropriated tribal annuities serves as an eye-opener for all involved: "The Indians learned a lesson therefrom, and *they were not the only learners*" (*W*, 33, emphasis added). In the redirection of the educational processes in Muscogee territory, the teacher becomes the student, learning to evolve beyond a conditioned emotional response to what is foreign to her own culture. While *Stiya* aims to transform Native students, *Wynema,* at least in part, works to reeducate white readers, as they experience through the example of the white teacher the difficult process of confronting their own reflexive racism. The lessons here are not simply ethnographic, though Wynema works to teach her teacher (and Callahan, her readers) about some of her tribe's traditions. They also call attention to the white supremacy underlying feelings like disgust in order to promote a more self-conscious and progressive politics.

Genevieve's reeducation allows her to be a voice for Native political resistance in the text, a role Callahan undoubtedly hoped her non-Native readers might adopt as well. A discussion in which the teacher argues against allotment confirms her political awakening. Under the 1887 General Allotment Law, also known as the Dawes Severalty Act, tribal properties were redistributed in individual allotments, resulting in a monumental loss of tribal lands, first when surplus acreage was made available to railroad companies and white settlers and later when tax burdens forced many Native owners to sell their parcels. Womack reads Genevieve's protest and Wynema's initial support of the allotment policy as eliding a history of Muscogee activism against the policy and denying Natives a voice of protest.[45] To be sure, Genevieve's domination of the discussion, along with her patronizing attitude toward "the poor, ignorant savage" who would be hurt by the policy, suggests a protest on behalf of Native rights that is nonetheless firmly rooted in a sense of white superiority (*W*, 28). Yet the white woman's revised perspective, making possible an alignment with progressive Muscogee political stances, sets an important example. Once Genevieve begins to appreciate the integrity and value of racial and cultural differences, she becomes the voice in favor of tribal self-governance that she could not have been at the outset of the novel. Like Genevieve, readers of the novel might learn to "read" the unfamiliar culture in ways that foster progressive political action on behalf of Native people.

There are more literal reading lessons in the novel. Beginning with the allotment discussion, *Wynema* weaves into its sentimental plot paraphrases and direct quotations from journalistic, historical, and political sources, resulting in a text that, as Piatote points out, reimagines the generic possibilities of the sentimental novel.[46] Genevieve references pro-allotment editorials and the report of the secretary of the interior, as well as Alexander Pope's "Essay on Man" and the history of the Greek struggle for independence from the

Turks (*W,* 51–52, 58). On a scandal in which unscrupulous U.S. officials appropriated tribal annuities, Gerald quotes at length the oral history presented by a tribal elder (*W,* 31–32). Gerald, Genevieve, Wynema, and others read about growing tensions at Wounded Knee in papers like the *Muskogee Daily Phoenix* (*W,* 72–73). They learn of the slaughter of Native men, women, and children in the *Saint Louis Republic* and the *Cherokee Telephone,* and they have the story confirmed in a Lakota woman's eyewitness account (*W,* 97–98). The range of sources gathered here—embracing the mainstream white press and western literature and history but also Muscogee and Cherokee journalism, Muscogee oral narratives, and Lakota testimony—models a wider reaching, more autonomous reading practice than is demonstrated in Wynema's earlier reading of canonical English fiction and drama.[47]

Unlike Wynema's earlier sentimental reading of English literature and Genevieve's initial reading of Muscogee culture, the reading of these texts is critical. Genevieve, for example, turns an analytical eye on the secretary of the interior's report on allotment. The secretary, Genevieve quotes from a newspaper, "suggests that the period now allowed a tribe to determine whether it will receive allotment be placed under the control of the President, so that it may be shortened if *tribes give no attention to the subject or cause unreasonable delays;* and discountenances the employment of attorneys by the Indians to aid in negotiations with, or to prosecute claims against, the government.' This sounds like the lands will be allotted whether Indians like or no" (*W,* 51–52). Genevieve's close reading belies the notion that assimilation programs like the Dawes Act were ever intended to promote Native autonomy, as the law actually afforded the federal government fuller control over tribal properties. Moreover, this reading demonstrates for Wynema how *not* to become lost in texts. Wynema's initial view of allotment, like Genevieve's initial response to Muscogee culture, seems a programmed echo of the racist rhetoric of the day. She complains, "so long as our land remains as a whole, in common, these lazy Indians will never make a move toward cultivating it" (*W,* 51). But reconsidering the matter in light of Genevieve's interpretation of the report, Wynema determines she has been "a superficial thinker" on the subject (*W,* 52). As

Alves contends, "Wynema learns that she must read between the lines that are written by others . . . to understand with increasing acuity that the newspaper reports and school lessons she receives are not *the* truth so much as someone's *version* of the truth."[48]

The episode itself reflects the entrenched racism of nineteenth-century American reform movements: Genevieve remains patronizing, instructing Wynema in the proper critical stance, and Wynema begs forgiveness for her mistake. And yet in crucial ways the scene demands a revised understanding of what Callahan believed reading should entail for both white and Native readers. Whereas the reading in (and of) *Stiya* encourages unthinking admiration for white culture and disgust for Native ways, reading in *Wynema* involves gathering information from multiple sources, reading beneath the surface, and carefully thinking through the political implications of textual representations.

"Not Pocahontas": Reading and Native Authority

Reading critically, Callahan suggests, supports progressive politics because it involves questioning the relationship between texts and sociopolitical agendas. But if Wynema learns to read a government report critically, might she also learn to read literary texts the same way? And can her sentimental critique supply a model for reading *Wynema,* a novel in which a conventionally sentimental happy ending shares space with accounts of the real-life tragedy of a massacre of hundreds of indigenous people? To begin to answer these questions we need to look again at Wynema's reading practice, specifically the reading that is woven through her sentimentally charged love story. Wynema falls in love with and marries Genevieve's brother, Robin. The romance parallels that of Genevieve and Gerald, but for Wynema and Robin the difference of race calls attention to inequities that the conventions of sentimental romance will not meliorate. Because the miscegenous love story unfolds in the context of the heroine's sentimental reading, it tests the capacities of conventional reading practices to address racism.

The romance blossoms when Wynema accompanies Genevieve on a visit to her home in the East, and it is sealed over a conversation that touches on romantic stories of womanly self-sacrifice. Robin finds Wynema sitting in a tree reading Tennyson's "Lancelot and Elaine" (1859), a text she later carries with her back to Indian Territory, where Genevieve will tease, "Elaine? How sentimental!" (*W*, 67). At first glance, Wynema's reading of the English idyll is little more than a sign of her suitability for marriage to a white man. She is "totally absorbed" by the text, a state that suggests both her comfort with white culture and her apparently easy incorporation into it (*W*, 61). Like his sister, Robin values Wynema's sentimental reading for the ways it ties her to white culture. In fact, he interprets the Muscogee woman's emotional response to "Lancelot and Elaine" as evidence of her attachment to *him*. When Wynema cries over Lancelot's separation from Elaine, Robin believes she associates it with their own eventual parting when she returns home. The presumed overlap of emotional responses here reflects the ways sentimental reeducation depends on a transfer of affection. Sympathy for white figures in a text evolves into attachment to white people (and culture) outside of it. In a circle of affect that begins with the text, reading about a white romance produces Wynema's tears, the currency of sentimentality, and the tears move Robin to propose marriage. In other words, reading sentimentally figuratively and literally weds Wynema to white culture.

And yet this scene emphasizes Wynema's understanding of the difference between reading about romance and entering into a mixed-race relationship in the nineteenth-century United States, and in doing so it presents an alternative to the absorptive, uncritical reading of sentimental texts. Robin can idealize their romance as analogous to Lancelot's and Elaine's, but Wynema notes the unavoidable difference that race makes. Of the proposed marriage, she asks: "Robin what would our parents say? Would your mother accept a little black Indian for a daughter?" (*W*, 62). The question registers an otherness too incontrovertible, in the eyes of mainstream society, to be resolved through sentiment. It points to the inability of sentimental reeducation to move the two lovers beyond the limitations of a fundamentally racist society. Wynema's cultural orientation poses no obstacles to the union, for surely a Muscogee girl who reads Tennyson shows sufficient assimilation to be incorporated into white society. Yet in the eyes of members of the dominant society, the heroine's race fixes her difference and thus her incompatibility with the idealized domesticity presented in literary sentimentalism. Wynema's hesitation demonstrates that while "totally absorbed" in a text, she is not "lost" like Stiya; even as she experiences a deep emotional response, she retains a critical perspective on her own marginalized situation in relation to the romance in the idyll. Her question shows a sophisticated understanding of the relationship between text and context.

Robin quickly dismisses Wynema's qualms: "My sweetheart must not call herself names" (*W*, 62). Nor does the novel dwell extensively on the problem of integrating Wynema into the white Weir family: the story subsequently skips ahead "some years" to a domestic scene in which Robin's mother joins the happy, multiracial household of Robin, Wynema, and their infant daughter (*W*, 71). Still, Robin's scolding intimates that for him racial reconciliation will be accomplished by an imaginative sacrifice of an indigenous identity, a "name" ("black Indian") he deems too shameful to be spoken aloud. Wynema's hesitation and Robin's response both obliquely register the artificiality of sentimental reconciliation. Sentimental ideals of multiracial unity aside, racialized hierarchies remain very much in play in this particular attempt to erase a troublesome difference.

As if to press the point that the sentimentally inflected romance will not place Native and non-Native lovers on an equal footing, Robin seals the engagement by throwing his arms around Wynema and kissing her repeatedly against her will. His physical domination gives credence to Wynema's sense that she will be subordinated in a marriage to a white man. Robin's apology for this transgression comes, naturally, in the form of a sentimental text, a letter that begs forgiveness but expresses no regret: "I'll promise never, *no never* to be guilty of the same offense again—if I can help it." Wynema "reperuse[s] and kisse[s] the billet"; the letter becomes a stand-in, like Stiya's newspapers, for the absent white authority figure (*W*, 64). But she reads white-authored texts decidedly more self-consciously than did Stiya, for once again she raises and leaves lingering questions about the ability of sentimental texts to overcome racism. When she returns home, Wynema receives another letter from Robin. Genevieve, remarking on the "sentimental sighs and pale cheeks" its reading elicits, guesses that her brother and student are engaged (*W*, 68). When she asks why Wynema has not told her of the engagement, Wynema's reply returns to the incontrovertible difference of race structuring U.S. society: "Oh, because—because, I feared you might not like it—that the engagement might not please you" (*W*, 68). That is to say, even as she responds emotionally to white-authored texts like "Lancelot and Elaine" and Robin's letter, Wynema retains a critical understanding of the cultural context of her own romance and the residual impediments to a true sympathetic union of racial others. Reading produces the tears of sentimental affiliation, but tears do not dilute the social and political reality of racial division. In placing white-authored texts at the center of this interracial love affair, Callahan lays bare the false promises embedded in the reading promoted by sentimental reeducation.

As Robin's physical domination suggests, *Wynema* registers an awareness of structures of power defined by gender as well as race difference. Robin's substitution of "my sweetheart" for the racially identifying name Wynema gives herself affirms the gendered power structures manifested in his forced kisses. In marriage, Wynema will be his possession. This mainstream view of marriage requires Wynema to sacrifice not only her identity, as indicated in Robin's rejection of her self-naming as Indian, but also her personal autonomy. The conversation surrounding the proposal fittingly references two models for womanly sacrifice in conventional European American literature: Tennyson's lily maid of Astolat, who dies unrequited in her love for Lancelot, and Pocahontas, who risks her life for the white colonist John Smith.[49] Yet Callahan invokes these stories only to reject the plot of womanly self-sacrifice they contain.

When Robin begs Wynema to descend from the tree, she asks, "Did you never read that Pocahontas could leap from one tree to another like a squirrel?" (*W*, 61). As Charlotte J. Rich notes, when Wynema compares herself to Pocahontas, she does so by emphasizing the heroine's independence, signified by her ability to leap from tree to tree, rather than her willingness to give up her life for a white man.[50] Wynema offers Robin a lesson in how to read more critically. He should read the Pocahontas story as a representation of the Native woman's power, she suggests, not in the conventional way as a celebration of self-sacrifice. Importantly, Robin recognizes the difference between Wynema and the mythic heroine. "Yes, but you are not Pocahontas, and I am not John Smith, though I wish I were. . . . For then you would jump down and save me—from toiling up this tree" (*W,* 61). Despite the appeal of myths of female sacrifice to a white man like Robin, the quick admission that Wynema's story is not Pocahontas's story signals Callahan's refusal to graft conventional sentimental plots onto nineteenth-century contexts of race and gender relations. Like Sigourney's long poem "Pocahontas," Callahan's scene takes up the beloved national myth only to repurpose it as an instrument of protest. The reference to the story becomes an opportunity to refuse the romanticized dominant cultural narrative of female and Native sacrifice.

Conversations about allotment and women's rights frame the couple's romantic exchanges, drawing further attention to the political realities of race and gender oppression that mainstream sentimental stories obscure. Before her tree-top flirtation, Wynema lectures Robin on the importance of women's suffrage, insisting that "one day, the 'inferior of man,' the 'weaker vessel' shall stand grandly by the side of that 'noble lord of creation,' his equal in *every* respect" (*W,* 45). The ironic use of common figures of speech reflects Wynema's ability to read conventional expressions critically. Irony countermands the conventional sentimentalism of the romance and rejects the idealization of female sacrifice in conventional myths and literature. The point here is that Wynema can respond emotionally to sentimental stories about white and Native women without losing sight of the social and political implications of their plots—or her own situation within a racist and patriarchal society that would incorporate her into a romantic fantasy of Native subjugation and self-negation.

Suspicious Reading, Sentimental Critique, and "The Indian's Story"

Initiating decades of critical attention to American literary sentimentalism, Ann Douglas famously criticized the form for its "failed political consciousness."[51] Critics who take a literary nationalist approach to Native American literature make a related complaint when they charge Native writers who adopt conventional literary modes with conceding to the dominant culture. Elizabeth Cook-Lynn, for instance, condemns Native writers who "have moved away from nationalistic concerns in order to gain the interest of mainstream readers."[52] Seeking a Native literature and literary criticism rooted in tribal culture, Womack finds a fatal flaw in *Wynema* in its replacement of Creek sensibility with white literary formula. Yet the fact that the novel aims to reeducate readers complicates dismissals of its sentimentalism. Womack's interpretation disallows the possibility that a Native woman could analyze her own situation as an assimilated writer working in a conventionally feminine, predominantly white literary tradition, or that she could use this position as a platform to reverse the direction of sentimental reeducation and thereby challenge political and social structures that subjugate both Natives and women. Juxtaposing *Wynema* with a propagandistic work like *Stiya* reveals the complexity of Callahan's political and aesthetic project. While *Stiya* promotes the assimilating subject's purely emotional responses to texts as an instrument of assimilation, *Wynema* represents reading *by* and *of* white and Native characters as a means of critical resistance. In this sense, Callahan's work can indeed be seen as the Native "act of nation building" that Womack seeks.[53]

Callahan's investigation of the ways emotional responses to texts relate to structures of power anticipates recent scholarly debates about reading, affect, and political agency in sentimental literature. Much of this discussion focuses on the political consequences of conventional reading and writing practices. Since Jane Tompkins's promotion of the "cultural work" performed by nineteenth-century women's sentimental fiction, a relatively simple question has motivated discussions about the genre: does it do good cultural work or bad?[54] Many critics join Wexler in identifying the insidious effects of reading sentimental literature and culture in a white, masculinist society, pointing to the ways sentimentalism promotes in readers, for instance, "sentimental possession," "disciplinary intimacy," or "imperial domesticity."[55] My analysis of sentimental reading follows such critiques and extends Wexler's analysis of sentimentalism's role in shoring up dominant political and social structures, especially in fictions like *Stiya,* which are overtly calculated to do so. But I take seriously Cindy Weinstein's caution against monolithic interpretations of sentimental novels that fail to appreciate both the ideological variability and aesthetic complexity of this body of texts. Weinstein's assertion that some sentimental texts "have the capacity to interrogate their generic foundations" widens the interpretive frame for examining a body of writing that critics often homogenize, suggesting how writers could work both within and against the parameters of literary convention.[56] Callahan did not adopt sentimental convention unconsciously or uncritically; rather, she attempted to reconcile sentimental affiliation and critical detachment in order to challenge the racial hierarchies imposed by nineteenth-century sentimental reeducation.

This attempt to rethink the ways texts produce feeling and knowledge also has bearing on broader academic conversations about affect and critical interpretation—in other words, on our own reading practices as scholars. In the past several years, theorists have begun to question the primacy of a "hermeneutics of suspicion," the interpretative style associated with French philosopher Paul Ricouer that privileges detachment, skepticism, and demystification as approaches for uncovering meanings otherwise hidden within a text.[57] As an interpretive strategy, suspicious reading positions itself against reading that surrenders to the full play of emotions a text can evoke, emotions like sorrow, excitement, or delight. Suspicious readers do not get drawn into or manipulated by texts but presumably maintain the critical distance that allows for a clear-eyed understanding of literature's secrets and subtexts. To put it another way, the suspicious reader (also known as the critic) is distrustful not just of texts but of the feelings they evoke. Nativist and feminist critics often harbor suspicions of highly affective print conventions like sentimentalism, which would seem to hide texts' more insidious social and cultural effects. Such critics work to demystify conventional literary works by peering beneath their affective registers.

Yet there is good reason to be suspicious of suspicious reading. To begin with, as Rita Felski points out, the disavowal of affect is disingenuous, because a hermeneutics of suspicion has its own affective register—distrust is, after all, a feeling.[58] Moreover, Eve Kosofsky

Sedgwick argues that our critical habits of skeptical detachment can have stultifying effects: "They may have made it less rather than more possible to unpack the local, contingent relations between any given piece of knowledge and its narrative/epistemological entailments for the seeker, knower, or teller."[59] The implicit idea that affect and critique are mutually exclusive, that reading with feeling means reading without political awareness or agency, limits our understanding of the ways literary conventions can be deployed in the interest of structural change. Sedgwick and Felski are joined by other theorists, including Michael Warner, Sianne Ngai, and Michael Millner, who have begun to break down the dichotomy between critical and emotionally responsive reading in productive ways.[60] Their work suggests a role for reading that produces sensations like desire and grief in the construction of critical and democratic public spheres. If we allow that critique can intersect with emotional sensations in our consumption of texts, we can better illuminate, in Sedgwick's words, "the many ways selves and communities succeed in extracting sustenance from the objects of a culture—even a culture whose avowed desire has often been not to sustain them."[61]

Wynema offers an opportunity to explore the intersections of emotional response and critical knowledge most strikingly in its final chapters. The last section of the book has troubled modern readers because it shifts so abruptly from the sentimental romance plot to accounts of the massacre at Wounded Knee, and then back again to what appears a hastily rigged happy ending.[62] On the surface, the shifts suggest authorial uncertainty: a polemic on the slaughter of defenseless Lakota men, women, and children and a warning about retribution is followed, seemingly illogically, by a description of the heroine's blissful, multicultural family and community. The sentimental closing scene seems designed to make us forget the horror of Wounded Knee or the protests against it. The inconsistency begins to make sense, however, if we understand *Wynema* as attempting to reconcile sentimental affiliation and critical resistance through her characters' and her readers' affective and critical consumption of a multitude of texts. Recognizing the ways sentimental critique unites emotional attachment and critical resistance—producing love without sacrificing truth—should help us come to terms with the novel's strange mix of polemic and sentimental impulses.

If we allow that sentimental and critical reading practices are not mutually exclusive, we can begin to see Callahan as imagining a kind of reparative reading of literature and culture. "Reparative reading" is Sedgwick's antidote for suspicious (or "paranoid") reading. Reparative reading makes space for feelings of attachment, sadness, pleasure, surprise, and hope in the production of knowledge. "Additive and accretive," rather than demystifying, it is an interpretive practice that serves as a balance against the critical imperative which, among other things, disavows affective ways of knowing about and engaging with structures of power.[63] I do not want to overstate the connection between reparative reading and what I am calling sentimental critique in *Wynema*. Certainly, Callahan was not developing an affect theory *avant la lettre*. Yet there is an unmistakable resonance between the goal of sentimental critique and an interpretive aim to "use one's own resources to assemble or 'repair' the murderous part-objects [fractured by the dominant culture] into something like a whole."[64] Paul Kelleher directly links reparative reading and sentimental reading when he describes Sedgwick's thinking as evidence of "a *sentimental turn* for queer theory."[65] Importantly, in calling for reparative reading, Sedgwick argues that approaches that allow for affective engagement and those that engage a suspicious detachment need not be mutually exclusive; the best theory allows them to "interdigitate" in "the ecology of knowing."[66] The end of *Wynema,* which encourages critical and affective responses to the Wounded Knee massacre as it brings together emotion-laden scenes and cool editorial commentary, offers an opportunity to explore just such a tessellated ecology.

Since the massacre occurred near the time of the novel's publication, Callahan likely included chapters on Wounded Knee as a way of educating her readers about what had happened. She did so in a way that calls for a sentimental critique of mainstream accounts of the event. The chapters require readers to respond with both affect and critical detachment, to feel for victims but also to analyze representations for what they conceal or expose about the nation's ugliest realities. Information about Wounded Knee comes to Wynema and her friends, and so to Callahan's readers, through a variety of Native- and non-Native-authored texts. Much discussion surrounds these texts, as Wynema and others sift through them to find, in the words of one Native-authored editorial, "facts and figures and not mere sentimentalism" (*W*, 98).

With the extended family gathered, Gerald reads aloud a newspaper account of the starvation on the Sisseton and Wahpeton reservations as tribe members wait for promised government aid. He then quotes an editorial attacking the Ghost Dance religion and advocating a U.S. military assault on its practitioners. As critics have pointed out, the Native-authored letter that Gerald next quotes shifts narrative authority from white to Native voices as it presents a radical critique of Christian hypocrisy and a defense of the Ghost Dance as "a better religion—a religion that is all good and no bad" (*W*, 73).[67] Thus, the range of positions Gerald presents requires that Callahan's characters and readers read widely and critically to construct a response to the massacre. Carl Peterson, the white missionary friend of the Weir and Keithly families, articulates the conclusion such reading will produce: clearly the Lakota are the victims of a government determined "to starve and slaughter this defenseless people" (*W*, 74).

Callahan's readers also learn about Wounded Knee through a sentimental subplot about two fictional victims, the warrior Wildfire and his wife, Miscona. Wildfire determines to die with honor rather than submit to the U.S. government, and Miscona refuses to leave her husband's side. In the ensuing attack they are killed, leaving their infant orphaned.[68] The narrator presents the story with melodramatic flourishes aimed at bringing the reader to tears. The text describes the lovers dying side by side, "free at last, and the little papoose sweetly sleeping between them" (*W*, 90). If the tragedy calls for an emotional response, however, it also supplies crucial lessons in reading critically. Traveling to the plains, Carl tells Wildfire that if he submits to U.S. military forces he will be protected. Wildfire reacts to the government's promise as a story that must be read with suspicion. How can he be sure, he asks, that acts of treachery against his tribe will not be repeated? Before readers weep over Wildfire's death, they confront the dangers of responding to sentimental texts purely affectively.

Wildfire's suspicion is especially sharp in light of a recent attack in which a contingent of whites murdered Chief Few Tails and his followers. The chief's wife, wounded in the attack, could barely express to Wildfire and his companion what happened, but the story is told in the resulting scene of carnage. Wildfire explains,

> Yes those bleeding, gaping wounds[,] those eyes glaring in death, those stiff bodies lying where they fell, told a story—a story far more eloquent and impressive than human lips could have uttered. Do you want to know what that story was, Carl Peterson?—you who come here and warmly talk of peace? Well, it was this: they told me we had suffered long enough at the hands of the white man; they cried out for revenge; they told me to fight the pale-faces until they or I lie bleaching in the sun, as those dead bodies were; but they told me *never,* NEVER listen to a tale of peace, even if told by a friend. Peace! Let those talk of peace who live in quiet homes, who are surrounded by friends and loved-ones, happiness and affection; but peace is not the watchword of the oppressed. (*W,* 81–82)[69]

Like *Stiya, Wynema* deploys the power of the visual here, but with a wholly different purpose. The pictures on the walls of Stiya's home and the photographs in the novel itself are part of the educational instrument that promotes unthinking capitulation to white authority but disguises its effects. The picture of carnage that is seared in Wildfire's memory, in contrast, is a more transparent text, one that makes plain the costs of absorption in dominant cultural narratives. Wildfire reads a moral in the scene of slaughter. The sentimentally inflected "tale of peace" told by a white ally covers over a reality of systematized racism. Reading beneath the surface of this tale reveals the profound economic and social inequities that maintain the distance between the privileged in their quiet homes and the vulnerable and oppressed, pushed to the margins of society. To read the promises of white authorities naively, to experience them as "mere sentimentalism," is to suffer. As she did by having Wynema reeducate her teacher, Callahan here overturns orthodox structures of authority. Wildfire instructs his white friend on the disingenuousness of white claims and the need for a critical approach, and an enlightened Carl admits, "it was all so, yea, and more" (*W*, 84).[70]

The call for a critical reading practice aside, this scene remains sentimentally charged. Wildfire's story of racial violence generates a cross-racial exchange of feeling. "Carl knelt among his Indian friends and lifted his voice, full of tears, in earnest, fervent supplication to the 'All-Father,'" praying in English and Lakota. He notices the men "were all much touched, and Wildfire's eyes were moist with feeling" (*W*, 85). While Wildfire's story produces shared tears, however, the gathered Native men remain "not in the least shaken in their purpose" of resistance (*W*, 86). The scene encourages a reading mode both affiliative and confrontational. It suggests that emotional connection across racial lines, among characters *in* the novel or in the experience of readers *of* the novel, need not entail a loss of self or result in compliance with dominant structures of power. This deployment of sentiment evokes sympathetic affiliation without eliminating Native autonomy or mitigating Native resistance.

The integration of sentimental and critical responses here reflects the self-consciousness with which Callahan approached her own account of a national crime. It gives her an opportunity to register a final protest against the reading and writing by non-Natives that underwrote U.S. national policies and contributed to injustices like the massacre at Wounded Knee. Like Wildfire, the narrator juxtaposes a Native perspective on the massacre with the story produced by the dominant culture:

> "But," you ask, my reader, "did not the white people undergo any privations? Did not the United States army lose two brave commanders and a number of privates?" Oh, yes. So the papers tell us; but I am not relating the brave (?) deeds of the white soldier. They are already flashed over the world by electricity; great writers have burned the midnight oil telling their story to the world. It is not my province to show how brave it was for a great, strong nation to quell a riot caused by the dancing of a few "bucks"—for *civilized* soldiers to slaughter indiscriminately, Indian women and children. Doubtless it was brave, for so public opinion tells us, and it cannot err. But what will the annals of history handed down to future generations disclose to them? Will history term

> the treatment of the Indian by the United States Government, right and honorable? Ah, but that does not affect my story! It is the Indian's story—his chapter of wrongs and oppression. (*W*, 92–93)

As did Sarah Wakefield, Callahan registers awareness of the clash between her story and mainstream stories "the papers tell us," the stories "the annals of history" will preserve. But unlike Wakefield, she emphasizes the ways such official narratives require the cooperation and consent of an unthinking "public opinion." The narrator models a corrective to this kind of automatic absorption of texts by penetrating the racism underlying rhetoric deployed in the context of such indiscriminate killing. The punctuation of "brave (?)" and "*civilized*" announces the narrator's repudiation of the official narrative and the settler colonialist regime it sustains. The biting irony here reflects a more sophisticated reading of widespread reports and demands careful attention to "the Indian's story."

The novel thus intervenes in its own generic configuration by promoting a more nuanced sentimental reading, even of its own idealized, sentimental ending. The final chapter describes a bustling western town named for Wynema, a home to whites and Natives in "happy families" "nestled close together" (*W*, 103). Wynema herself resides at the center of a multiracial family that now includes Wildfire and Miscona's orphaned daughter. Two other Wounded Knee orphans have joined the community, one adopted by Genevieve and Gerald, the other by Carl and his wife, Winnie (Robin's and Genevieve's sister).[71] An elderly survivor of the Wounded Knee massacre, Chikena, also resides there. Equal relations of consanguinity and consent bind Natives and non-Natives together in domestic tranquility.

But two dark prophecies temper this happy ending. Following Wounded Knee Carl predicts "terrible retribution in store for our Government on account of its treachery and cruelty to the Indians" (*W*, 102). "Wrong is always punished," he warns. "There will be wars and pestilence, anarchies and open rebellions. The subjects of the Government will rise up in defiance of the 'authorities that be' " (*W*, 102). Soon after, Chikena advises the novel's heroine, "Wynema, thou child of the forest, make haste and seek with me the happy hunting-grounds of our fathers, for not many years of oppression can your people stand. Not many years will elapse until the Indian will be a people of the past" (*W,* 104). What is striking in these prophesies, delivered by a white man and a Lakota woman, is the refusal to allow the happy ending to wipe away responsibility for past and future indigenous suffering. Chikena's warning recites a sentimental Vanishing American narrative, to be sure, and the stereotypical language she uses reflects concession to dominant cultural protocols for representing non-assimilated Native people. Yet the emphasis on "oppression" revises the expedient story of inevitable Native disappearance. As I argue in chapter 2, mainstream stories of Vanishing Americans, such as James Fenimore Cooper's *The Last of the Mohicans,* ask that readers feel for the grieving victims of settler colonization but erase from memory the social and political conditions that have caused Native suffering. Chikena's vision holds whites accountable in ways conventional recitations do not: it is the suffocating weight of racial tyranny, rather than the inevitable tide of "progress," that will precipitate the disappearance of Native life and culture. The jeremiadic tone of Carl's assessment breaks into the conventionally sentimental mode at the end of the novel as well, making Native people not passive victims but agents of resistance who will "rise up in defiance" against their oppressors.

The contrast between the happy domestic scene and the grim prophesies is jarring. While some read such ruptures as evidence of a mixed-race, assimilated writer's conflicted sensibility, the emphasis on reading practices throughout the novel suggests we should give Callahan more credit.[72] In this closing, she conveys her sense of the dangers of writing and reading "mere sentimentalism," even the sentimentalism of her conventionally happy ending, without political awareness. The qualifier is important: sentimentalism threatens Native autonomy when feeling is all it produces. Callahan's story, "the Indian's story," asks instead for a sentimental reading that generates emotion even as it encourages interrogating representations in the context of real-world tragedies.

Wynema offers strikingly metatextual insights into the implications of texts and reading in the context of U.S. race relations. Certainly, the novel bears the imprint of the pro-assimilationist thinking that produced *Stiya* in its sometimes stereotyped depictions and its elevation of white, middle-class subjectivity. But rather than simply asking readers to read in order to "feel right" about what happened to Native people in the halls of mission schools or on the plains of Wounded Knee, Callahan insists that her readers read differently. She attends to the conventional reading and writing practices that operated in the racial conflicts of her day, revealing the limitations of sentimental reading as an answer to the "Indian question." As an alternative, she endorses a more effective model of reading for political resistance. Her novel illustrates how texts categorized as sentimental may in fact turn the form inside out, offering a critique from within that questions the intentions of conventional literature and the implications of purely affective reading. As such it educates us about the ways popular literary forms can be used to intervene in political crises and the ways writers and their readers can find new methods for mediating racial and national conflicts.

Far from being compromised by its generic investments, then, *Wynema* begins to theorize literary sentimentalism as an instrument of protest, to explore a methodology for critical engagement with and through convention that can serve a politics of resistance. I have been arguing throughout this book that nineteenth-century women writers protesting Indian policy were more acutely conscious of the limitations of textual convention than we have recognized. Sarah Wakefield and Lydia Sigourney registered the conflicts between their activist intentions and the established forms of expression—trial testimony, captivity narrative, petition, Indian lament poetry—into which their protests were channeled. Wakefield's adoption of a mainstream literary mode devolves into an epistemological muddle, as she recognizes that dominant cultural conventions influence what she knows of her truth as much as how she conveys her truth to others. Sigourney negotiated the contradictions between protest and conventional literary modes more successfully. In sentimental poems like "The Cherokee Mother" and "The Indian Girl's Burial" she challenges the integrity of white sympathy for Indians. With the long poem "Pocahontas," one of her last works to address "the Indian question," she indicts as deeply compromised the very sentimentalism she engages.

But with *Wynema* Callahan goes further than recognizing the limitations and contradictions of literary convention. Against a national assimilation effort that used literary sentiment and sentimental literacy to discipline the marginalized, she presents models of affective reading and writing that preserve autonomy and promote critical reflection and resistance. To accommodate her protest, she stretches the contours of both the sentimental assimilationist novel and the practice of reading sentimentally.

Where Callahan found space for Native critical resistance in the assimilationist novel, the Cherokee editor and writer Ora Eddleman located it in an equally unlikely place: the mass-circulated commercial magazine. Emerging in Indian Territory just a few years after publication of *Wynema,* the magazine *Twin Territories* at once appealed to a broad national audience and presented itself as an instrument of Native expression and activism. As I argue in the following chapter, Eddleman capitalized on features of the commercial magazine—its seriality, its heterogeneity, and its capacity to organize and discipline communities of readers—to resist mass culture's role in subjugating Native peoples. Like Callahan, Eddleman found ways to make her generic investments pay political dividends. Hers was in many ways an even more ambitious undertaking.

CHAPTER FOUR

Talking Back

Ora Eddleman's "Indian Magazine" and Native Publicity

"Lo, the poor Indian, with pastepot and shears! The teepee exchanged for the sanctum, war paint for printer's ink, and the scalping knife for the blue pencil. It is a Cherokee woman who has wrought this marvel, and the paper she edits is called the Twin Territories."[1] The anomalous being described in this February 8, 1902, *Pittsburgh Press* profile was twenty-two-year-old Ora Veralyn Eddleman, the editor and owner of the first mass-distributed commercial magazine published by Native Americans.[2] *Twin Territories: The Indian Magazine* had been launched in 1898 by Eddleman's sister and brother-in-law, Myrta and Walter Sams, who hired the then-teenager as editor. Eddleman purchased the magazine soon after, and aside from two years in which it was under different ownership, she presided over it until it ceased publication in 1904 (fig. 3).[3] Her status as a Native woman magazine editor attracted the attention of the *Kansas City Journal, New York Times, Inland Printer, Timely Topics, Harper's Weekly,* and *Out West Magazine,* each of which lauded her achievement in terms only slightly less patronizing than the *Pittsburgh Press.*[4] The Kansas City newspaper took note of Eddleman's fluent English and her knowledge of subjects ranging from art to political economy, with which, it said, "she is surprisingly familiar."[5] Charles Fletcher Lummis of *Out West Magazine* declared her magazine "fully as creditable as many published by her white sisters."[6]

FIGURE 3. *Two Native Men on Horseback*. In *Twin Territories* 4, no. 3 (March 1902), cover. Courtesy DeGolyer Library, Southern Methodist University.

Eddleman would go on to edit a column in *Sturm's Oklahoma Magazine* and write essays for *Good Housekeeping* and *Harper's Bazaar*.[7] In the 1930s, she reinvented herself for a new medium: answering calls and letters from listeners as the "Sunshine Lady," she pioneered talk radio and Native broadcasting in a highly successful program on Casper, Wyoming, station KDFN.[8] But she remained best known as "an Indian woman editor."[9]

It is ironic, then, that Eddleman was no Indian, at least according to federal officials who stripped her of her Cherokee identity in

1896. Eddleman's great-great-grandparents, an Irish man adopted into the Cherokee tribe and a Cherokee woman, had emigrated west with other members of the tribe between 1817 and 1819. In the last decade of the century, Eddleman's mother, Mary Daugherty Eddleman, moved her large family from Texas to Muskogee, Indian Territory, with the express purpose of reaffirming tribal ties.[10] To be officially enrolled as Cherokee citizens, however, the family was obliged to apply to a U.S. government board. The Eddlemans' lengthy written appeal connected them to some of the most prominent figures and events in Cherokee history. Affidavits from tribe members testified to their involvement in tribal affairs and their familial connections to the father and uncle of a recently deceased Cherokee chief.[11] Yet the Dawes Commission, the three-member panel established to finalize tribal rolls in Indian territories, denied the application. A federal appeals court upheld the decision that defined every member of the Eddleman family as non-Native.

As jointly constructed in mass media and government bureaucracy, Eddleman was an impossibility, a stereotypical "tepee Indian" who at the same time was not quite Native enough. Different as the competing definitions of the editor were, however, they participated in the same dominant cultural project of managing Native people by commandeering the processes of racial and tribal identification. As Jamaica Kincaid reminds us, "to name is to possess."[12] Descriptions like the one in the *Pittsburgh Press* profile sustained the social order through stereotypes that fix racial difference and reinforce boundaries. Naming Eddleman "the poor Indian" mitigated the threat posed by a Native editor wielding an instrument of mass media. The federal enrollment decision also supported established social structures by naming. The detribalization of individuals and families was common in the era of allotment, when the federal government took control of Native resources to distribute them as it saw fit. U.S. enrollment policies granted allotments of tribal lands only to those individuals with a sufficient (perceived) degree of Native ancestry. By commanding the terms of racial and tribal identification, the U.S. government restricted Native access to tribal properties, culture, and belonging.

In the pages of *Twin Territories*, Eddleman challenges these efforts to define her as either "tepee Indian" or non-Native. An editorial published soon after the appearance of the profile in the *Pittsburgh Press* complains about the ways the mainstream media "dwell[s] at length upon the idea that [the magazine's] editor is an Indian girl[,] 'the daughter of a full-blood Cherokee squaw,' to quote one esteemed exchange." Eddleman goes on,

> It is true that the editor of TWIN TERRITORIES is of Indian blood—a Cherokee and prouder of that than any distinction she may attain, but she is not a "full-blood Cherokee squaw," nor is she the daughter of one. Cherokee squaws, in the sense intended, are of times long past.
>
> This for the benefit of those misled ones who have enquired of the editor "Do you speak English?" "Will you send me a picture of you in your native dress?" "Is your magazine printed in Indian?" "Are you not afraid to go among the homes of Indians?" To these we would say, read TWIN TERRITORIES. It represents the people of the two Territories known as "The Twins"—one of the best countries under the sun.[13]

The racism underlying praise for the Cherokee woman's editorship reveals itself in an obscenity, "sq—w," that connotes primitivism, submission, and sexual victimization.[14] Eddleman means to put the term and "the sense intended" to rest, along with racist assumptions about "savage" indigenous life. At the same time, her declaration that she is "a Cherokee and prouder of that than any distinction she may attain" registers her rejection of the Dawes Commission decision that stripped her of tribal identity. In fact, Eddleman continued to identify as Cherokee, sometimes using her traditional name, Tucheta, and often expressing pride in her Native heritage.[15] Neither the war-paint-and-scalping-knife savage members of the mainstream press describe nor the non-Cherokee the U.S. government denominated, the editor insists on the right to define herself.

Eddleman's focus on descriptions of her mother's "full blood" intimates an opposition, as well, to specific institutional practices of racial identification in the Dawes era. While her response corrects the record on her genetic heritage, it also rejects the essentializing standards of blood quantum in federal policy. Like "sq—w," the adjective "full-blood" functions as part of a subjugating system. Indian policy of the Dawes era aligned an abstract, racialist "sense" of indigenous people—as primitive, dependent, and doomed—and pseudoscientific ideas about the biological essence of racial identity. In insisting she is proudly Cherokee even if not "full-blood," Eddleman counters the dominant culture's standards of tribal belonging by representing herself as an assimilated, mixed-race person who remains deeply connected to her tribe and "the people."

Eddleman's objection anticipates current debates among tribal leaders, government agents, academics, and individuals about how to assess Native and tribal belonging, whether through biological kinship, historic ties to community, cultural orientation, or other criteria.[16] It is neither my intent nor my place to enter into such debates here. Rather, I want to reveal how the editor contested dominant cultural authority to define the terms of those debates. For Eddleman, the question was not simply "Who is an Indian?" but "Who decides?" Through her magazine she presented Native identity as both richly varied and self-determined. In this chapter I argue that Eddleman's adaptations of the commercial magazine genre facilitated resistance against mainstream efforts to categorize and manage Native people as they redefined what it meant to be a Native American at the turn of the twentieth century.

Attention to the ways Eddleman reclaimed an indigenous right of self-definition can reveal the capacities of a conventional print form to scaffold Native political resistance. That scaffolding entails de- and reconstruction: Eddleman both critiqued mainstream print culture and remade the popular magazine form, protesting U.S. Indian policy by taking up, appraising, and transforming an instrument that underwrote it. Where Sigourney's, Wakefield's, and Callahan's interventions into conventional print forms could be oblique, Eddleman's were direct and explicit. She attacked mainstream media for circulating ideas about indigenous people that facilitated their oppression. At the same time, she capitalized on the magazine form's capacity to counter dominant ideologies. Eddleman converted the correspondence column, typically a means of granting a voice and a sense of community to readers, into a mechanism for disciplining white consumers and asserting Native authority. Through a regular photographic feature, she challenged popular visual practices that structured race and class, making possible a reconfiguration of Native, middle-class womanhood. And in her own fictional contributions to the magazine, Eddleman offered variations on the racial passing story that insisted on indigenous rights of racial and tribal self-definition and economic autonomy. Through such transformations, Eddleman turned the commercial magazine into a platform for Native protest.

Mass Culture, Magazine Heterogeneity, and the Native Public Sphere

Like Callahan's *Wynema,* Eddleman's *Twin Territories* addressed both Native and non-Native readers. It contributed, along with a number of Cherokee-produced newspapers, to the explosion of Native print media after removal, a development that kept those in Indian territories informed and provided a forum for debates about political issues affecting them.[17] *Twin Territories* was distinct, however, because it was a commercial magazine not tied to a tribal government, religious organization, or school, and because it was directed at readers both inside and outside of Indian territories. The magazine was profit-driven, launched, as Eddleman recalled in an editorial, "First, because there is not a publication of its kind. . . . Second, because there *ought* to be money in it."[18] Notwithstanding its cover assertion that it was "Published for the Indians of Indian Territory and Oklahoma," it appealed to a national readership in order to generate income from subscriptions and advertising. To a certain extent Eddleman saw the magazine's content as a commodity that should be tailored to meet demands far and wide. "Our first object will be to entertain our readers," she wrote. "We want everybody who reads TWIN TERRITORIES to read it eagerly, and to be interested in what they read. If there is something lacking which you think would be of interest, write us."[19]

The effort to attract a national audience required what Eddleman's contemporary Chauncey Yellow Robe (Sicangu Oyate Lakota) called "commercializing the Indian" for white consumption.[20] In many ways, *Twin Territories* conformed to dominant cultural expectations about the exotic Native. At the same time, the magazine was largely assimilationist and capitalistic, celebrating the ways Native people in Indian territories had adopted dominant cultural values and confirming, to some extent, established cultural hierarchies. It showcased examples of successful Native "progress" such as thriving schools, churches, and businesses, and it urged Native peoples' cooperation with allotment policy as a path to prosperity. One editorial proclaims faith in an assimilationist trinity: "Enlightenment, Christian people, ENTERPRISE! Those are the three levers which have brought order out of chaos: have relegated the unprincipled 'squatter' to the background: have reared flourishing colleges on the site of bark tepees, and caused this earthly abiding place to blossom as a rose."[21]

Such content shares space, however, with traditional indigenous tales, tribal histories, poetry in Native-English patois, and political reports on pan-tribal strategies for challenging federal authority. The magazine published the proceedings of intertribal meetings and reported on the work of tribal delegations to Congress. It featured commentary by leaders in tribal government, including Joshua Ross, a noted Cherokee educator and delegate; Pleasant Porter, chief of the Muscogee (Creek) Nation; and Robert L. Owen, a prominent Cherokee lawyer and lobbyist. As much as it promoted assimilation, the magazine also worked to protect and nurture traditional Native and tribal culture. *Twin Territories* was one of the first places where the works of traditionalist Muscogee poet and humorist Chinnubbie Harjo (Alex Posey) appeared in print.[22] The magazine showcased other Native authors as well, among them Mabel Washbourne Anderson (Cherokee), James Roane Gregory (Yuchi), Charles Gibson (Muscogee), and Henry B. Sarcoxie (Delaware). Beyond appealing to a broad audience, it provided a national stage for specifically indigenous cultural and political expression.

The mix of content and perspectives in the magazine reveals the complex interplay between mass and local culture, commerce and political expression, and racial display and tribal authenticity in Native Americans' involvement in commercial media at the end of the nineteenth century. *Twin Territories* materialized when the development of American mass culture multiplied the possibilities for communicating with broad audiences. The same moment saw intensified attacks on sovereignty and rights, conditions that made Native public expression critical. The need for forums for Native expression was especially urgent in Indian and Oklahoma Territories during implementation of allotment. The so-called Five Civilized Tribes (the Cherokee, Chickasaw, Choctaw, Muscogee, and Seminole peoples) had been initially excluded from the provisions of the Dawes Severalty Act, but pressure on Washington to make 20 million acres of tribally held lands in Indian and Oklahoma Territories available to white "boomers" led to an 1893 Indian Office appropriation bill that extended allotment. The bill empowered the Dawes Commission to finalize tribal enrollments in order to process allotments in the territories. In substantially limiting tribal membership, the federal enrollment operation further shrank land bases and undermined tribal power and culture. Native sovereignty was challenged not just by the U.S. government's seizure and redistribution of tribally held properties, then, but also by its takeover of tribal enrollment procedures. The Eddlemans were not alone in being stripped of their tribal citizenship: of more than 300,000 individuals who applied to the Dawes Commission for enrollment, nearly two thirds were denied.[23]

American mass culture played a significant role in such national efforts to dispossess and disempower Native people. Wild West shows, dime novels, and photographs produced in the allotment era circulated representations of "savage Indians," reinforcing assumptions that indigenous peoples were in need of government management. As Native activists pointed out, the alliance between mass media and federal policy could be overt. Yellow Robe, for example, denounced the Indian Bureau's support of performances and films that perpetuated racist stereotypes of Native people.[24] Yet this period also saw an expansion of Native involvement in the production of mass culture. The U.S. government had ceased treating with Native people in 1871, erasing Native diplomatic standing and authority to negotiate the terms of federal actions affecting tribes. With official channels for Native expression closed, mass-media forms provided an alternative. Yellow Robe seems to embrace the potential of mass media in the prologue to the 1930 film *The Silent*

Enemy (in which he appears), insisting, "This picture is the story of my people."[25]

If mass culture colluded with U.S. efforts to control and contain Native people, it also offered new possibilities for Native resistance. Analyzing the connections between the birth of American mass culture at the turn of the century and the emergence of a Native public sphere, Nancy Bentley argues that other leading figures of Yellow Robe's generation, including Charles Eastman (Santee Dakota), Zitkala-Ša (Yankton Sioux), Standing Bear (Ponca), and Geronimo (Apache), worked to leverage mainstream cultural forms in "an effort at post-diplomatic expressivity, an attempt at world building that looked to the mass communicability of Native styles and signifiers as the materials for securing greater recognition and protection for Native societies." Bentley locates a "generative tension" in Native peoples' mobilization of mass cultural forms as a means of resisting the systematic dismantling of indigenous political authority. Although commercialized racial spectacles like Wild West shows contributed to oppression, "their distinct vantage on the space of mass culture . . . meant that Native Americans saw possibilities for using the energies of mass culture in the service of their own post-diplomatic analysis and expression."[26]

In identifying the ways indigenous people used mass cultural forms to protect and promote Native societies, Bentley departs from recent critical trends that emphasize mediation in Native-authored texts in English. Scholars frequently interpret texts that combine dominant cultural and indigenous styles and perspectives as efforts to address racial conflicts by smoothing out difference. Texts produced by Native women, especially, seem to invite this kind of critical reading, a tendency that should not be surprising given the dominant cultural celebration of figures like Pocahontas and Sacagawea. Cheryl Walker, for example, devotes a chapter of her book on nineteenth-century Native American literature to "Sarah Winnemucca's Mediations."[27] Similarly, Dee Garceau's chapter in a critical anthology on Native women's lives is titled "Mourning Dove: Gender and Cultural Mediation."[28] Studies of Native periodical writing from this period also forward the idea of Native women's facilitating relations between Natives and non-Natives. Focusing on Native women contributors to *American Indian*

Magazine (1916–20), Carol Batker argues that they worked "to keep in play a dialectic between integration and separatism, cultural adaptation and preservation."[29]

Like *American Indian Magazine, Twin Territories* addressed a mixed audience and promoted both progressive assimilation and the preservation of Native culture.[30] Yet to claim that Eddleman used the magazine to mediate cultural differences would be to ignore her frequently oppositional editorial stance. At times, the editor seems to wish to foreclose the possibility of interracial dialogue altogether. In the correspondence department, "What the Curious Want to Know," Eddleman's answers to white letter writers are sometimes so dismissive as to shut down the lines of communication. "Really, I ought not to pay attention to your questions," she writes in response to a correspondent's stereotyping views of Native culture.[31] When another correspondent planning at trip expresses fear of being attacked in the Wild West, Eddleman sniffs, "I'd rather not advise you at all."[32] Alexia Kosmider contends that "What the Curious Want to Know" reflects Eddleman's strategy "to bridge the boundaries that separate 'whites' from 'Indians,' emphasizing Indians who are well educated, similar to whites."[33] But antagonistic "advice" hardly seems calculated to ease conflicts.

Even advocating assimilation was not necessarily a mediating strategy for Eddleman. She characterized assimilation as a means of competing rather than complying with whites, as expressed in a 1902 editorial: "We must learn of our white neighbor and his ways must be our ways, his impulses must stir our emotions and stimulate our energies. We must strive to keep pace with him in his onward march. Why should we not be his rival as well in the grand chase on the high road to prosperity as on the hunter's path? If it is education that has placed him in his advanced station in life, why should not we be as powerful as he?"[34] "Mediation" is an inapt term for such a rallying cry.

In fact, many Native American studies scholars have registered their discomfort with critical emphasis on mediation in English-language texts produced by Native people. They point to the inherent asymmetry of interpretations that privilege acts of transculturation, accommodation, and resolution over expressions of Native political and cultural resistance. Reading for mediation can result in downplaying critical confrontations. For Siobhan Senier, it "can have a disturbing way of keeping Euro-Americans at the center of the discussion; it can frame American Indian writing mainly in terms of what the writing can do for non-Indian readers."[35] Similarly, Robert Allen Warrior (Osage) takes issue with "uncritical praise" of writings by Zitkala-Ša and others in *American Indian Magazine* that emphasize integrationist political positions at the expense of attention to the considerable inter- and intraracial conflicts of the progressive era.[36] For Jace Weaver (Cherokee), celebrating such cultural negotiations can be "another way of asserting Western universalism against native peoples."[37]

If the contradictions in *Twin Territories* are not efforts to mediate, how should we understand them? And how can we reconcile the magazine's mass distribution and commercialism with its stated claim to speak to and for indigenous people? Answering these questions requires an appreciation of the heterogeneity and contestation that constitute a public sphere, as well as attention to ways the magazine form, in particular, accommodates tensions critical to publics and counterpublics. In a moment of political crisis in which the dominant culture compels consent through legal and extralegal pressures, any platform that encourages a multiplicity of views can create the "generative tensions" essential to the emergence of a Native public sphere. The inherent multiplicity of the magazine form accommodates meaningful public deliberations as other print forms do not. Eddleman's editorship of *Twin Territories* reveals the ways the conventions of the commercial magazine—heterogeneity of perspectives, capacity to organize or discipline readers, recontextualization of popular visual forms, and potential for accreting themes over time through seriality—might be exploited in order to claim an indigenous right to self-definition and political expression.

To make this claim is to enter into longstanding debates about the promises and perils of expression through commercial print media. Descriptions of publics frequently grapple with the question of what mass cultural products like magazines do *to* and *for* their producers and consumers. Print periodicals helped to engender the public sphere Jürgen Habermas describes emerging in the eighteenth century, when the circulation of English "moral weeklies" like the *Tatler,* the *Spectator,* and the *Guardian* stimulated public discussions among bourgeois readers in coffeehouses and salons. These kinds of texts allowed for a distribution of knowledge and opinion that had previously been concentrated in high-ranking individuals, state institutions, and the church, and in this way they helped produce liberal democratic agency. Readers became informed, shared opinions, and drew conclusions in ways that granted them agency.[38]

But Habermas argues that with the increased commercialization of periodicals in the nineteenth century, print culture began encouraging individuated reception of texts and performances and discouraging rational-critical argumentation in the public arena. The "structural transformation" of the public sphere—that is to say, its dissolution—occurred when subjects began consuming mass-media texts and performances privately and passively, a practice that undermined the democratic circulation of opinions. For Habermas, developments in modern mass media "deprive [consumers] of the opportunity to say something and to disagree"; the unwritten rule imposed on consumers is "Don't talk back!"[39]

Subsequent scholars have found much to object to in Habermas's conception of the public sphere. Feminist and Marxist theorists remind us that, contrary to the utopian vision of an eighteenth-century realm in which social status had no bearing, the bourgeois public denied women, the underclass, and people of color the right to participate in its deliberations. Critics also oppose Habermas's indictment of commercial mass-media forms and his privileging of the role of high cultural or "literary" materials in the production of publics. A number of recent books in media and cultural studies explore how new kinds of deliberative publics (or counterpublics) might be formed around emergent mass cultural, post-literary media.[40]

Studies of popular periodicals offer particularly rich analyses of the development of counterpublics, as scholars have begun to show how commercial magazines in the nineteenth century indeed "talked back" to the dominant public.[41] Coming full circle from Habermas's celebration of print weeklies, some scholars see challenges to established structures of power in the rise of the magazine industry. Recent interest in nineteenth- and early twentieth-century American and British periodicals has been fueled in part by a sense that magazines amplify voices on the margins. As Jean Marie Lutes explains, "Precisely *because* writing published in periodicals lacks the prestige and status of the bound book, it is an essential source for scholars who seek insight into writers who—by virtue of their gender, race, ethnicity, class, sexual orientation, or other factors—have lacked access to the most privileged venues of American letters."[42] Scholars have called attention to the shifting demographics of editors, writers, and readers, as women and racial minorities increasingly produced and consumed magazines.[43] For Matthew Schneirov, turn-of-the-century magazine culture contributed to "the dream of a new social order."[44]

In attending to the ways the marginalized use mass cultural print forms like magazines to constitute counterpublics, Habermas's critics have emphasized the value of public contestation. Rejecting the notion of a singular public—"*the* public"—Nancy Fraser posits a nexus of multiple publics that exist in competition with each other as well as in opposition to the "official" white, patriarchal public sphere. Competition among multiple publics is necessary for a healthy democracy, Fraser insists, because "in stratified societies, arrangements that accommodate contestation among a plurality of competing publics better promote the ideal of participatory parity than does a single, comprehensive, overarching public sphere." Contestation is a key characteristic of Fraser's concept of subaltern counterpublics. She takes issue with the very notion of an *a priori* set of "common concerns" on which participants in the public sphere ostensibly deliberate, for "what will count as a matter of common concern will be decided precisely through discursive contestation." Fraser thus distinguishes between public deliberations, processes that "tend to operate to the advantage of dominant groups and to the disadvantages of subordinates," and public contestations, which "help expand discursive space" to make room for the competing interests and identities that make up a diverse society.[45]

Other critics capitalize on this distinction between an official public sphere that strives for consensus and the contestant counterpublics at its margins. In her analysis of the black counterpublic sphere at the turn of the twentieth century, Catherine R. Squires objects to the idea that all members of a counterpublic share the same ideologies and engage in political resistance in the same ways. Such a view obscures the heterogeneity of constituents within marginalized groups and the range of opinions that variously relate to those of the dominant public.[46] While Fraser emphasizes "interpublic relations," discursive contact among different publics, Squires calls for further consideration of "intrapublic" engagement and contests.[47]

Bringing together Fraser's and Squires's lines of thinking sheds light on the ways a magazine like *Twin Territories* might support a Native counterpublic by structuring contestations both *across* and *within* publics. The magazine form is exceptionally well-suited to disrupting the drive for consensus and producing exchanges that construct the counterpublic. Attention to its productive tensions challenges the critical view that mass culture (often described, like the public, as a singular entity, "*the* mass culture") extinguished the flame of critical public discourse. As Margaret Beetham points out, the magazine form is radically heterogeneous, mixing different kinds of written and visual texts created by different people for varied purposes and in a range of contexts. Moreover, the genre embodies a temporal multifariousness that underlines distinctions among its different components and contributors. A magazine is not a singular manuscript produced in a defined historical moment but a number of issues appearing over time. Inevitably, a magazine's articles, poems, stories, and illustrations exist in dialogue with one another, both within a given issue and across a periodical run. Beetham usefully describes the periodical as having a "double relationship to time. Each number of a periodical is both of its moment and of a series, different and yet the same as those which have gone before."[48] While there is a certain imperative for consistency across issues (in terms of the title, general format, and regularity of publication), periodicity aligns with diversity of content and authorship to encourage the debates of public life in ways other textual forms do not.[49]

Beetham draws on communication theories of seriality to distinguish between "closed" forms, those that assert dominant structures of meaning by closing off alternatives, and "open" forms that "refuse the closed ending," making them potentially disruptive. She points to several features that make the magazine "open": "It resists closure because it comes out over time and is, in that respect, serial rather than end-stopped. Its boundaries are fluid and it mixes genres and authorial voices; all this in a time-extended form seems to encourage readers to produce their own readings."[50] Beetham's distinction has bearing on the evolving understanding of counterpublics as heterogeneous systems, platforms for contestation that resist social pressure for consensus. It suggests the need to pay close attention to the dynamic conjunctions that occur in magazines as a way of exploring the possibilities of democratic pluralism in the modern era.

Eddleman's "Indian Magazine" is heterogeneous and "open" not just in its multimediality, plural authorship, and seriality but also in the diversity of political perspectives that its content, producers, and audiences bring into conjunction. The heterogeneity of *Twin Territories* makes it a rich ground for the production of both inter- and intrapublic exchange on issues important to people in Indian territories. Differing opinions about assimilation and traditionalism, for example, find articulation across multiple issues of the magazine. Muscogee writer Charles Gibson argues in an April 1902 essay that assimilation will result in, as his title indicates, "The Passing of the Indian": "The Indian is now being hurried into civilization, and also to his doom."[51] Six months later, an essay with the same title, by white businessman and ethnographer Montague Chamberlain, counters Gibson's prediction with one more sanguine: the assimilated Native "will pass into our American civilization, and will be a strong factor in the life of our nation."[52] The repetition of the title calls the reader's attention to difference more than consensus, as Chamberlain reconfigures Gibson's passing *out of* existence as a kind of racial passing *into* mainstream society. There is no question about where Eddleman stood in this debate. She championed assimilation and occasionally expressed her frustration with traditionalists who refused to adopt mainstream practices. And yet in placing these two essays in explicit dialogue (a headnote preceding Chamberlain's essay refers readers to Gibson's), she reproduces ongoing negotiations within and outside of Native communities about the possibilities and threats of assimilation.

A dialogue emerges more dramatically in "The Comanches, or 'Prairie Indians,'" a serialized "imaginary conversation between a Comanche Indian and his friend, Mr. Progress," which allegorizes ongoing debates between progressives and traditionalists. In the series, "Mr. Progress" urges his Comanche friend to release himself from attachment to the past. His Native interlocutor "Wild Tiger" counters, "The pleasures which you say civilization and education brings to the white man are woes and tribulations to the Indian."[53] Such imagined debates in the pages of *Twin Territories* help to establish the Native community as a public—that is, as an entity constituted by the layering of different ideas, opinions, and responses, or, in Michael Warner's terms, by the "concatenation of texts through time."[54]

Of course, not all mass-media texts encourage inter- and intra-public debate in this way. As Yellow Robe's complaint about collusion between the state and the culture industry indicates, sensationalistic representations of Native people in commercial mass media supported racial hierarchies and fortified efforts to repress those on the margins. Bias in the mainstream press reinforced ideas about indigenous peoples that in turn propped up U.S. projects aimed at undermining tribal sovereignty. Anticipating Yellow Robe, Eddleman often criticized the mainstream press for circulating damaging stereotypes of Native people. At the beginning of its fifth year of publication, she offers a history of the magazine that emphasizes its mission to counter the false representations of Natives being circulated in other magazines and newspapers:

> When in many ways these territories, particularly Indian Territory, were being misrepresented by false reports and gross exaggerations, when the truth about the Indians of the Five Civilized Tribes was being withheld and in its place glowing accounts of the "wild Indian Territory inhabitants" were being published in many eastern and northern publications for the benefit of those who were becoming interested in this part of the world, Twin Territories came on the scene, and, with a few other periodicals that realized the harm that was being done to a great people and a great country, has tried faithfully to portray the true condition of things, the real advancement of the Indian people, and to help in whatever measure it could to place the civilized Indian and his

> home in a true light for the people interested, but who had been, alas, wrongly informed.[55]

Native periodicals like *Twin Territories,* Eddleman insists, bear a counterpublic obligation not just to create a forum for internal and intercultural "talk" but to "talk back" to other print institutions.

Eddleman's serialized short story "Only an Indian Girl" thematizes this conflict between mainstream and indigenous print culture as it establishes Native communities as publics characterized by reasoned, open debate. The story revolves around a romance between a misguided white publisher and a self-possessed Native journalist. Morrison, owner of a New York newspaper, travels west at his doctor's orders. Carrying his prejudices about Native people with him to Tahlequah, Indian Territory, he is surprised to find a vibrant, politically complex community. Even more to his astonishment, he meets an independent young Cherokee woman, Danny Gray, who is a talented writer. Initially dismissing Danny as "only an Indian girl," Morrison finds himself drawn to her self-reliance and intelligence. Morrison's conversion narrative is not unlike that of the white teacher in *Wynema,* with Danny reeducating Morrison and helping him see the error of his ways. Danny pokes fun at Morrison's racist notions of Indian Territory, joking that he "must keep a sharp lookout for the Indians, who crave the white man's scalp," and the newcomer has to concede that he has been a "fool" and a "blockhead" in his assumptions about life and culture in the territories.[56] Native-run territory newspapers also contribute to Morrison's conversion: as he reads eloquent editorials and reports, he comes to appreciate the deliberativeness of the inhabitants and the complexities of their political debates. His reading enlightens him about a highly divisive Cherokee tribal election in which traditionalist and progressive interests clash—about the contestations, that is, of a dynamic Native public.[57]

Contained within the romance story is a critique of dominant mass media and an insistence on the need for Native intervention in its narratives. Learning that Morrison is a newspaper man, Danny's father voices concern that the New Yorker may be in Tahlequah to "write up the country." "We have all sorts of things written about us by men who like to create sensations," he worries aloud. "If they'd tell the truth we wouldn't mind so much, but they make us out too bad."[58] Like Yellow Robe in his critique of Wild West shows, Mr. Gray sees mainstream media outside of Indian territories as circulating damaging stereotypes. As the representative of the mainstream press, Morrison needs the correction that the Native journalist, Danny, supplies. The story's conventional happy ending has Danny accepting Morrison's offer of employment as an assistant editor and principal writer, as well as, subsequently, his marriage proposal. Morrison learns to see in different ways, but he also comes to understand the need to bring Native voices into mainstream media in order to "tell the truth." The story does more than just establish Tahlequah as a dynamic, democratic public; it also reimagines mass media's role in amplifying a diversity of public and counterpublic voices. In strikingly metanarrative gestures, "Only an Indian Girl" articulates the need to include Native voices in dominant cultural print outlets as a means of counterbalancing the circulation of stereotypes and untruths about Native people.

"Read up a Little": Disciplining Non-Natives

Beyond critiquing mainstream media, *Twin Territories* censures and disciplines mainstream readers. The correspondence column "What the Curious Want to Know" began appearing in *Twin Territories* in December 1900 and became a regular feature in 1902, when Eddleman returned to her post as editor after a hiatus. In that year, it appeared near the middle of most issues and occupied a full page or more, suggesting its central importance to the magazine. The column was signed "B.A.N." initially, and "Yours Candidly" in subsequent appearances, but the editorial voice is clearly Eddleman's.[59] The feature is significant for the ways it dismantles an economy of knowledge that privileged white understanding and for its brash repudiation of the media conventions that made Native lives and properties objects of white consumption.

"What the Curious Want to Know" is unconventional in its refusal to empower correspondents as participants in a conversation about Native issues. Periodicals may be seen as more social than other text forms because they conventionally encourage interaction among readers, writers, and editors.[60] Correspondence columns, which became more prominent in British and American periodicals at the end of the nineteenth century, typically invite readers to be part of a conversation in the pages of magazines, offering them a sense of community and granting them a public voice. Accordingly, scholars have mined letters from readers of nineteenth-century magazines for evidence of community building and individual empowerment.[61] Eddleman's correspondence column, in contrast, isolates and disempowers a group of readers. It addresses almost exclusively "our subscribers in the states," non-Native readers from cities like Chicago and New York and small towns up and down the East Coast.[62] While elsewhere she encouraged local readers' interaction with her magazine, in this department Eddleman disciplined the "curious" outsiders who would insert themselves into tribal communities and exploit their human and material resources.[63]

One of the most obvious ways Eddleman disciplined non-Native readers was by silencing them. Unlike other correspondence columns of the period, "What the Curious Want to Know" omits readers' questions, publishing only Eddleman's answers. Her responses sometimes, but not always, indicate the nature of inquiries. A typical entry answers "Doubting Thomas, Edinburg, Massachusetts" this way: "Yes, it is certainly true that the majority of the Indian girls of this country can easily stand as the equal of their white sisters, in point of beauty and education. Many of the Indian girls are finished in music and art. (b) Who told you that? It is not true."[64] By not publishing the original queries and instead selectively referencing them, the Native editor essentially authorizes herself to speak for white correspondents. And by picking and choosing the queries she paraphrases—leaving readers to wonder, for example, what foolish question prompted the second answer to "Doubting Thomas"—she denies correspondents control over their own discourse. These nonlocal, non-Native correspondents can neither form imagined communities among themselves as readers of *Twin Territories* nor contribute content to the periodical. Eddleman's management of outsiders' words makes her column counterpublic in an unexpected way, by effectively denying members of the dominant public entry into critical conversations within Indian territories.

Moreover, the department constructs non-Native information-seekers in ways that expose their materialistic self-interests, thereby refusing the possibility of a monolithic public oriented around "common concerns." The department's title reflects the magazine's commercialism in its suggestion that it supplies what consumers "want." Yet from the outset, Eddleman objected to non-Native readers' demands for information, demands fed by the "false reports and gross exaggerations" circulating in the mainstream press. In a note introducing the department in 1900, Eddleman complains that "columns filled with . . . ridiculous and sensational fabrications" in northern and eastern newspapers suggest there are fortunes to be made in Indian territories. These reports had led eastern profit-seekers to harass tribal officials with their queries. With "What the Curious Want to Know," Eddleman reluctantly takes on the task of addressing these queries:

> Even now *Twin Territories* would not dwell on this subject were it not for the fact that the chiefs of the several tribes of Indians and Indian Agents are continually in receipt of letters written by verdant youths and cast-off old bachelors living in the northern and eastern states who haven't brains enough to discern the truth nor comprehension enough to judge human nature, who are the misguided victims of the stories referred to in this article. What ordinary common sense youth reared in the western country would ever be guilty of entertaining the foolish idea that anywhere among any people could be found a wealthy maiden foolish enough to purchase a husband?[65]

This description does more than insult the people who necessitate a department like "What the Curious Want to Know." It also defines the motivations of most of the "curious" as pure greed, rather than harmless interest. Eastern youths and old bachelors are curious about Indian territories because they want to acquire a Native wife and obtain her allotted land. Indeed, answers to white men determined to find a propertied Native bride appear frequently in the department (along with at least two answers to white women hoping to marry Native men).[66] Notwithstanding Eddleman's assurance in a subheading that "All questions relative to this country and the Indians whose home it is will be cheerfully answered," her introductory comment makes "What the Curious Want to Know" a censure of her audience outside of Indian territories.[67] It reflects an underlying goal of the department: to expose the popular interest in Native people and culture as symptomatic of non-Natives' desire to possess, in both abstract and concrete ways, Native bodies and properties.

Some of the questions addressed in "What the Curious Want to Know" seem innocent enough. Correspondents might ask about the invention of the Cherokee alphabet or the meaning of "Muscogee," for example, and Eddleman responds courteously, if succinctly, to such queries.[68] But most entries reflect correspondents' self-interest, their desire for land, business opportunities, and Native artifacts. Eddleman tersely redirects or dismisses many requests for information of this kind. "Yes, you can lease land here. . . . Write to one of the real estate agents who advertise in Twin Territories," she tells "Farmer's Boy, Payton, Ind." In the same column she informs "Curio Collector, Ebensburg, New Hampshire," that the artifacts he or she seeks are not for sale.[69] She puts off the unambiguously named "Hustler, Altoona, Ill.," who apparently wants to gauge the market for newspapers in the territories: "Yes, there are three—one daily and two weeklies. It is a good town, but does not need another newspaper yet."[70] But her business-like tone does not mitigate the cumulative effect of a stream of grasping queries from profit-seeking outsiders, and at times her impatience erupts in sarcasm. When "Milliner, Oakhill, New York," asks if it is true that Indians like beads on their hats, Eddleman makes no effort to contain her annoyance: "What do you take us for? Where have you been the last half century? Seriously, I wouldn't advise you to come here with a stock of millinery. . . . The poor Indians'll manage to get head-gear in some way or other, without you. . . . It would be a pity to have you sacrifice yourself to come way out here in order to educate them to wearing up-to-date hats. It wouldn't pay you, my dear madam—but you might learn a whole lot!"[71] The sting of the response lies in its canny reversals. The non-Native subject is presented as the one who is out of step with progress; the milliner may intend to teach Native people about fashion but she has much to learn herself. More broadly, the comment challenges an economy of knowledge in which Native people are subject to instruction from whites on all matters, from fashion to farming practices, and it establishes Native authority over the distribution of information about Indian territories.

Again and again in the department Eddleman calls attention to her non-Native correspondents' ignorance, and she takes a commanding tone that belies her own youth. "You talk in conundrums, John, my dear boy," she chides one letter writer. "If you want an answer from me 'through the male,' as you write it, send a stamp—or a messenger boy!"[72] She castigates would-be suitors of Native women: "So you, too, are willing to sacrifice yourself for a 'squaw,' provided she's not too ugly, and has land? I've no patience with your kind."[73] If the emphasis on the ignorance of white correspondents reverses structures of knowledge, the use of acerbic humor here and elsewhere performs another reversal: it makes white outsiders, those consumers of mainstream representations of Native people, sources of entertainment for Native readers who know better.

"What the Curious Want to Know" suggests an antidote to the kind of mindless consumption of print media that threatens democratic publics and counterpublics: the non-Native reader is advised, "Educate yourself."[74] "It seems to me that any person of average intelligence would know by this time that Indian girls aren't so hard up for suitors as to be willing to offer themselves and their lands and money," Eddleman chastises a correspondent. "You're away off track. Read up."[75] To "Indian Territory's Admiring Friend, Geneva, N.Y.," she responds, "I don't know whether to advise you to come here or not. . . . If you should come, and the Indians here 'ate you up,' then you'd blame me, and I don't want to be responsible. However, I'll say this much—if the shocks of sudden surprises are shattering to your nerves, don't come to Indian Territory with your present idea of its wildness. Read up a little."[76] The repeated admonishment to "read up" comes with qualifiers. Eddleman reminds readers that getting at the truth about Native people requires discriminating among conventional print sources. In her answer to "Curiosity, Wellsville, N.Y.," she at once critiques mainstream print culture and presents her own magazine as the most reliable source for information. "You have evidently been reading some of the many falsehoods about this country," she writes.

"Read TWIN TERRITORIES regularly and get the truth, and you won't ask such foolish questions."[77] Like Callahan's *Wynema,* Eddleman's "What the Curious Want to Know" prescribes a critical reading practice, but more than the novel this correspondence department privileges Native print media as most qualified to convey the truth about indigenous life and identity.

Counterarchives of Native Womanhood

Twin Territories is heavily illustrated, and photographic images throughout the magazine provide another way for Eddleman to resist non-Native attempts to circumscribe and exploit Native life. At the turn of the century, commercial photography both defined the possessive individualism of white Americans and subjugated racial others. Portrait photography extended an aristocratic tradition of self-representation to middle-class whites, allowing them to advertise dominant cultural values of individualism and materialism. At the same time, institutional images of criminals, "scientific" catalogues of racial "types," and romanticized pictures of indigenous people helped to solidify boundary lines between whites and others by presenting visual evidence of biological difference and the inferiority of non-whites. Nineteenth-century photography was "a system of representation capable of functioning both *honorifically* and *repressively,*" as Allan Sekula puts it in his comparison of middle-class portraits and criminal mug shots.[78] In the regular feature "Types of Indian Girls" (sometimes titled "Types of Indian Women"), Eddleman reconfigures commercial photography to disrupt that system. The department presents a "counterarchive" of images that at once claims a space for Native females in the middle class and challenges essentializing representations of indigenous exoticism and inferiority. Considered in the context of commercial studio photographs of both white and Native women in Indian territories, "Types of Indian Women" can be recognized as a way of contesting the multilayered visual-cultural systems that structured social hierarchies at the turn of the century.

In identifying "Types of Indian Girls" as a counterarchive, I draw on Shawn Michelle Smith's comparative methodology for understanding the ways photographic displays construct race or contest racialized social structures. Smith reads W. E. B. Du Bois's archive of photographs of African Americans, collected for the Paris Exposition of 1900 in volumes titled *Types of American Negroes* and *Negro Life in Georgia,* against competing photographic practices that reinforce predominating structures of race and class. Juxtaposing Du Bois's collections with middle-class portraiture and the photographic catalogues produced by biological racialists reveals that "visual culture was fundamental not only to racist classification but also to racial reinscription and the reconstruction of racial knowledge in the nineteenth and early twentieth centuries."[79] As Smith points out, the title of *Types of American Negroes* echoes the essentializing terms of scientific taxonomies that sought to codify racial "types" according to physiognomic traits (Francis Galton's eugenicist catalogues are a prime example). Yet Du Bois's archive confounds scientific racialism by representing African Americans with a vast diversity of phenotypes, including dark and light skin and eyes, in order to register the contingency of race. At the same time, the archive presents subjects in conventional middle-class poses and uses settings and props that signal high economic standing in order to insist on African Americans' inclusion in the middle class.

Du Bois refused, in other words, to "type" the American Negro as essentially other.[80] Eddleman's similarly titled "Types of Indian Girls," which appeared two years before Du Bois's archive, also deploys the conventions of commercial portraiture to emphasize its Native subjects' middle-class belonging, and it simultaneously works against an industry of racial display that defines Native people as exotic and archaic. Eddleman thus reconfigured commercial photographic representation, a technology of white, middle-class affirmation and Native subjugation at the turn of the century, as an instrument of protest.

Commercial photographers moved west in droves in the later decades of the nineteenth century, establishing studios in rapidly developing towns and cities. They were aided by a number of technological advancements that made photography easier and more profitable. Smaller film cameras lessened the difficulty of transporting equipment, dry-plate technology minimized exposure time, and advances in printing allowed for cheaper reproduction. (Another innovation, the half-tone process developed in 1880, benefited *Twin Territories* by facilitating printing of photographs in newspapers and magazines without the use of engravings).[81] Economic shifts within and outside of the territories, meanwhile, made studio portraiture a lucrative business.

Professional portrait photography was a mechanism of middle-class, white personhood in Indian territories as elsewhere. Economic boom times produced a steady stream of middle-class customers. For the newly emigrated, a studio portrait could nicely demonstrate success in the territories, through both the subject's fine clothing and the fact that he or she could afford the services of a professional photographer. Middle-class portraits conveyed more abstract qualities as well. Traditionally, portraitists use formal conventions like settings and poses to capture the individuality of the subject, "the fragile architecture of a human character that has never existed before and will never exist again." In a typical pose in commercial portrait photography, subjects look not directly into the camera lens but slightly at angle and into the distance, with an expression that communicates introspection and emotional gravity.[82] As Smith argues, the commercial photographic portrait marks out social boundaries by bestowing interiority on a select group: accessible only to those who can afford it, it makes interior essence the exclusive possession of members of the privileged classes.[83] The middle-class studio portrait facilitates, in Sekula's words, "the ceremonial presentation of the bourgeois self."[84]

A carte de visite taken around 1900 by Stillwater, Oklahoma Territory, photographer Henry Madison Wantland illustrates the conventions that established middle-class identity in this period. The photograph depicts an unidentified young woman whose starched white blouse, silk skirt, and fashionably oversized hat advertise solid economic standing (fig. 4). The contrast between the dark hat and light blouse plays against a muted gray backdrop to draw attention to the sitter's face and eyes. The backdrop's soft floral wall pattern subtly evokes the decor of a Victorian drawing room. The only prop is what appears to be a tightly folded handkerchief the woman holds in one hand, proof, perhaps, of her retention of feminine refinement in what many Americans thought of as the Wild West. The woman's contemplative gaze, directed somewhere over the photographer's shoul-

FIGURE 4. Henry Madison Wantland, *Carte de Visite Single Portrait of a Young Woman Sitting,* ca. 1900. Courtesy © Dickinson Research Center, National Cowboy and Western Heritage Museum, Oklahoma City, Oklahoma.

der, projects thoughtfulness and serenity. All of these details grant the subject of the portrait the depth of character and context of material comfort that constituted middle-class belonging.

But middle-class portraiture was not the only source of profits for professional photographers in Indian territories. Studios also supplied the high demand for images of the "vanishing race" of Native Americans. Art and commercial photography industries at the turn of the century at once capitalized on and perpetuated the idea that "the

Indian as he has hitherto been is on the point of passing away," as Theodore Roosevelt put it in his foreword to Edward S. Curtis's famous photography collection *The North American Indian* (1907–30).[85] The popular appetite for souvenir "Indian pictures" was enormous. Studio photographers reproduced such images on stereographs, postcards, and cabinet cards (images mounted on cardboard that often advertised the photography studio on the bottom or reverse side), and they sold hundreds of thousands between 1890 and 1920.[86] So popular were these representations that William Henry Jackson, one of the most successful commercial photographers in the West, formed a partnership with a Detroit company to produce colored lithographs at a rate of two hundred prints an hour. It is not clear whether or how much Native individuals were paid to sit for photographs intended for the market—Jackson reported paying Native models "a small recompense"—but certainly they did not share in the profits when their likenesses were sold many times over.[87] If middle-class portraits signaled white subjects' economic authority, then the scores of souvenir Indian pictures produced in the same period reflected Native peoples' economic exploitation.

More than this, souvenir Indian pictures supported racial and social hierarchies by recirculating stereotypes of Native people as exotic, archaic, and tied to nature. For Richard W. Hill, Sr. (Tuscarora), the indigenous subjects in such photographs appear "enveloped in a romantic stillness and removed in time."[88] Staging and props contributed to the sense that Native people had been left behind in a rapidly modernizing world. Subjects appear in traditional clothing, sometimes holding bows or other accouterments and posed against painted backdrops of outdoor scenes. Boulders or tree branches might be brought into the studio to fill out the visual field, and in some cases subjects sat or stood on mats made to resemble grass (fig. 5). In two images produced in the Fort Sill, Oklahoma Territory, studio of photographer George A. Addison around 1895, young indigenous women lean awkwardly on massive tree stumps. Taking up nearly a third of the visual field and emphatically cut short, the stumps are not just signs of Native people's place in nature; they are also powerful metaphors for a kind of truncation of human progress (figs. 6 and 7). As contrived as such contexts are,

FIGURE 5. George A. Addison, *Young Kiowa (?) Woman in Buckskin Dress with Elk Tooth Decoration, Bow and Arrow,* ca. 1895. Courtesy © Dickinson Research Center, National Cowboy and Western Heritage Museum, Oklahoma City, Oklahoma.

FIGURE 6. George A. Addison, *Young Indian Woman with Fringed Shawl,* ca. 1895. Courtesy © Dickinson Research Center, National Cowboy and Western Heritage Museum, Oklahoma City, Oklahoma.

they fulfilled cultural expectations of the primitive, natural, and vanishing Native other.

Such staging does much to "type" Native people as anthropological specimens, rather than as individuals. Whereas middle-class portraits might be shot with minimal props and against indistinct backdrops, these artifices play a more prominent role in souvenir

FIGURE 7. Studio of George A. Addison, *Studio Portrait of Indian Girl with Elaborate Dress,* ca. 1895. Courtesy © Dickinson Research Center, National Cowboy and Western Heritage Museum, Oklahoma City, Oklahoma.

Indian pictures. The muted floral wallpaper and the handkerchief in Wantland's portrait only whisper a context, encouraging the viewer to focus on the subject's expression as a reflection of her individuality. The painted backdrops and oversized stumps in the Addison studio photographs, in contrast, make an explicit connection between the subject and an (artificial) extra-domestic space. The prominence of studio embellishments suggests that these subjects, lacking self-evident distinctions of personality, require a strong visual narrative to represent them adequately.[89] Native subjectivity fades in the face of such representation, as the elaborate contrivance of a "natural" setting denies the models their individuality. As is evident in the identically staged images of women leaning against stumps, individual Native subjects become little more than variations on a theme.

The way the models are posed in such photographs further reduces the sense of personhood. Blank, forward expressions and direct gazes at the camera suggest documentation rather than portraiture. These images are not made to capture the subject's interior self but to preserve evidence of a disappearing culture, albeit as defined by dominant cultural expectations. The subjects' standing poses were likely intended to highlight the beading, needlework, and fringing on their traditional clothing. Yet because the women are not identified on the photograph by name or tribe, there is little differentiation of specific cultures. Instead, the repetition of poses and props effectively genericizes Native identity. In contrast to the individualized subject of Wantland's photograph, the Native women in the souvenir pictures are made representatives of an entire race.

As different as they are, then, middle-class photographic portraits and souvenir Indian pictures joined in the larger project of affirming racial and social hierarchies. In "Types of Indian Girls," Eddleman co-opts both of these photographic conventions in order to disrupt the social structures they supported. The department presents studio portraits of Native women living in Indian territories. Captions identify subjects by name and tribe, occasionally offering additional details about an individual's interests and family. The department's title notwithstanding, subjects presented here are not "types" but individuals of merit and distinction. An editorial comment accompanying the third installment of "Types of Indian Girls" insists that "just ANYBODY can't get their picture in TWIN TERRITORIES. She must be a pure-minded, respectable girl."[90] These criteria for selecting subjects for the department followed requirements of middle-class womanhood in their emphasis on feminine virtue, but they deviated from mainstream codes in two important ways: rich and poor women, even "the poorest girl in the Territory," might be included among those represented, and, as a headnote introducing the first installment announces, "pictures of Indian women, only, will appear."[91] The department thus extends the representation of individuality, of "pure-minded and respectable" character, to Native people and the underclass. At its most basic level, "Types of Indian Girls" grants Native women the subjectivity and self-possession they were denied in other commercial representations.

Many of the photographs reproduced in the department closely follow the conventions of middle-class studio portraiture. Subjects sit against neutral gray or black backdrops, and they are shot from the shoulders up, a composition that draws attention to the face and gaze. The close framing of these conventionally posed portraits provides a view of subjects' Victorian clothing and hairstyles without making them defining characteristics. At first glance, the portraits of Native women in mainstream middle-class attire might appear to function as little more than advertisements for the assimilative "progress" of Indian territories, much like the images of bustling schools and successful businesses elsewhere in the magazine. Kosmider argues accordingly that Eddleman's presentation of indigenous womanhood in "Types of Indian Girls" draws on European American ideals mostly to endorse them, in the process erasing its subjects' Native and tribal identity.[92]

But such a reading assumes that Native women in European American dress somehow forfeited their Native identities—in effect, that Native being inheres in the kinds of clothing and props that commercial photographers like Addison used to define Native subjects. The captions for the individual photographs reject this racialized logic by underscoring subjects' tribal affiliations. In the July 1902 installment of "Types of Indian Girls," for example, the caption for the photograph of Leota Crabtree describes her as "a beautiful young girl who is proud of her Creek blood."[93] The emphasis on pride in tribal origins echoes Eddleman's own editorial assertion of her Cherokee heritage and suggests that the appearance of assimilation does not cancel out Native identity.

At the same time, the poses of the subjects solidify their middle-class belonging. In her portrait in the same installment, Ella Monahwee sits at a slight angle to the camera. Holding her chin high and serenely gazing into the distance, she projects dignity, intelligence, and strong character, even a kind of nobility. In contrast to the women in souvenir Indian photographs, she is as an individual, not an artifact. The caption under her portrait emphasizes that she has "only a fraction of white blood, mingled with that of the Creek tribe," affirming that middle-class individuality is as much the possession of Natives as non-Natives (fig. 8).[94]

The recurrence of the "Indian blood" idiom in the two captions gives pause because it seems to invoke the federal government's standard of blood quantum as a measure of Native identity. For the Dawes Commission, the degree of Native descent was biologically defined but fully legible in an applicant's appearance. Rather than relying on self-reporting or existent tribal rolls, the commission largely worked by assessing subjects' outward presentation and behavior. In interviews with thousands of applicants, commissioners looked at dress, language, and social conduct for signs of Nativeness. Rose Stremlau's analysis of Dawes Commission records reveals that applicants whose appearance or behavior was thought to approximate dominant cultural norms—those who dressed and acted "white"—were assigned a lower blood quantum, while those who displayed what were perceived as Native social and cultural values were assigned a higher blood quantum.[95] Because only subjects deemed at least one-half Native qualified for allotments, the ironic result was that many Native people were penalized, in terms of loss of property and rights of tribal citizenship, for looking and acting like middle-class whites—that is, for exhibiting the assimilation that the Dawes Act was intended to encourage.

Not surprisingly, using visual impressions as empirical evidence for racial and tribal identity often resulted in wildly inaccurate judgments. On the basis of appearance and behavior, full siblings were sometimes assigned different degrees of blood quantum.[96] Another problem arose because of the way the commission conflated tribe and race: the offspring of a "full-blood" Muscogee mother and a "full-blood" Seminole father, for instance, might be designated one-half Indian of the Muscogee tribe.[97] Such errors

204 TWIN TERRITORIES.

TYPES OF INDIAN GIRLS.

A Beauty of the Cherokee Tribe, Miss Helen Severs.

Miss Ella Monahwee, in whose veins flows only a fraction of white blood, mingled with that of the Creek tribe.

Miss Leota Crabtree, a beautiful young girl who is proud of her Creek blood.

FIGURE 8. "Types of Indian Girls." In *Twin Territories* 4, no. 7 (July 1902), 204. Courtesy Library Division, Western History Collections, University of Oklahoma Libraries.

expose the arbitrary nature of the system and the illogic of defining tribal identity as a biological fact revealed in observable traits. It is unclear whether members of the Eddleman family appeared in person before the Dawes Commission. It is likely, though, that Eddleman's preference for European American clothing and hairstyles would have suggested to Dawes authorities that she lacked enough Cherokee "blood" to qualify for tribal citizenship.

Eddleman's presentation of individuals who approximate European American identity in dress but are Muscogee by "blood," however, rejects the idea that indigenous essence inheres in appearance. The insistence that Monahwee has only a fraction of "white blood" despite her middle-class appearance challenges Dawes Commission systems of assessment. Eddleman's own photographic presentation did the same. The portrait accompanying her essay in *Good Housekeeping* shows her in European American dress and hairstyle, yet the caption underneath identifies the author as Cherokee and includes her tribal name.[98] A more souvenir-esque portrait of Eddleman published in *Twin Territories* with the caption "An Indian Huntress Costume" presents her in dress that is anything but traditional.[99] These presentations confound ideas about the legibility of Native identity. Like the portraits in "Types of Indian Girls," they refute the surveillance system used by U.S. officials to manage Native people.

In most installments of "Types of Indian Girls," Eddleman uses the formal conventions of the photographic portrait to construct a Native, middle-class identity. As the image of the editor as an "Indian Huntress" suggests, though, she occasionally deploys the souvenir Indian picture to the same end. In the March 1902 edition of *Twin Territories,* "Types of Indian Girls" features three photographs. The lower third of the page presents oval portraits of two Cherokee women, Nanny Blackstone and Erna Eddleman (Ora Eddleman's sister). Captions identify each subject by name and tribe. Above these pictures is a larger, rectangular one, a nearly full-length portrait, with the caption "ANNIE, (a beautiful Kiowa girl, dress valued at $300)" (fig. 9).[100] The women in the portraits at the bottom of the page wear Victorian dresses and hairstyles, and each sits with her body turning slightly away from the camera and her

FIGURE 9. "Types of Indian Girls." In *Twin Territories* 4, no. 3 (March 1902), 69. Courtesy DeGolyer Library, Southern Methodist University.

gaze directed into the distance in the conventional style of middle-class portraiture. In stark contrast, the model in the photograph at the top, Annie Berry, wears a ceremonial buckskin dress and adopts an unusual standing pose, with elbows bent and hands at the back of her head. Despite their very different presentations, the captions remind readers that Native identity inheres in a diversity of visual presentations. Erna Eddleman and Nanny Blackstone are as Cherokee as Annie Berry is Kiowa. The variety of poses and dresses in these photographs reflects the diversity of "types" among the "Indian Girls" in the territories.

By repurposing the image of Berry, Ora Eddleman appropriates the souvenir Indian picture to change its meaning. The photographer of the Berry portrait, William E. Irwin, produced hundreds of images of Native people in his Oklahoma Territory studio, including at least two other shots of Berry (identified by the studio as "Kiowa Annie") in the same dress.[101] Such photographs appeared on cabinet cards for the commercial market. Berry's unusual pose in this particular picture must have been intended to showcase for non-Native consumers the fringe work and elk-teeth decoration on her dress. Taken on its own, the posture would seem to objectify Berry by presenting her as little more than a mannequin for displaying traditional Kiowa clothing.

Eddleman, however, uses the image to make Berry something other than artifact. By presenting it with the portraits of the other Native women, she insists on Berry's middle-class personhood. The grouping of images encourages the viewer to connect Berry's strong gaze to those of Erna Eddleman and Blackstone, all suggesting a depth of character. At the same time, the composition of the page challenges mainstream values that privilege assimilation over traditionalism. Ora Eddleman makes the Berry image the most prominent one: the model's body fills much of the frame of the picture, just as the picture takes up the majority of the space on the page. Placing the image above the other two creates a triangle, with Berry at the apex. The composition of the page is echoed in the angle of the subject's arms and the way her long, dark hair frames her face, drawing further attention to her powerful stare but also reiterating her place of prominence. Eddleman thus grants the Kiowa young woman—here "ANNIE" rather than "Kiowa Annie"—the individuality and subjectivity Irwin denies her.

Meanwhile, the striking detail in the caption that Berry's dress is "valued at $300" emphasizes the Kiowa girl's middle-class standing. The detail not only testifies to Berry's considerable wealth; it also contests assumptions that traditionalist indigenous people—those whose appearance and behavior would suggest their status as fully Native—were unqualified to manage property and income. As David Treuer has said in describing contemporary enrollment controversies, "Blood quantum has always been about 'the stuff.'"[102] Dawes Commission calculations of tribal heritage determined which applicants would receive allotments, but they also established restrictions on allottees' legal rights to transfer or lease their lands, on the assumption that those of "full blood" were less capable of managing property than those of mixed Native and white descent. The Five Tribes Act of 1906 specifically upheld these restrictions even as it eased the trust status on land held by allottees of mixed heritage.[103] Thus blood quantum evolved into a means of determining Native landholders' competency to make decisions about their property—a system, in other words, for maintaining boundaries of both race and class. By presenting a young woman who appears fully Kiowa and who is at the same time represented as having considerable economic power, the portrait of Berry repudiates the U.S. government's racialized system of property control.

It is important to remember that Eddleman did not advocate resisting federal enrollment processes. While many tribal groups organized for opposition, refusing in large numbers to cooperate with the Dawes Commission, editorials in *Twin Territories* urged compliance in the hope that closing the rolls would bolster Native political and economic power and lead to national citizenship for Native people and a restoration of tribal autonomy. A June 1900 editorial looks forward to the ratification of Cherokee and Muscogee allotment treaties as a precursor to the creation of a Native territorial or state government, as "then will be inaugurated a state of affairs which will bring quiet and push to this country, such as has not been seen in any other land."[104] Eddleman would go on to marry a white man employed by the Dawes Commission. Yet in "Types of Indian Girls," Eddleman protests the assessments that underwrote allotment. By pairing images of middle-class, assimilated female subjects with captions proclaiming their "Indian blood," she rejects the operating idea that racial and tribal identity is written on the surface of the body. And by emphasizing a traditionally attired Kiowa woman's substantial wealth, she contests U.S.

government efforts to limit the property rights of Native people according to their presentation as "fully" indigenous.

Fictions of Identity

Wealthy Native girls like Annie Berry populate the short stories Eddleman wrote for *Twin Territories,* and there, too, she used the magazine to oppose the authority of the white supremacist gaze to control Native bodies and properties. I turn now to some of these stories to suggest how they reconfigure racial and tribal identity to free it from the dominant culture's regulatory surveillance. A recurring plot in Eddleman's fiction involves an indigenous woman whom whites misidentify or fail to recognize as Native. Given her personal experience, stories about members of the dominant culture misreading race and identity would have had special significance for Eddleman. These plots not only destabilize the white systems that define Native and tribal personhood; they also, in their revelations of characters' true identities, forward images of Native women who are, like the young women in "Types of Indian Girls," culturally and economically empowered. In many ways, such stories contest the federal takeover of tribal enrollment and the U.S. government's control of Native individual and tribal resources.

Eddleman's short stories almost always feature situations in which white characters misread or misunderstand Native life and culture. Like those in *Wynema,* white characters in Eddleman's fictions undergo processes of reeducation under the tutelage of amused Native friends. The interaction between Morrison and Danny Gray in "Only an Indian Girl" provides one example. Another occurs in "Lucy and I as Missionaries," in which two white women teachers from the East, who resolve to "go to some nice, heathenish place and convert the people," land in the bustling metropolis of Muskogee, Indian Territory.[105] When one of the women learns that the charming gentleman with whom she is chatting at a social event is Native, her first impulse is to run from the room. The reaction elicits her interlocutor's laughter, along with his reassurance that she has nothing to fear.[106] Scenes like this invert racialized structures of authority in the same way that "What the Curious Want to Know" does: they make whites childlike figures in need of instruction as well as spectacles for Native peoples' entertainment.

A more dramatic example of the pattern of white misperception, recognition, and reeducation appears in a story in which a Native woman assumes a false identity. As "Aunt Mary's Christmas Dinner" opens, a white family anticipates the arrival of an orphaned Native girl they have agreed to take into their home. Wondering out loud about the girl, whom they dub simply "Cherokee," Aunt Mary and her two nephews rehearse mainstream stereotypes of Native people as impoverished, infantile, and backward. Assuming their charge is a poor young child, Aunt Mary has purchased toys and dolls for her. One nephew, Joe, imagines "Cherokee" "wearing a little red shawl and buckskin moccasins . . . rais[ing] the mischief when we try to convert her into an up-to-date little girl"; his brother Frank mutters, "I'll bet that little 'Injun' will be a fright, with her uncivilized ways." Blinded by racial stereotypes, the family does not recognize the young woman, Nannie Jenkins, when she arrives. Joe reports not seeing "anyone who resembles an Indian in the least" at the train station, and when Nannie makes her own way to the house and knocks on the door, the family mistakes her for a cook. Because she "can't resist a joke," Nannie acts the part over several days, passing as non-Native (though what race or nationality the family attributes to their new servant is never stated). Nannie discloses her true identity over Christmas dinner. Joe, who in the meantime has become smitten with the "cook," then reveals his love for her, and Aunt Mary and Frank welcome her into the family.[107]

The story concludes with an idealized, multicultural domestic scene, but its plot points to the extra-domestic problem of whites claiming the authority to identify and categorize Native people. The white family members' initial confidence that they will easily identify the Cherokee girl by her appearance and behavior perform in small the essentializing assumptions that underlay the Dawes Commission's enrollment procedures. The family's subsequent failure to recognize Nannie exposes the flimsiness of dominant cultural systems for defining tribal and Native identity according to a visual calculus. Eddleman's story of a Native woman's identity performance denies whites the capacity to categorize Native people.

At the same time, Nannie's deception shifts authority to the Native subject. Ironically, the masquerade as domestic servant grants Nannie a kind of power over Aunt Mary and her nephews. Serving meals as the cook, she eavesdrops on their further speculations about "Cherokee," thus entering into the closed space where dominant cultural discourse organizes racial and social hierarchies. Facilitated by the family members' faith in the legibility of race, the hoax in effect reverses the racializing gaze, allowing Nannie to scrutinize the family from a privileged position of invisibility. Nannie's "joke," a version of the trickster's shape-shifting, gives the Cherokee woman the upper hand. More strikingly, Nannie's authority is resignified in economic terms. She decides to reveal her true identity when she overhears Frank bewailing his financial ruin. Because she loves Joe, she volunteers to clear Frank's debts using her own substantial funds. As it turns out, Eddleman's Native heroine is not just smarter and more "up-to-date" than the family members suppose; she is also wealthier. The combination of her epistemic and economic authority upends conventional social structures of power.

Eddleman deploys a similar strategy in her serialized story "A Pair of Moccasins." In it, the Native girl Chinka is rescued from a train wreck by a white businessman. Given the English name Eloise, she is sent to a boarding school in the East, where one of her classmates is the businessman's daughter, Veda. Veda does not recognize the girl her father rescued and instead, like the newspaperman Morrison, sees "only an Indian girl." Eloise and Veda are cast in a play as a queen and her maid, respectively. Veda is outraged, refusing to play servant to someone she sees as her racial inferior. But she is chastened when she learns of Eloise's connection to her father and, more pointedly, of the Native girl's economic power. Eloise reveals that she has used her own money to save Veda's father from financial ruin and make possible the white girl's education. Unwilling to play the role of someone economically dependent on a Native person, Veda finds herself occupying that very identity in reality, and as a result she has a change of heart and begs Eloise's forgiveness.[108]

Like "Aunt Mary's Christmas Dinner," "A Pair of Moccasins" exposes the entanglements of race and class within systems of racial categorization. In the first story, confusion about Nannie's identity stems in part from the family's assumptions of her impoverishment, while in the second, Veda's race hatred comes to a head over the suggestion that she perform a class role she deems unnatural. The denouements that reveal the Native characters' true identities also establish their economic power. In connecting revelations of Native identity and Native financial autonomy, these stories confront progressive-era policies that used assessment of appearance and behavior to control Native property. Allotment aimed at assimilating Native people by introducing them to capitalist values of possessive individualism, but in practice it entailed seizures of tribal lands and the imposition of unprecedented restrictions on the property of Native individuals. The two stories of mistaken identity deny whites authority over both Native identity and Native property.

In this way, these stories shed light on a more general emphasis in *Twin Territories* on Native property and economic success. The magazine's pages are filled with photographs of fine homes, profiles of successful Native farmers and businessmen, and portraits of richly attired Native women like Annie Berry. The emphasis on materialism—like the unabashedly commercial aspirations of the magazine itself—certainly reflects compliance with dominant cultural values. Yet Eddleman's representations of financially successful Native heroines also explode the crude conflation of race and class on which justifications for federal intervention in tribal affairs depended. Encountering such characters repeatedly in the pages of *Twin Territories* encouraged readers to see Native economic empowerment in new ways, as more politically resistant than accommodationist. That "Aunt Mary's Christmas Dinner" and "A Pair of Moccasins" were published in close succession reflects the ways thematic repetition in the magazine accretes meaning over time. The discursive interplay of such stories complicates the dominant cultural understanding of racial and class identity.

Still another story of mistaken identity focuses explicitly on dominant cultural efforts to read race. In "The Honor of Wynoma, a Thanksgiving Story by a Cherokee Girl," a Native woman's white fiancé encourages her to pass for white in a visit to the fiancé's family home.[109] Passing narratives, in which a person benefits by performing a racial identity other than the one assigned by society, have a long tradition of troubling the waters of racial categorization in America. The works of African American writers from Hannah Crafts to Danzy Senna explore the profound implications of crossing the color line by passing. Fictions of Native passing are rarer, and the context of a dominant cultural obsession with identifying and categorizing Native people makes Eddleman's passing story doubly significant. The Dawes Commission assumption that it could quantify Native-ness through observation reflected an abiding faith in the legibility of race. To tell a story of racial passing is to strike at the foundation of that faith—and, in turn, to oppose the official policies it underwrote.

Passing narratives destabilize dominant cultural systems for categorizing others according to race, but they also tend to validate certain kinds of racial identity and belonging. In African American passing narratives, a character's performance as a member of the dominant race is nearly always represented as costly because it requires the sacrifice of cultural belonging. To take a prominent example, in Nella Larsen's *Passing* (1929), Clare Kendry, a black woman passing for white, finds herself longing for the African American community from which she is necessarily estranged by her racial performance. The novel would seem to represent the politics of passing as profoundly contradictory: Clare's ability to cross the color line exposes the contingency of racial categories, while her feeling that her "true" place is in the black community reaffirms those categories. Gayle Wald addresses this paradox by reading passing narratives not as evidence of the transcendence of or capitulation to dominant racial imperatives but as ways to "explore—through negative as well as positive example—the possibility that these imperatives might be reclaimed or refashioned as sources of collective mobility and 'racial' affirmation." Put another way, though passing exposes race as a fiction, it simultaneously constructs racial identity as both real and a potential source of political agency.[110]

While this approach to African American passing narratives proves useful for understanding a story of Native passing, the history I have sketched in this chapter suggests that the implications of racial performance (in passing) and racial affirmation (in the revelation of identity) would have been quite different for Native people at the turn of the century than for African Americans. The complications of passing multiply when federal bureaucratic systems deny thousands of indigenous people their tribal identity, effectively forcing them to "pass" as white, as a means of weakening Native communal and political bonds and Native people's individual and collective power. In this context, affirming racial identity according to different criteria than those imposed by the dominant culture represents an expression of political resistance. Eddleman's editorial self-naming—as not "full blood" but nevertheless "Cherokee[,] and prouder of that than any distinction she may attain"—defies the Dawes Commission's assignment of her identity as non-Cherokee and asserts her right of self-definition. Similarly, the Native passing narrative at once undermines dominant cultural efforts to categorize indigenous people and grants Native characters authority to reconfigure definitions of identity. By exposing the flimsiness of systems that attribute race to observable characteristics, the passing narrative supports racial and tribal community-building and Native empowerment. "The Honor of Wynoma" mobilizes the passing narrative to disrupt dominant cultural systems of knowledge and racial categorization; more importantly, it makes possible a Native heroine's assertion of identity and tribal belonging on her own terms.

In the story, "blood" codes white racist subjugation of Native people, while the act of passing confounds the surveillance on which racism relies. The white Mrs. Boynton is outraged when she learns that her son, Horton, has fallen in love with a young Native woman in the West. Reading of Horton's plans to marry, she asks, "Must our first grandchildren have the blood of savages in their veins?" Later she declares, "I could never bear for him to marry a girl with a drop of Indian blood."[111] Her responses reflect the language of racial categorization being deployed in federal enrollment and allotment processes. Ironically, the "drop of Indian blood" that horrifies Mrs. Boynton would be nowhere near enough to earn recognition of tribal belonging from the Dawes Commission. Nonetheless, in both Mrs. Boynton's expression of anxiety and Dawes enrollment procedures, whites exert authority over racial others by adhering to the essentialist idea that racial differences are legible and quantifiable.

Passing challenges this authority. Horton conspires with his sister to present his mixed-race sweetheart, Wynoma Littleheart, as his sister's white classmate. Brought home for the Thanksgiving holiday, "'Noma" charms Mrs. Boynton, and the elder woman determines her bright, vivacious houseguest is a perfect match for her son. Mrs. Boynton pronounces Wynoma "our kind" and arranges for her to be thrown together with Horton at every opportunity. "When he meets you and mingles again among civilized people, I hope he will forget this wild Indian girl," she tells Wynoma.[112] Despite her confidence in her ability to identify the perfect daughter-in-law, Mrs. Boynton cannot recognize the "blood" she presumes defines the line between "civilized" and "wild," between Native people and "[her] kind."

Like Nannie, Wynoma performs an identity that allows her to enter into the closed circle of white privilege and be witness to the discourse that buttresses it. So comfortable is Mrs. Boynton in Wynoma's presence that she confides her horror at the news of her son's engagement. "Think of it, I, to receive a low born Indian girl as my daughter? The very thought makes me shudder. You can perhaps realize how I feel."[113] The appeal for empathy suggests that the discourse of race has inclusive as well as exclusive functions: it works to reinforce the boundaries that keep the racial other out, but it also builds a community based on a presumption of shared hatred of the racial other.

The essentializing logic on which this fantasized community is based ricochets back on white privilege in Wynoma's disclosure of her true identity. Appalled at Mrs. Boynton's racism, she breaks off her engagement with Horton and reveals herself to his mother as "'the low-born Indian girl' your son loves." She turns the language of "blood" against the white woman in her promise to cut all ties to the family: "You will find that, although some white blood is mingled with that of my Indian ancestors, I can still be unrelenting, brave and true to my promise."[114] Fictions of blood, Wynoma demonstrates, cut both ways. Wynoma's subsequent exit from the Boynton home is paradigmatically disruptive: she literally removes herself from the white gaze that attempts to categorize and qualify her.

The passing performance destabilizes the essentializing systems through which racial boundaries are delineated, restructuring racial relations. Again, Eddleman uses the pattern of misunderstanding and revelation to upend conventional power dynamics. Mrs. Boynton recognizes how she has been "ignorant and prejudiced." She renounces her racism and welcomes Wynoma as "my daughter's equal, yes, in some respects, my daughter's mother's superior!"[115]

But before this happens, Wynoma articulates how the experience of passing has conditioned a reaffirmation of Native identity according to new terms. The scheme devised by her fiancé has resulted in a profound sense of loss for the heroine. "I can't help feeling like there is a forlorn, mistreated little Indian girl out there in my Western home who has been deceived by herself and her lover," Wynoma tells Horton. The experience of passing has solidified her commitment to an identity, rooted in place and community, that transcends romantic love. She resolves to "go back and tell [the lost Native girl] that at least she has her old self back again, if she did give up her—lover."[116]

The language of identity loss and recovery is especially poignant in the context of the Eddlemans' homecoming and the Dawes Commission's denial of the family's application for enrollment. Like the other stories of mistaken identity, "The Honor of Wynoma" dismantles dominant cultural systems that bestow or deny Native identity at will. It ends not just with a restructuring of racialized hierarchies but with an expression of Native identity that conflates "blood" with "honor" as a primary artifact of tribal belonging. "I should have owned my Indian blood, and accepted the consequences," Wynoma tells Horton in the midst of her ruse. "As it is, my honor has asserted itself in time. I shall go no further. If you could not take me in the face of your mother's prejudice and opposition, you are not deserving of me, and it is best that we part."[117] The comment establishes "Indian blood" as a metaphor for pride in Native and tribal identity, rather than the material evidence of race. Getting "her old self back again" means reasserting ties to family and community, Wynoma's "Western home," and defending indigenous honor.

As she does in "Types of Indian Girls," in "The Honor of Wynoma" Eddleman reclaims and reconfigures "Indian blood" to establish a definition of indigenous personhood rooted not in genetic heritage (and its ostensibly corresponding appearances and performances) but in historic and communal connections, in ties to an originary people and place. In this way she anticipates the work of contemporary Native writers, artists, and activists who challenge standards of Native authenticity imposed by the dominant culture by reimagining the terms of those standards. The concept of "memory in the blood" developed by N. Scott Momaday (Kiowa) is a well-known, if controversial, example of this kind of challenge.[118] As Chadwick Allen argues, Momaday's phrase appropriates and transforms the U.S. government's essentializing system of classification, turning "blood" into a trope for an indigenous identity drawn from, among other things, "the assertion of an unmediated relationship to indigenous land bases (whether or not those lands remain under indigenous control)" and an imaginative communion with the tribal past.[119] Thus Wynoma's connection to her "Western home" reanimates her "old self"; both landscape and history are woven into the honor of tribal membership. In Eddleman's reimagining, as in Momaday's trope, "Indian blood" loses its materiality to become a remembered trace that transcends boundaries of time and space and persists in the face of assimilation, dispossession, and subjugation.

Eddleman's short stories in *Twin Territories* are concerned with varied attempts by non-Natives to identify and categorize Native people. The editor recognized these attempts as threats to tribal sovereignty, economic autonomy, and indigenous personhood. Like other features of "The Indian Magazine," Eddleman's fiction aims not just to deny whites the right to define Native people but also to establish on Native terms what it means to be Native. These stories assert the indigenous right to "own . . . Indian blood" in the face of dominant cultural efforts to wrest it away from its possessors.

I have been interested throughout this book in the ways Native and white women fracture an alliance between mass cultural forms and dominant political and cultural systems of oppression in the nineteenth century. But I hope to suggest as well the present-day implications of Eddleman's and Callahan's more radical transformations of print conventions. By deploying and transforming the assimilationist romance novel and the commercial magazine to make them do the work of resistance, Eddleman and Callahan lay the groundwork for later Native women writers and artists to indigenize and thereby politicize conventional print forms—a development that is the subject of my epilogue.

Epilogue

Toward a Theory of Feminist Indigenist Reinvention

This book has brought together four very different writers in order to expand the sense of nineteenth-century women's aesthetic and political expression. Sarah Wakefield, Lydia Sigourney, S. Alice Callahan, and Ora Eddleman challenged both the political regimes and the generic expectations of their times. The white war refugee turned memoirist, the white professional sentimental poet, the Muscogee (Creek) teacher and author of assimilationist romance, and the Cherokee commercial magazine writer and editor took up, tested, critiqued, and to some extent reimagined established popular genres in order to voice protest. I have used a cross-cultural approach to identify shared practices in the deployment of literary conventions as an expression of dissent. But this is not to universalize women's experiences fighting oppression or to generalize their writing strategies. In these last few pages, I want to concentrate on the distinctions that have emerged in my case studies and to suggest their implications for understanding the aesthetics and politics of Native American women's creative protest in the present moment—when tribal communities and Native women continue to challenge racist and sexist public policies and, at the same time, when transformations in publishing practices have expanded opportunities for Native women to control the terms of their own aesthetic production and political expression. The literary protests of Native women writers in the late nineteenth century illuminate feminist indigenist reinventions of the twentieth and twenty-first, reinventions wonderfully embodied in the recent comic book production of Kickapoo writer, artist, and activist Arigon Starr.

If my case studies suggest a shared project of generic and political intervention across the nineteenth century, they also underline the difference race makes. After all, Wakefield's and Sigourney's frustrations with being silenced in official forums are a far cry from Callahan's and Eddleman's personal suffering under U.S. policies of the Dawes era. Then, too, Callahan and Eddleman experienced a double marginality that Sigourney and Wakefield did not know. Indigenous women face a burden of political, economic, and sexual oppression that began with the imposition of Western gender hierarchies through colonization and extended through legislation like the Dawes Act, which required Native women to be married in order to receive allotments. Simply put, the stakes of protest are higher for Native women than for the non-Native women who commiserate with them, and the imperative for protest is far greater.

As a result, my four subjects also varied in the degree of their creative agency, the extent of their transformations of print conventions, and the potency of their political dissent. There is a vast distance between Wakefield's frustrated struggles with a "diseased imagination" and Callahan's recuperative model of sentimental critique. In one sense, Wakefield's anxiety about the pressure of culturally determined modes of knowing and expressing, her sense that she could not escape the culturally determined emotional responses that scaffold injustice, was answered by Callahan's call for reading that is at once affective and fiercely critical. Sigourney obliquely condemned the anonymous white readers of Indian lament poetry, who consumed scenes of Native suffering under a pretense of sympathy, by representing them as unfeeling voyeurs at a Native burial. Eddleman went further, publicly calling out the ignorance and racism of individual white correspondents whose mainstream reading had trained them to see Native people as a commodity. The end of Sigourney's "Pocahontas" tacitly admits the poem's own complicity in colonial erasure, its failure to extract itself from sentimental and nationalist mythologies. Eddleman's "The Honor of Wynoma," in contrast, culminates in the main character's assertion of indigenous self-possession and her repudiation of dominant racial and class codes. All of my subjects chafed against the limits of print conventions, but Eddleman and Callahan opened the contours of those conventions more effectively and protested more assertively. The Native writer-activists critiqued the conventions they engaged directly, and they claimed latitude for reinventing traditional forms of expression and thereby subverting established structures of power in ways that their non-Native counterparts did not.

I have covered a good deal of historical ground in this book, moving from debates over removal in the early decades of the nineteenth century to struggles to maintain tribal political and cultural sovereignty at century's end, but shifts in women's political involvement over time do not explain these differences. To be sure, women exerted more influence on policies affecting Native people in Callahan's and Eddleman's day than in Sigourney's and Wakefield's. Women were so involved in public conversations about allotment that Senator Henry Dawes avowed the policy was "born of and nursed by" the Women's National Indian Association (WNIA).[1] But the WNIA was a white woman's organization, as well as a conservative one; Native women remained shut out of most discussions of public policy, and their objections to policies like allotment and education for assimilation were rarely given a hearing. By the progressive era, the campaign for women's suffrage had made major inroads in states and territories in the West, which were earliest to grant white women the right to vote. Yet it would take many more decades and a series of legislative measures—the Citizenship Act of 1924, the Nationality Act of 1940, and the Voting Rights Act of 1965—to fully enfranchise Native women. To state the obvious: one of the differences race makes is the significant lag time between the granting of political rights to white women and to women of color.

Rather than positioning Callahan and Eddleman at the end of a universalizing arc of women's political advancement, we should recognize them as foundational figures in a tradition of specifically indigenist literary reinvention—and as writers who might help us theorize in new ways contemporary Native women's creative activism and the interplay of indigenous politics and aesthetics. In the introduction to their anthology of Native American women's writing, *Reinventing the Enemy's Language,* Joy Harjo (Muscogee, Cherokee) and Gloria Bird (Spokane) describe a tradition of Native women taking up and constructing anew the literary genres and styles imposed on them by colonization. "We are coming out of one or two centuries of war, a war that hasn't ended," Harjo reminds us. "Many of us at the end of the century are using the 'enemy language' with which to tell our truths, to sing, to remember ourselves during these troubled times." Speaking in the enemy tongue involves loss, yet Bird insists that when Native women writers appropriate the colonizers' language and textual forms, "something is happening, something is emerging and coming into focus that will politicize as well as transform literary expression." Colonization forces Native women to adopt non-Native modes of expression, but "when we began to create with this new language . . . we named it ours, made it usefully tough and beautiful."[2]

What is striking here is the description of Native women's literature as not just reinventing mainstream forms of expression but also erasing an artificial line between the aesthetic and political significance of texts. The language that emerges when Native women write in the enemy's tongue is both aesthetically satisfying and politically effectual, "beautiful" and "usefully tough." Elizabeth Archuleta (Yaqui) suggests that attention to the ways Native women take up and alter non-Native literary forms can lead to a deeper understanding of Native feminist literature: "Analyzing Indigenous women's appropriation, reinvention, and use of English and writing as rhetorical sites of power allows us to begin conceptualizing alternative methodologies for articulating an Indigenous feminist theory."[3] I would add that it also helps us to rethink the relations between generic convention and activism in ways that illuminate the metatexual dimensions of Native women's literary protests, in the past and today.

The history of Laguna Pueblo author Leslie Marmon Silko's *Almanac of the Dead* (1991) exemplifies the ways beautiful and usefully tough new forms can emerge when Native women writers repurpose dominant cultural genres to voice protest. Silko set out to write a conventional novel about drug trafficking in her hometown of Tucson, Arizona. The book would be "something that could be sold at the bookstand in the supermarket," she thought, "a very short, simple, commercial novel, something that anyone could read, not political, something that I would call a cops-and-robbers novel about the cocaine smuggling."[4] Research for the book led Silko to investigate corruption in the Tucson police force and the Central Intelligence Agency's involvement in the international drug trade. Her writing coincided with her increasing involvement in advocating for Native rights, immigration reform, poverty relief, and racial equality. She took a break from work on the novel to protest the election of Arizona Governor Evan Mecham, among whose right-wing policies was the cancelation of Martin Luther King, Jr., Day. She also stopped writing for months in order to create an imposing graffiti mural expressing her opposition to the militarization of U.S. borders and the economic injustices of unfettered capitalism. Her outrage inflected her writing, and the book, initially intended to be a short, marketable thriller, was reshaped into a response to social and political injustice on a grand scale, a nearly eight-hundred-page fictional condemnation of half a millennium of colonial violence and theft.

Monumental in the scope of its indictment and horrifying in its representation of an apocalypse of exploitation, torture, and ruin, *Almanac of the Dead* explodes assumptions and expectations—assumptions about the historic foundations of the international drug trade and global ecological disasters, certainly, but also expectations for writing by a celebrated Native woman author. It remains, not surprisingly, one of the most controversial works of fiction of our time, a far cry from the supermarket paperback Silko envisioned and a radical departure from her previous works (to the disappointment of some readers).[5] In interviews, Silko has described the evolution of the book from a "not political" thriller into an almost indescribable work of rage and resistance as a process beyond her control, one in which buried histories and spirits seeped into her consciousness and spilled onto the page.[6] And yet the novel's conceptual origins in a conventional print genre suggest a deliberate politicization of mainstream literary protocols. It is not that Silko rejected the thriller form as inadequate for the work of political opposition. Rather, she took up the genre and exploded its contours, radicalizing obligatory features like conspiracy plots and action scenes to amplify her opposition to global injustice. Silko's resistance to the political status quo is matched by her refusal to stay within the bounds of generic requirements.

Silko's explosive repurposing registers the breadth of possibilities for a specifically indigenous remaking of conventional print forms. Scholars have recognized the ways Native writers frequently reinvent conventional literary genres by breaking down their boundaries in unexpected ways. Native writers incorporate practices like oral narrative and performance into their English-language novels; they interweave poetry and prose, autobiography and ethnography, image and word. Dean Rader cites a prevalence of multigeneric and intertextual books by contemporary Native poets as evidence of Native "compositional resistance," the refusal to follow the rules imposed by European American standards of literary expression. Defying generic boundaries serves an indigenous oppositional politics, Rader says: "Native writers go intrageneric because it is a revolutionary project that subverts the means by which cultural dominance is created and fostered."[7]

Although Rader does not explore the gender implications of compositional resistance, it is worth noting that the majority of his examples of genre-bending poetry collections are written by women: Silko, LeAnne Howe (Choctaw), Luci Tapahonso (Navajo), and Louise Erdrich (Ojibwe). While Native men also write in ways that challenge generic boundaries—Sherman Alexie (Spokane, Coeur d'Alene), who rounds out Rader's list, is a prime example of someone who amalgamates prose, poetry, music, film, and other genres—the prevalence of women doing so points to a Native female tradition of literary reinvention. In marshalling poetry to articulate protest, the Native women poets Rader references rethink the genre itself. Theirs is both a political and aesthetic revolution.

Callahan and Eddleman participated in the same radical project. Callahan's incorporation of news stories into her novel crossed generic boundaries, while her protocol for reading both affectively and critically amounted to a reinvention of sentimentalism itself. Her transformations of the genre resisted the insidious operations of education for assimilation that underwrote settler colonization. In her magazine, Eddleman repurposed normative conventions like middle-class portraiture and souvenir Indian representations to challenge mainstream assumptions about Native identity. She deployed textual instruments like the correspondence column and the passing narrative to claim indigenous rights to self-definition and autonomy. As in the contemporary examples Rader cites, these writers demonstrated self-awareness about the interplay between form and content and a desire to expand the parameters of conventional literary expression to make room for protest. To conclude, I briefly turn to work that might be considered a legacy of Callahan's and Eddleman's de- and reconstructions of popular print conventions, a shining example of feminist indigenist generic revision: Starr's comic book series *Super Indian.*[8]

The multitalented Starr is arguably the most "intrageneric" Native person publishing and performing today. Where Eddleman moved from a successful career in magazine writing, editing, and publishing to a pioneering role as a radio talk-show host, Starr ranges even more widely across media. She is a highly respected singer, songwriter, and musician and the recipient of three Native American Music Awards; a playwright whose comedy *The Red Road* has garnered numerous honors; and an actor with noted appearances on the stage and in television. Her work as a comic book writer and artist emerged from her career in performance. The stories that became *Super Indian* were commissioned as a series of audio plays for the Native Radio Theater Project. After writing and performing in these nationally broadcast plays, Starr began producing *Super Indian* as a regularly updated Web-based comic. Rezium Studios, the production company Starr founded with editor Janet Miner, has since published the first two volumes in hardcopy.

Most of Starr's performance work focuses on Native issues, but the comic book form offers a unique opportunity to bring these issues to broader audiences. Starr is a founding member of the Indigenous Narratives Collective, a group that advocates for Native comic and graphic novel creators and supports Native comics as a means of challenging stereotypes and initiating social change. In interviews she has said that the comic book allows her to use humor and visual art to delve into issues of Native identity, community, and representation in a way that is accessible to mainstream readers.[9] At the same time, the short length of the comic book and opportunities for self-publishing in the digital age make it possible to bypass the popular culture industry and retain authority over production. Publishing a comic series in Web installments allows Starr to build an audience for hardcopy print versions, and it preserves her creative control over content and distribution.[10]

With *Super Indian,* Starr appropriates a conservative commercial medium to accommodate a distinctly indigenous activism. Like the captivity narrative, the Indian lament poem, the didactic assimilation romance, and the commercial magazine, the comic book would seem an unpromising vehicle for oppositional politics, especially feminist indigenous protest. Typically produced on an industrial scale for wide distribution, comic books tend to promote established cultural values. Mainstream comic books circulate debasing stereotypes of race, ethnicity, nationality, and gender; celebrate U.S. nationalist and imperialist power; and confirm white patriarchal privilege. Several scholars point to the ways commercial comic books represent Native peoples, in particular, through a matrix of dehumanizing types: the living artifact of the past, the mystic guide, the child of nature, the semi-civilized sidekick, the hypermasculinized Indian warrior, the hypersexualized Native princess.[11]

But the comic book form's fragmented narratives and mix of visual art and text engender tensions that can be exploited to articulate a countercultural point of view. In recent years, writers and artists marginalized by race, gender, sexuality, or class have taken up this conservative form in work that challenges both hegemonic social structures and established protocols of expression. When repurposed, forms like comics and graphic novels can encourage an awareness of the ways textual convention colludes with dominant cultural authority. As Hillary L. Chute argues, creating comics from the margins of society can produce "a constant self-reflexive demystification of the project of representation."[12] Charles Hatfield describes the producers of alternative comics as expanding the possibilities of the art: "Out of a struggle with the conventions of serial publication, they have created breathtaking experiments in narrative structure and density."[13] The decentered position of minority writer-artists and their engagement with a convention that typically works to subjugate them results in a politically inflected and deeply self-conscious revision. Assessing the comic book tradition and altering or redirecting its styles and structures, marginalized writer-artists have radicalized a conventional form.

Entirely written, drawn, lettered, and colored by Starr, *Super Indian* adapts the tropes of the commercial superhero comic to critique and revise the form from within. Although she asserts her natural drawing style is closer to that of artists like Matt Groening than anyone else, *Super Indian* shows the heavy influence of industrially produced superhero entertainments like the *Batman* television program and the *X-Men* comic book series.[14] The lettering and visual styling; the rendering of a muscle-bound, tights-clad superhero; and the plots involving secret identities, loyal sidekicks, and mad scientists in *Super Indian* all resemble features of the mainstream comic books produced by DC Comics and Marvel Comics that Starr read as she was growing up.[15] Yet Starr's version of the form leaves room for playful exposure of its stereotypes and clichés while at the same time investing its conventions with a distinctly indigenous and feminist political sensibility.

Super Indian: Volume One opens with a frontispiece send-up of conventional representations of Indians in comics. The first panel shows a buckskin-clad Native figure on horseback, silhouetted against a yellow sun. The accompanying text mimics the romanticized rhetoric of conventional comic books: "The ancient ones foretold of a mighty native warrior who would return to aid his people in their darkest hour of need." After three more panels depicting this figure fighting enemies, protecting babies, communicating with animals, and even using his mystic powers to hover in mid-air, Starr tosses the clichés aside in the last panel on the page. Over a close-up of the romanticized figure, now winking at the reader, the narrator concedes, "that warrior and his story are told in another comic book" (fig. 10).[16] By opening with a playful swipe at comic book stereotypes, *Super Indian* invites readers to question the conventional comic protocols that dehumanize Native people. Readers become

FIGURE 10. Arigon Starr, *Super Indian: Volume One,* frontispiece. "Super Indian" created by Arigon Starr. © 2012 Wacky Productions Unlimited. Used with permission.

FIGURE 11. Arigon Starr, *Super Indian: Volume One,* title page. "Super Indian" created by Arigon Starr. © 2012 Wacky Productions Unlimited. Used with permission.

collaborators, brought into Starr's project by the Native figure's conspiratorial wink, in the deconstruction of a popular genre.[17] The opening does not throw out conventional comic traditions; rather, it negotiates without crossing the line between homage and parody. Similarly, the title page that follows pays tribute to a paragon of superhero tradition in its depiction of the chiseled protagonist, dressed in a blue and red costume and sporting a large red letter "S" on his chest, even as the hero's long hair and the letters "NDN" on his prominent belt buckle signal something new (fig. 11).[18] These initial moves are metatextual and reparative: they encourage a critical awareness of racism in conventional comic books while at the same time opening the comic book form to the possibilities for a specifically indigenous expression.

The opening prepares for the politicization of the mainstream comic in the pages that follow. Starr's central hero is the mild-mannered Hubert Logan, a janitor on the fictional Leaning Oaks Reservation who transforms into Super Indian when his community is threatened by evil forces. A counterpart introduced in *Super Indian: Volume Two,* Phoebe Francis, is the overworked employee of a company that offers Native-style outdoor adventures. Urged on by ancient spirits when her tribe is under attack, she becomes the superhero Laguna Woman, also called Ka'Waika Woman. Hubert and Phoebe break the mold of Native characters in mainstream comic books in many ways, not least of which is their thoroughly contemporary reservation existence. Far from artifacts frozen in the past, they represent a thriving reservation geek culture. Hubert has a second secret life as the controversial blogger Rez Boy, and Phoebe gets lost in *Never at Dusk,* a fantasy novel series that follows the passionate adventures of a group of modern-day werewolves and vampires. Beyond just countering stereotypes of Indians found in mainstream comic books, Starr's emphasis on her protagonists' side interests performs an intervention into other mass-cultural forms. The Native characters' blogging and fandom decolonize twenty-first-century digital and print media, insisting on the inclusion of Native people as producers and consumers. That *Never at Dusk* is a wicked parody of Stephenie Meyer's *Twilight* series, with its romanticized depictions of Native culture and its appropriation of Quileute tribal traditions, reminds readers of the imperative for critiquing representations of Native Americans in mainstream media. At the same time, by having Phoebe dream she appears as a character in *Never at Dusk,* Starr dramatizes Native peoples' interventions in the forms of popular culture that (mis)represent them.[19]

Popular phenomena like the *Twilight* series are not the only threat to contemporary Native identity and culture, of course, and Starr organizes her plots around the broader assaults to Native tribes and individuals that result from ongoing settler colonization. Corruption among U.S. and tribal officials administering reservations, economic injustice, cultural appropriation, federally imposed standards of tribal citizenship and Native identity, and the organized theft of tribal resources all figure in her comics. Starr's villains resemble the maniacal evil-doers familiar to mainstream comic fans, but they reflect the particular dangers U.S. policies and practices pose to Native existence in the twenty-first century. "The Anthro" is a German professor who uses a mysterious crystal to transform into a giant and capture human "specimens" for his collection of Native artifacts. Wampum Baggs, the white leader of a conglomerate known as the "Circle of Evil," was a keen student of tribal traditions who stole a powerful wampum belt; he now plots to take over first the reservation and then the world.[20] The fanged and fantastically named Blud Kwan'tum literalizes assaults on Native personhood that began with the federal imposition of blood quantum as a measure of tribal citizenship during the Dawes Era. A Bureau of Indian Affairs employee descended from Spanish conquistadors, Kwan'tum is cursed by an Aztec shaman when he tries to steal sacred gold. To stay alive, he needs a constant supply of the blood of enrolled Native Americans. He stages a sham blood drive at Leaning Oaks so that he can use transfusions to become a "full blood" and control the reservation. Drained of blood, Kwan'tum's victims become his dead-eyed servants.[21]

Constructed as elaborate puns, the villains in *Super Indian* signify the many weapons wielded by U.S. cultural and political authorities to dominate Native Americans. Here and elsewhere, Starr's emphasis is on various kinds of consumption of tribal identities and resources, consumption that, vampire-like, depletes Native people of their life force. Conventional print forms can facilitate that consumption. Starr's opening salvo at comic book stereotypes and her satire of the fantasy-romance industry's representations of tribal traditions underline the ways popular culture exploits and distorts Native identity. But Starr is also interested in reversing that dynamic. The *Super Indian* comics perform a complex cultural critique that suggests what can happen when Native people turn the tables and consume the mainstream print conventions that would consume them. Dominant cultural forms can be destructive, but when Native producers creatively redirect and transform them, they become powerful means of resistance.

The tale of Super Indian's origins thematizes the dangers and rewards of this consumption. As a boy, Hubert gained his superpowers when he ate commodity cheese tainted with an experimental substance, "rezium," developed by the U.S. government. The same commodity cheese empowered one of Hubert's archenemies, Derek Thunder, who grows up to tyrannize the Leaning Oak community as Wampum Baggs's brutal deputy.[22] The backstory registers a protest against the ways the United States poisons its indigenous inhabitants with cheap surplus foods, of course, but it also serves as a useful allegory for Starr's aesthetic and political project. Popular print convention, like tainted commodity cheese, is powerful stuff. It can threaten Native life and culture, but when its energies are absorbed, digested, and redirected, it can also empower. It makes sense, in that regard, that Starr's production company is named "Rezium Studios." In making her comic book, she harnesses the radioactive power of a popular convention to advocate for Native people. More than just critiquing it, Starr manages to reclaim the highly consumable and consuming form of the superhero comic as a vehicle for articulating indigenous dissent.

These preliminary comments on *Super Indian* should suggest the ways contemporary Native women writers and artists extend a vital political and cultural intervention that began much earlier. My aim in this book has been to show how unconventional politics may be performed in what would seem the least likely print forms, in genres ranging from captivity narratives to commercial magazines. Like Starr, the nineteenth-century writers I have examined took up conservative genres to voice dissent. As they channeled protest against U.S. Indian policy into forms that otherwise sustained dominant cultural and political projects, they became acutely aware of formal constraints that limited female and Native expression and reinforced white, patriarchal ways of thinking and knowing. Their works became occasions for critiquing the very cultural forms they took up.

Yet the women writer-activists I have analyzed did not leave it at that; they also strove to politicize the conventions they adopted, albeit with various degrees of success and satisfaction. This was a risky undertaking, to be sure. The struggle against the constraints of convention left Wakefield tangled in a representational knot, unable to move beyond dominant interpretations to allow the truth of her experiences in the Dakota Conflict to be heard or comprehended. For Sigourney, the effort to make literary convention accommodate protest ended in an acknowledgment that, despite her best efforts, her reform did not go far enough. More attuned at the very beginnings of their writing careers to the complicity of mainstream print convention with political authority, Callahan and Eddleman offered explicit resistance to generic requirements and accomplished more dramatic transformations. Like Starr, these two Native activist-writers managed to be *in* convention but not *of* it, and their achievement suggests the potential in popular print for amplifying indigenous political expression, even as it registers the need to continually push against the requirements of genre.

Still, for all of the writers I have examined here, the imperative for protest generates fascinating and important creative interventions. Wakefield, Sigourney, Callahan, and Eddleman each recognized the strictures of the textual conventions they engaged. Their frustrations with such constraints kindled forceful critiques as well as imaginative adaptations of form. Their efforts should make us rethink assumptions of both the rigidity of literary convention and the anti-aesthetic nature of political dissent, in the nineteenth century as today. I hope that the foregoing chapters provoke conversations not just about how nineteenth-century Native and non-Native women protested Indian policy but also about the mutually determining relationship between politics and art. As Hannah Arendt has said, "the conflict between politics and art . . . cannot and must not be solved."[23] The conflict cannot be solved because the struggle against political oppression and the necessity to find new ways to express dissent are always inextricably entwined. It *must* not be solved because the friction generated when art meets politics has the potential to craft new, unconventional modes of expression—modes of expression that can, in turn, begin to remake the world.

Notes

Introduction: Aesthetics, Politics, and Literary Convention

1. "Our Editorial Comment," *The Indian's Friend,* March 1888, quoted in Lori Jacobson, " 'Shall We Have a Periodical?': *The Indian's Friend,*" in *The Woman's National Indian Association: A History,* ed. Valerie Sherer Mathes (Albuquerque: University of New Mexico Press, 2015), 71. Throughout this book, a number of terms designate racial and cultural identities. I use "Native" and "non-Native" when taking a present-day perspective in order to centralize Native identity and offset the default normalization of European American culture. In the context of nineteenth-century life and culture, I use the term "Indian" to be consistent with the language of the period (hence "Indian policy") and in reference to particular cultural constructs (such as "Indian lament"). I use "white" to refer to specific communities and movements, as in the white women's anti-removal campaign. The adjectives "indigenous" and "European American" also appear. I try to specify tribal designations for indigenous individuals and communities as much as possible. I acknowledge the inadequacy of all of these identifiers to capture specific experiences of race, culture, nationality, and community.
2. Exceptions include Nina Baym, "Reinventing Lydia Sigourney," *American Literature* 62, no. 3 (1990), 385–404; Sandra Zagarell, "Expanding 'America': Lydia Sigourney's *Sketch of Connecticut,* Catharine Sedgwick's *Hope Leslie,*" *Tulsa Studies in Women's Literature* 6 (1987), 225–46; Paula Bernat Bennett, *Poets in the Public Sphere: The Emancipatory Project of Women's Poetry, 1800–1900* (Princeton, N.J.: Princeton University Press, 2003), 59–60; and Karen L. Kilcup, *Fallen Forests: Emotion, Embodiment, and Ethics in American Women's Environmental Writing, 1781–1924* (Athens: University of Georgia Press, 2013), 40–52.
3. S. Alice Callahan, *Wynema: A Child of the Forest,* ed. A. LaVonne Brown Ruoff (Lincoln: University of Nebraska Press, 1997), ix.
4. Kathryn Zabelle Derounian-Stodala, *The War in Words: Reading the Dakota Conflict through the Captivity Literature* (Lincoln: University of Nebraska Press, 2009), 4.
5. Letter to an unknown recipient, January 22, 1885, quoted in Siobhan Senier, *Voices of American Indian Assimilation and Resistance: Helen Hunt Jackson, Sarah Winnemucca, and Victoria Howard* (Norman: University of Oklahoma Press, 2001), 30.

6. Callahan, *Wynema,* ix; Sarah Wakefield, *Six Weeks in the Sioux Tepees: A Narrative of Indian Captivity,* ed. June Namias (Norman: University of Oklahoma Press, 1997), 86.
7. Robert Allen Warrior, *Tribal Secrets: Recovering American Indian Intellectual Traditions* (Minneapolis: University of Minnesota Press, 1995); Craig S. Womack, *Red on Red: Native American Literary Separatism* (Minneapolis: University of Minnesota Press, 1999); Jace Weaver, Craig S. Womack, and Robert Allen Warrior, *American Indian Literary Nationalism* (Albuquerque: University of New Mexico Press, 2006). See also Craig S. Womack, Daniel Heath Justice, and Christopher B. Teuton, eds., *Reasoning Together: The Native Critics Collective* (Norman: University of Oklahoma Press, 2008), and Daniel Heath Justice, *Our Fire Survives the Storm: A Cherokee Literary History* (Minneapolis: University of Minnesota Press, 2006).
8. James H. Cox, *Muting White Noise: Native American and European American Novel Traditions* (Norman: University of Oklahoma Press, 2006), 4.
9. Craig S. Womack, "The Integrity of American Indian Claims: Or How I Learned to Stop Worrying and Love My Hybridity," in Weaver, Womack, and Warrior, *American Indian Literary Nationalism,* 161.
10. Lisa Brooks, "Afterword: At the Gathering Place," in ibid., 244.
11. Jace Weaver, "Splitting the Earth: First Utterances and Pluralist Separatism," in ibid., 47.
12. Simon J. Ortiz, "Towards a National Indian Literature: Cultural Authenticity in Nationalism," in *Nothing but the Truth: An Anthology of Native American Literature,* ed. John L. Purdy and James Ruppert (Upper Saddle River, N.J.: Prentice Hall, 2001), 120. The essay was originally published in 1981.
13. Weaver, "Splitting the Earth," 73–74. Although Jace Weaver identifies as an American Indian literary nationalist, he describes his most recent projects, on the transatlantic circulation of Native people, wealth, technology, and commodities, as taking "a hard cosmopolitan turn," suggesting a narrowing of the gap between nationalist and other approaches. Jace Weaver, "Turning West: Cosmopolitanism and American Indian Literary Nationalism," in *The Native American Renaissance: Literary Imagination and Achievement,* ed. Alan R. Velie and A. Robert Lee (Norman: University of Oklahoma Press, 2013), 33.
14. Jill Carter, "Blind Faith Remembers . . . This Ain't No Love Story, This Ain't No Masque: *Princess Pocahontas and the Blue Spots* as Transformative Ritual for the Grandmothers, the Ones Who Remain, and for the Ones Who Are Yet to Come," in *Performing Worlds into Being: Native American Women's Theater,* ed. Ann Elizabeth Armstrong, Kelli Lyon Johnson, and William A. Wortman (Oxford: Miami of Ohio University Press, 2009), 25.
15. Cox, *Muting White Noise,* 5, 65. Cox's latter comment is in reference to *Green Grass, Running Water,* the novel by Thomas King (Cherokee).
16. Cox, *Muting White Noise,* 13.
17. Jace Weaver, *That the People Might Live: Native American Literatures and Native American Community* (New York: Oxford University Press, 1997), 43.
18. Senier, *Voices of American Indian Assimilation and Resistance,* 17, 20, 19.

19. Walter Benjamin, "The Author as Producer," in Benjamin, *Reflections: Essays, Aphorisms, Autobiographical Writings,* ed. Peter Demetz, trans. Edmund Jephcott (New York: Harcourt Brace Jovanovich, 1978), 221.
20. Jane Tompkins, *Sensational Designs: The Cultural Work of American Fiction* (New York: Oxford University Press, 1986), xv, xvi.
21. Cindy Weinstein, *Family, Kinship, and Sympathy in Nineteenth-Century American Literature* (New York: Cambridge University Press, 2004), 5.
22. Elizabeth Maddock Dillon, "Sentimental Aesthetics," *American Literature* 76, no. 3 (2004), 495.
23. Eric Cheyfitz, *The Columbia Guide to American Indian Literatures of the United States since 1945* (New York: Columbia University Press, 2006), 103.
24. Elizabeth Cook-Lynn, "American Indian Fiction Writers: Cosmopolitanism, Nationalism, the Third World, and First Nation Sovereignty," *Wicazo Sa Review* 9, no. 2 (1993), 26–36; Cook-Lynn, "American Indian Intellectualism and the New Indian Story," in *Natives and Academics: Researching and Writing about American Indians,* ed. Devon A. Mihesuah (Lincoln: University of Nebraska Press, 1998), 111–38; Womack, *Red on Red.*
25. Angela Calcaterra, "It Needs Not the Display of Language: Aesthetics and Politics in Early Native American Writing," *Early American Literature* 49, no. 2 (2014), 502.
26. Cook-Lynn, "American Indian Intellectualism and the New Indian Story," 132–33.
27. Louis Owens, *Mixedblood Messages: Literature, Film, Family, Place* (Norman: University of Oklahoma Press, 1998), 4.
28. Robert Dale Parker, *The Invention of Native American Literature* (Ithaca, N.Y.: Cornell University Press, 2003), 2.
29. Calcaterra, "It Needs Not the Display of Language," 502.
30. Eliza Richards, *Gender and the Poetics of Reception in Poe's Circle* (Cambridge: Cambridge University Press, 2004), 68; Womack, *Red on Red,* 116, 114.
31. David Treuer, *Native American Fiction: A User's Manual* (Saint Paul, Minn.: Graywolf Press, 2006), 4, 49, 65, 195.
32. Matthew L. M. Fletcher, "*Native American Fiction* Tough on Indian Culture," *Indian Country Today Media Network,* August 3, 2007, http://indiancountrytodaymedianetwork.com. The lengthiest of the negative assessments is Arnold Krupat, "Culturalism and Its Discontents: David Treuer's *Native American Fiction: A User's Manual,*" *American Indian Quarterly* 33, no. 1 (2009), 131–60.
33. Adrienne Rich, "Permeable Membrane," *Virginia Quarterly Review* 82, no. 2 (Spring 2006), www.vqronline.org.
34. Cindy Weinstein and Christopher Looby, "Introduction," in *American Literature's Aesthetic Dimensions,* ed. Cindy Weinstein and Christopher Looby (New York: Columbia University Press, 2012), 2. In American literary studies, these efforts include Christopher Castiglia and Russ Castronovo, eds., "Aesthetics and the End(s) of Cultural Studies," special issue of *American Literature* 76, no. 3 (2004), and Emory Elliott, Louis Freitas Caton, and Jeffrey Rhyne, eds., *Aesthetics in a Multicultural Age* (New York: Oxford University Press, 2002). In Native American studies, they include Chadwick

Allen, *Blood Narrative: Indigenous Identity in American Indian and Maori Activist Texts* (Durham, N.C.: Duke University Press, 2002); Matthew Herman, *Politics and Aesthetics in Contemporary Native American Literature: Across Every Border* (New York: Routledge, 2010); and Dean Rader, *Engaged Resistance: American Indian Art, Literature, and Film from Alcatraz to the NMAI* (Austin: University of Texas Press, 2011).

35. Parker, *The Invention of Native American Literature,* 2.
36. Benjamin, "The Author as Producer," 221, 224, 228, 230.
37. James Baldwin, "Everybody's Protest Novel" (1949), in *James Baldwin: Collected Essays,* ed. Toni Morrison (New York: Library of America, 1998), 11, 13, 16, 14.
38. Ibid., 18, 15, 12.
39. Ibid., 18.
40. Benjamin, "The Author as Producer," 223.
41. Baldwin, "Everybody's Protest Novel," 12.
42. Lauren Berlant, *The Female Complaint: The Unfinished Business of Sentimentality in American Culture* (Durham, N.C.: Duke University Press, 2008), 59, 60.
43. Benjamin, "The Author as Producer," 231–32.
44. Baldwin, "Everybody's Protest Novel,"12, 15.
45. Benjamin, "The Author as Producer," 236.
46. Berlant, *The Female Complaint,* 64.
47. Barbara Harlow, *Resistance Literature* (New York: Methuen, 1987), 28–29.
48. Rita Felski, "After Suspicion," *Profession* (2009), 30.

1. Nameless Outrages: The Dakota Conflict, Rape Rhetoric, and Sarah Wakefield's "Captivity" Narrative

1. Useful studies of the Dakota Conflict include Duane Schultz, *Over the Earth I Come: The Great Sioux Uprising of 1862* (New York: St. Martin's Press, 1992); Roy W. Meyer, *History of the Santee Sioux* (revised edn., Lincoln: University of Nebraska, 1993); C. M. Oehler, *The Great Sioux Uprising* (1959; reprint, New York: Da Capo Press, 1997); and Michael Clodfelter, *The Dakota War: The United States Army versus the Sioux, 1862–1865* (Jefferson, N.C.: McFarland, 1998).
2. "Chaska" is a Dakota cognomen for a first-born son. Sarah Wakefield, *Six Weeks in the Sioux Tepees: A Narrative of Indian Captivity,* ed. June Namias (Norman: University of Oklahoma Press, 1997), 145n25. Chaska's given name is represented with various spellings in the historical record; I adopt the version Namias uses in the modern reprinting of Wakefield's narrative. The term "Dakota" encompasses a number of different bands belonging to a subgroup of the Sioux people, and I use it here for consistency with period representations.
3. Ibid., 53. Subsequent references are cited parenthetically.
4. Charles S. Bryant and Abel B. Murch, *A History of the Great Massacre by the Sioux Indians, in Minnesota, including the Personal Narratives of Many Who Escaped* (1863; reprint, St. Peter, Minn.: E. Wainwright and Son, 1872); Isaac V. D. Heard, *History of the Sioux War and Massacres of 1862 and 1863*

(New York: Harper, 1864); Harriet E. Bishop McConkey, *Dakota War Whoop; or, Indian Massacres and War in Minnesota, of 1862–3* (1863; reprint, Saint Paul: William J. Moses, 1864). The conflict was also described in Adrian J. Ebell, "The Indian Massacres and War of 1862," *Harper's New Monthly Magazine* 27 (June 1863), 1–24. At least two dime novels fictionalized the event: Edward Ellis, *Indian Jim: A Tale of the Minnesota Massacre* (London: Beadle, 1864), and Ann Coleson, *Miss Coleson's Narrative of Her Captivity among the Sioux Indians!* (Philadelphia: Barclay, 1864). Ellis would go on to include a heavily biased nonfiction account in *The Indian Wars of the United States from the First Settlement at Jamestown, in 1607* (New York: Cassell, 1892).

5. Bryant and Murch, *A History of the Great Massacre,* iv; McConkey, *Dakota War Whoop,* 19.
6. Kathryn Zabelle Derounian-Stodola, *The War in Words: Reading the Dakota Conflict through the Captivity Literature* (Lincoln: University of Nebraska Press, 2009). Derounian-Stodola's valuable study treats the often competing accounts of the conflict produced by European Americans (including Wakefield) and Native Americans between 1862 and 1978.
7. "Heard's History of the Sioux War," *North American Review* 97, no. 202 (January 1864), 266.
8. Jane Grey Swisshelm, *Crusader and Feminist: Letters of Jane Grey Swisshelm,* ed. Arthur J. Larsen (Westport, Conn.: Hyperion, 1976), 194.
9. "The Indian War in Minnesota," *Saint Paul Pioneer,* October 23, 1862.
10. Priscilla Wald, *Constituting Americans: Cultural Anxiety and Narrative Form* (Durham, N.C.: Duke University Press, 1995), 3.
11. June Namias, *White Captives: Gender and Ethnicity on the American Frontier* (Chapel Hill: University of North Carolina Press, 1993), 225.
12. Derounian-Stodola notes the correct spelling is "Hepan"; I use "Hapa" to maintain consistency with Wakefield's narrative. Derounian-Stodola, *The War in Words,* 294n48.
13. Different versions of Wakefield's court testimony are available in *The Court Proceedings in the Trial of Dakota Indians following the Massacre in Minnesota in August 1862* (Minneapolis: Satterlee, 1927), 10–11, and in Case 3: We-chank-wash-to-do-pee, Records of Selected Cases Decided by the Military Commission Sitting in Minnesota, in Douglas Linder's transcription of handwritten records prepared by Isaac V. D. Heard, commission secretary, available at "Famous American Trials: The Dakota Conflict Trials," http://law2.umkc.edu. The quotes here are from Linder's transcription. The suggestion that Chaska's involvement in Gleason's murder was an act of mercy appears in the Heard records but not in the 1927 publication. Both sources err in their presentation of the verdict and its aftermath. *The Court Proceedings in the Trial of Dakota Indians* records the verdict as "Not Guilty," but Chaska's appearance on a list of condemned indicates the opposite. In Heard's records, Wakefield's protector is described as "sentenced to hang, but not executed"; however, he was indeed put to death. On the variant records of the proceedings, see Namias, *White Captives,* 222–25.

14. Case 3: We-chank-wash-to-do-pee. The other witness was Angus Robertson, a mixed-blood Dakota. Gary Clayton Anderson and Alan R. Woolworth, eds., *Through Dakota Eyes: Narrative Accounts of the Minnesota Indian War of 1862* (Saint Paul: Minnesota Historical Society Press, 1988), 183.
15. Scott W. Berg, *38 Nooses: Lincoln, Little Crow, and the Beginning of the Frontier's End* (New York: Pantheon, 2012), 289.
16. Louis H. Roddis, *The Indian Wars of Minnesota* (Cedar Rapids, Iowa: Torch Press, 1959), 155.
17. On the unfairness of the trials, see Carol Chomsky, "The United States–Dakota War Trials: A Study in Military Injustice," *Stanford Law Review* 43, no. 1 (1990), 13–95.
18. One prisoner was granted a last-minute reprieve, reducing the final number of condemned to thirty-eight. While many historians praise Lincoln for intervening, David Martínez (Gila River Pima) condemns the president's execution of the remaining prisoners as mass murder. David Martínez, "Remembering the Thirty-Eight: Abraham Lincoln, the Dakota, and the U.S. War on Barbarism," *Wicazo Sa Review* 28, no. 2 (2013), 5–29.
19. Letter from Sen. Morton S. Wilkinson, Rep. Cyrus Aldrich, and Rep. William Windom to Abraham Lincoln, quoted in McConkey, *Dakota War Whoop,* 282.
20. Ibid., 282–83.
21. Gov. Alexander Ramsey to Abraham Lincoln, August 26, 1862, Abraham Lincoln Papers, Manuscript Division, Library of Congress (Washington, D.C.: American Memory Project, 2000–2002), http://memory.loc.gov.
22. Shoshana Felman, "Education and Crisis, or the Vicissitudes of Teaching," in Shoshana Felman and Dori Laub, *Testimony: Crises of Witnessing in Literature, Psychoanalysis, and History* (New York: Routledge, 1992), 6.
23. Namias, *White Captives,* 232.
24. Most scholarship suggests rape was rare or nonexistent among eastern tribes but did occur among western tribes, likely as a result of contact with white warfare practices. There is disagreement, however, over the extent of the practice of raping captives. For conflicting viewpoints, see Thomas S. Abler, "Scalping, Torture, Cannibalism and Rape: An Ethnohistorical Analysis of Conflicting Cultural Values in War," *Anthropologica* 34, no. 1 (1992), 3–20; Lillian A. Ackerman, "Complementary but Equal: Gender Status in the Plateau," in *Women and Power in Native American North America,* ed. Laura F. Klein and Lillian A. Ackerman (Norman: University of Oklahoma Press, 1995), 87; Susan Brownmiller, *Against Our Will: Men, Women, and Rape* (New York: Simon and Schuster, 1975), 142; Alice Nash, "'None of the Women Were Abused': Indigenous Contexts for the Treatment of Women Captives in the Northeast," in *Sex without Consent: Rape and Sexual Coercion in America,* ed. Merril D. Smith (New York: New York University Press, 2001), 10–26; and Claudio Saunt, *A New Order of Things: Property, Power, and the Transformation of the Creek Indians, 1733–1816* (New York: Cambridge University Press, 1999), 151–53. Namias suggests more than two women may have been sexually abused in the Dakota

Conflict but notes "the rape issue is highly contested." Wakefield, *Six Weeks in the Sioux Tepees,* 129n5, 130n10.

25. Isaac V. D. Heard, quoted in Meyer, *History of the Santee Sioux,* 126.
26. Namias, *White Captives,* 235–37.
27. John G. Nicolay to Henry H. Sibley, December 9, 1862, Abraham Lincoln Papers.
28. Derounian-Stodola, *The War in Words,* 71.
29. Quoted in Wakefield, *Six Weeks in the Sioux Tepees,* 121–22.
30. In an earlier version of this chapter, I suggested that Riggs may have deliberately switched the confession of We-Chank-Wash-to-don-pee and Robert Hopkins. That conclusion seems wrong, given that Hopkins also had been removed from the list of condemned. Janet Dean, "Nameless Outrages: Narrative Authority, Rape Rhetoric, and the Dakota Conflict of 1862," *American Literature* 77 (2005), 119–20n22. As I point out below, Wakefield indicates Riggs met Chaska at Camp Release; however, Walter Bachman cites Riggs's handwritten notes to argue the clergyman did not know the prisoner well and could not have intentionally contributed to his death. Bachman, *Northern Slave, Black Dakota: The Life and Times of Joseph Godfrey* (Bloomington, Minn.: Pond Dakota Press, 2013), 267–72, 137n55, 135n34; personal communication with the author, January 10, 14, 2014.
31. Sarah F. Wakefield to Abraham Lincoln, March 23, 1863. Abraham Lincoln Papers.
32. Ibid.
33. Ibid. Derounian-Stodola concludes that the "Officer" referenced is Mankato jailer Joseph Brown, but there is evidence to suggest that Wakefield's husband had in mind Sibley himself, who was known to have fathered at least one child with a Mdewakanton woman. Derounian-Stodola, *The War in Words,* 72; George A. S. Crooker to Abraham Lincoln, October 7, 1862, Abraham Lincoln Papers; Bachman, *Northern Slave, Black Dakota,* 77n30.
34. A list of "friendlies" is included in Heard, *History of the Sioux War,* 187, and Reverend Moses N. Adams, "The Sioux Outbreak in the Year 1862, with Notes of Missionary Work among the Sioux," in *Collections of the Minnesota Historical Society* 9 (1901), 446–49.
35. Schultz, *Over the Earth I Come,* 76; John D. Bessler, *Legacy of Violence: Lynch Mobs and Executions in Minnesota* (Minneapolis: University of Minnesota Press, 2003), 47.
36. Case 3: We-chank-wash-to-do-pee.
37. Bryant and Murch, *A History of the Great Massacre,* 103–4; McConkey, *Dakota War Whoop,* 49. Bryant and Murch identify Chaska as "the Indian who had not fired" at Gleason but do not record his protection of Wakefield and her children.
38. Namias, *White Captives,* 253.
39. Ibid., 238.
40. June Namias, "Editor's Introduction," in Wakefield, *Six Weeks in the Sioux Tepees,* 5.
41. H. H. Sibley to Sarah Sibley, September 27, 1862, quoted in Namias, *White Captives,* 226.

42. Andrea Tinnemeyer, *Identity Politics of the Captivity Narrative after 1848* (Lincoln: University of Nebraska Press, 2006), xiii.
43. Namias, *White Captives,* 36.
44. Christopher Castiglia, *Bound and Determined: Captivity, Culture-Crossing, and White Womanhood from Mary Rowlandson to Patty Hearst* (Chicago: University of Chicago Press, 1996), 122–23. On the ways intimations of sexual assault became embedded in captivity narratives, see Gary L. Ebersole, *Captured by Texts: Puritan to Postmodern Images of Indian Captivity* (Charlottesville: University Press of Virginia, 1995), 216–21.
45. Castiglia, *Bound and Determined,* 122.
46. Ibid. See also Michelle Burnham, *Captivity and Sentiment: Cultural Exchange in American Literature, 1682–1861* (Hanover, N.H.: University Press of New England, 1997).
47. Memorial drafted by George A. Nourse, U.S. district attorney for the district of Minnesota, quoted in Bryant and Murch, *A History of the Great Massacre,* 465.
48. Quoted in Schultz, *Over the Earth I Come,* 253.
49. *The Court Proceedings in the Trial of Dakota Indians,* 15.
50. Quoted in Wakefield, *Six Weeks in the Sioux Tepees,* 130n10.
51. Kathryn Zabelle Derounian-Stodola and James A. Levernier, *The Indian Captivity Narrative, 1550–1900* (New York: Twayne, 1993), 129–30.
52. Sabine Sielke, *Reading Rape: The Rhetoric of Sexual Violence in American Literature and Culture, 1790–1990* (Princeton, N.J.: Princeton University Press, 2002), 2.
53. W. J. Cash, *The Mind of the South* (New York: Knopf, 1941), 117, quoted in Jacquelyn Dowd Hall, "'The Mind That Burns in Each Body': Women, Rape, and Racial Violence," in *Powers of Desire: The Politics of Sexuality,* ed. Ann Snitow, Christine Stansell, and Sharon Thompson (New York: Monthly Review Press, 1983), 335.
54. Sandra Gunning, *Race, Rape, and Lynching: The Red Record of American Literature, 1890–1912* (New York: Oxford University Press, 1996), 11.
55. Sielke, *Reading Rape,* 2, 5.
56. Lynn A. Higgins and Brenda R. Silver, "Introduction: Rereading Rape," in *Rape and Representation,* ed. Lynn A. Higgins and Brenda R. Silver (New York: Columbia University Press, 1991), 2.
57. Sielke, *Reading Rape,* 2.
58. Heard, *History of the Sioux War,* 101.
59. McConkey, *Dakota War Whoop,* 283.
60. Ibid.
61. Ibid., 286.
62. Ibid. Other politicians, military officers, and journalists warned of a white mob uprising should Lincoln spare any of the condemned. See Schultz, *Over the Earth I Come,* 257–58.
63. McConkey, *Dakota War Whoop,* 241.
64. Bryant and Murch, *A History of the Great Massacre,* 340.
65. Higgins and Silver, "Introduction," 3.
66. Namias, *White Captives,* 239. The only known copy of the first edition of *Six*

Weeks in the Sioux Tepees is held at the Beinecke Library of Yale University, New Haven, Conn.

67. Among those captives who wrote that Wakefield "prefer[red] Indian to civilized life" was Mary Schwandt. Namias, "Editor's Introduction," 30.
68. Burnham, *Captivity and Sentiment,* 2; Theresa A. Toulouse, *The Captive's Position: Female Narrative, Male Identity, and Royal Authority in Colonial New England* (Philadelphia: University of Pennsylvania Press, 2007), 11–12.
69. Michel de Certeau, *The Practice of Everyday Life,* trans. Steven Rendall (Berkeley: University of California Press, 1984), 93.
70. Bachman, *Northern Slave, Black Dakota,* 135n34; Derounian-Stodola, *The War in Words,* 69. It is worth noting how the loaded term "schizophrenic" resonates with the conclusion by Wakefield's peers that she was a "Mono Maniac." Kathryn Zabelle Derounian-Stodola, "'Many Persons Say I Am a "Mono Maniac"': Three Letters from Dakota Conflict Captive Sarah F. Wakefield to Missionary Stephen R. Riggs," *Prospects: An Annual of American Cultural Studies* 29 (2004), 1–24; *The War in Words,* 293–94n36.
71. "The Indian Expedition. Letter from General Sibley's Camp. Interesting Account of the Indian Trials," *Saint Paul Pioneer,* November 15, 1862.
72. Martha Hodes, "Introduction: Interconnecting and Diverging Narratives," in *Sex, Love, Race: Crossing Boundaries in North American History,* ed. Martha Hodes (New York: New York University Press, 1999), 1.
73. Namias, "Editor's Introduction," 28.
74. Derounian-Stodola devotes a chapter to Wakefield and another white woman caught in the uprising in *The War in Words,* 55–76. Christopher Castiglia discusses parallels between *Six Weeks in the Sioux Tepees* and Mary Rowlandson's captivity narrative in *Bound and Determined,* 55. Rebecca Blevins Faery describes Wakefield's narrative briefly in *Cartographies of Desire: Captivity, Race, and Sex in the Shaping of an American Nation* (Norman: University of Oklahoma Press, 1999), 215. Wakefield's text is included with a short introduction in the anthology *Women's Indian Captivity Narratives,* ed. Kathryn Zabelle Derounian-Stodola (New York: Penguin, 1998), 237–313.

2. "She Wept Alone": The Politics and Poetics of Lydia Sigourney's Indian Laments

1. Other popular anti-removal poems include "The Cherokees' Reply. To the Proposition That They Should Remove beyond the Mississippi," *Cherokee Phoenix, and Indians' Advocate,* September 23, 1829; Josiah Canning, "The Indian Gone," in *Poems* (Greenfield, Mass.: Phelps and Ingersoll, 1838), 167; and George Lunt, "The Lament of the Cherokee," in *Poems* (New York: Gould and Newman, 1839), 130–32.
2. [L. H. Sigourney], "The Cherokee Mother," *Cherokee Phoenix, and Indians' Advocate,* March 12, 1831. Unless otherwise noted, subsequent references are to this publication of the poem.
3. Max Cavitch, *American Elegy: The Poetry of Mourning from the Puritans to Whitman* (Minneapolis: University of Minnesota Press, 2007), 129.

4. On the anti-removal campaign as a foundational moment in American women's political activism, see Alisse Portnoy, *Their Right to Speak: Women's Activism in the Indian and Slave Debates* (Cambridge, Mass.: Harvard University Press, 2005); Mary Hershberger, "Mobilizing Women, Anticipating Abolition: The Struggle against Indian Removal in the 1830s," *Journal of American History* 86, no. 1 (1999), 15–40; Amy Dunham Strand, *Language, Gender, and Citizenship in American Literature, 1789–1919* (New York: Routledge, 2008); and Susan Zaeske, *Signatures of Citizenship: Petitioning, Antislavery, and Women's Political Identity* (Chapel Hill: University of North Carolina Press, 2003). On a prior anti-removal campaign by Cherokee women, see Tiya Miles, "'Circular Reasoning': Recentering Cherokee Women in the Anti-Removal Campaigns," *American Quarterly* 61, no. 2 (2009), 221–43.
5. Lydia Huntley Sigourney, "The Cherokee Mother," in *Nineteenth-Century American Women Poets: An Anthology*, ed. Paula Bernat Bennett (Malden, Mass.: Blackwell Publishers, 1998), 7n6. My discussion of Sigourney's reform poetics takes up Bennett's call to resituate nineteenth-century American women's poetry within the public debates that inspired it. Paula Bernat Bennett, *Poets in the Public Sphere: The Emancipatory Project of Women's Poetry, 1800–1900* (Princeton, N.J.: Princeton University Press, 2003).
6. "Letter to the Delegation of the State of Connecticut. From an Association of Ladies," *Cherokee Phoenix, and Indians' Advocate*, March 12, 1831.
7. For a different reading of the relationship between the letter and poem, see Karen L. Kilcup, *Fallen Forests: Emotion, Embodiment, and Ethics in American Women's Environmental Writing, 1781–1924* (Athens: University of Georgia Press, 2013), 48–49.
8. Cari Carpenter, *Seeing Red: Anger, Sentimentality, and American Indians* (Columbus: Ohio State University Press, 2008), 32.
9. Bennett, *Poets in the Public Sphere*, 59; Nina Baym, "Reinventing Lydia Sigourney," *American Literature* 62, no. 3 (1990), 385–404; Sandra A. Zagarell, "Expanding 'America': Lydia Sigourney's *Sketch of Connecticut*, Catharine Sedgwick's *Hope Leslie*," *Tulsa Studies in Women's Literature* 6, no. 2 (1987), 225–46; Kilcup, *Fallen Forests*, 40–52; Tricia Lootens, "Hemans and Her American Heirs: Nineteenth-Century Women's Poetry and National Identity," in *Women's Poetry, Late Romantic to Late Victorian*, ed. Isobel Armstrong and Virginia Blain (New York: St. Martin's Press, 1999), 243–60. For an earlier dismissal of Sigourney's poetry, see Ann Douglas, *The Feminization of American Culture* (1977; reprint, New York: Anchor, 1988), 83–84, 202–3.
10. Gordon S. Haight, *Mrs. Sigourney: The Sweet Singer of Hartford* (New Haven, Conn.: Yale University Press, 1930), 123.
11. The original version of "Indian Names," published in 1834, ends with a trenchant condemnation of removal that describes "unresisting tribes" forced into a "caravan of woe." Lydia Howard Huntley Sigourney, "Indian Names," in *The Heath Anthology of American Literature*, vol. B, 6th edn., ed. Paul Lauter et al. (Boston: Wadsworth, 2009), 1696–98. As Sandra A. Zagarell's footnote points out, these stanzas were left out of subsequent versions. Notably, the stanzas are omitted even in a contemporary anthol-

ogy of protest literature. Lydia Sigourney, "Indian Names," in *American Protest Literature,* ed. Zoe Trodd (Cambridge, Mass.: Harvard University Press, 2006), 55–56.

12. Eliza Richards, *Gender and the Poetics of Reception in Poe's Circle* (Cambridge: Cambridge University Press, 2004), 67.
13. Mary Louise Kete, *Sentimental Collaboration: Mourning and Middle-Class Identity in Nineteenth Century America* (Durham, N.C.: Duke University Press, 1999), 118.
14. Bryan Sinche, "Lydia Sigourney's Sailors and the Limits of Sentiment," *Legacy* 29, no. 1 (2012), 63.
15. Bennett, *Poets in the Public Sphere,* 59–60.
16. Lauren Berlant, *The Female Complaint: The Unfinished Business of Sentimentality in American Culture* (Durham, N.C.: Duke University Press, 2008), 41.
17. Ibid., 55.
18. Ibid., 56.
19. Ibid., 63, 64. Berlant's original name for this form of textual resistance was "postsentimentality," a term that suggests being beyond or past using the sentimental to effect change. "Countersentimentality" far better captures the possibility I want to explore here, namely that writers may self-consciously manipulate conventional sentimentality to construct an alternative sentimental protest. Lauren Berlant, "Poor Eliza," *American Literature* 70, no. 3 (1998), 655.
20. Michael B. Beckerman, *New Worlds of Dvorˇák: Searching in America for the Composer's Inner Life* (New York: Norton, 2003), 30–37.
21. W. J. Henderson, "Dr. Dvorak's Latest Work," *New York Times,* December 17, 1893, quoted in Beckerman, *New Worlds of Dvorˇák,* 32.
22. Beckerman, *New Worlds of Dvorˇák,* 4.
23. Dana Luciano, *Arranging Grief: Sacred Time and the Body in Nineteenth-Century America* (New York: New York University Press, 2007), 71–72. My discussion of the Native mourner as out of synch draws on Luciano's fascinating deliberations on the temporal in representations of indigenous sorrow.
24. Daniel F. Littlefield, Jr., and James W. Parins, eds., *Encyclopedia of American Indian Removal* (Santa Barbara, Calif.: Greenwood, 2011), 240.
25. On the proliferation of representations of Native loss and mourning in the removal era, see Lucy Maddox, *Removals: Nineteenth-Century American Literature and the Politics of Indian Affairs* (New York: Oxford University Press, 1991), 31–32; Lora Romero, "Vanishing Americans: Gender, Empire, and New Historicism," *American Literature* 63, no. 3 (1991), 385–404; and Renée L. Bergland, *The National Uncanny: Indian Ghosts and American Subjects* (Hanover, N.H.: University Press of New England, 2000), 3.
26. Andrew Jackson, "State of the Union Address, December 6, 1830," in *The Cherokee Removal: A Brief History with Documents,* ed. Theda Perdue and Michael Green (1995; reprint, Boston: Bedford Books, 2005), 127.
27. "The Indian's Lament," words and melody by John Wallace Hutchinson (Boston: Stephen W. Marsh, 1846), quoted in Michael Pisani, *Imagining*

Native America in Music (New Haven, Conn.: Yale University Press, 2005), 96. Other songs about Native mourning appear in Michael Pisani, "A Chronological Listing of Musical Works on American Indian Subjects, Composed since 1608," http://indianmusiclist.vassar.edu/.

28. James Fenimore Cooper, *The Last of the Mohicans* (New York: Penguin Books, 1986), 349.
29. On the Vanishing American topos, see Brian W. Dippie, *The Vanishing American: White Attitudes and U.S. Indian Policy* (Lawrence: University Press of Kansas, 1982).
30. Ibid., 13; Cavitch, *American Elegy,* 130–31.
31. Cooper, *The Last of the Mohicans,* 350.
32. Luciano identifies obdurate attachment to the past in nineteenth-century representations of mourning Native Americans, like that in *The Last of the Mohicans,* as a fatal melancholia, "an inability to move on in time." Luciano, *Arranging Grief,* 81.
33. Kete, *Sentimental Collaboration,* 3.
34. Cavitch, *American Elegy,* 23.
35. Judith Butler, *Precarious Life: The Powers of Mourning and Violence* (London: Verso, 2006), 22.
36. Cooper, *The Last of the Mohicans,* 349.
37. Ibid., 30, 33.
38. The other epigraph from one of Cooper's American contemporaries, from Fitz-Greene Halleck's poem "Marco Bozzaris" (1825), opens the final chapter and anticipates its funeral scene. The poem idealizes a hero's death in the 1821 battle for Greek independence.
39. William Cullen Bryant, "An Indian at the Burial-Place of His Fathers," in *Poems* (1836; reprint, New York: Harper and Brothers, 1840), 215–16.
40. Cavitch, *American Elegy,* 131.
41. Bryant, "An Indian at the Burial-Place of His Fathers," 215–16.
42. Gilbert H. Muller, *William Cullen Bryant: Author of America* (Albany: State University of New York Press, 2008), 89.
43. John Greenleaf Whittier, "The Indian Question," *Essex Gazette,* February 20, 1830, quoted in Barbara Cutter, "The Female Indian Killer Memorialized: Hannah Duston and the Nineteenth-Century Feminization of American Violence," *Journal of Women's History* 20, no. 2 (2008), 15.
44. J. G. Whittier, "The Vanishers," in *The Writings of John Greenleaf Whittier,* vol. 2 (Boston: Houghton and Mifflin, 1888), 50.
45. J. G. Whittier, "The Indian Girl's Lament," in *The Literary Souvenir; or, Cabinet of Poetry and Romance,* ed. A. A. Watts (London: Longman, Rees, Orme, Brown, and Green, 1831), 136–37, 134.
46. Mrs. L. H. Sigourney, "Indian Girl's Burial," in *Select Poems* (Philadelphia: Frederick W. Greenough, 1838), 137. The poem subsequently appeared under the title "Burial of the Indian Girl."
47. Ibid. On the inspiration for the poem, see Philip D. Jordan, "The Source of Mrs. Sigourney's 'Indian Girl's Burial'," *American Literature* 4, no. 3 (November 1932), 300–305.
48. [Catharine E. Beecher], "Circular Addressed to the Benevolent Ladies of

the U. States," *Christian Advocate and Journal and Zion's Herald*, December 25, 1829, 65, 66.

49. Portnoy, *Their Right to Speak*, 59.
50. Memorial of Sundry Ladies of Hallowell, Maine, Praying That Certain Indian Tribes May Not Be Removed from Their Present Place of Abode, January 8, 1830 (endorsed January 18, 1830), quoted in Portnoy, *Their Right to Speak*, 1.
51. Amy Kaplan, "Manifest Domesticity," *American Literature* 70, no. 3 (1998), 585.
52. *The Autobiography of Martin Van Buren* (Washington, D.C.: U.S. Government Printing Office, 1920), 275–76, quoted in Hershberger, "Mobilizing Women, Anticipating Abolition," 15.
53. Ronald N. Satz, *American Indian Policy in the Jacksonian Era*, 3rd edn. (Norman: University of Oklahoma Press, 2002), 21.
54. Jeremiah Evarts, *Cherokee Removal: The "William Penn" Essays and Other Writings*, ed. Francis Paul Prucha (Knoxville: University of Tennessee Press, 1981).
55. John A. Andrew III, *From Revivals to Removals: Jeremiah Evarts, the Cherokee Nation, and the Search for the Soul of America* (Athens: University of Georgia Press, 1992).
56. Francis Paul Prucha, "Introduction," in *Cherokee Removal*, 30.
57. Catharine E. Beecher, *Educational Reminiscences and Suggestions* (New York: J. B. Ford, 1874), 62.
58. Zaeske, *Signatures of Citizenship*, 23.
59. Strand, *Language, Gender, and Citizenship in American Literature*, 30.
60. William Lloyd Garrison, "Out of Place" (1830), in *Women and Social Movements in the United States, 1600–2000*, ed. Thomas Dublin and Kathryn Kish Sklar, http://womhist.alexanderstreet.com. Garrison later reversed his position on women's petitions. Portnoy, *Their Right to Speak*, 165.
61. Hershberger, "Mobilizing Women, Anticipating Abolition," 29.
62. Beecher, "Circular Addressed to the Benevolent Ladies of the U. States," 65.
63. Memorial of the Ladies of Steubenville, Ohio, against the Forceable Removal of Indians without the Limits of the United States (endorsed February 15, 1830), Petitions and Memorials Which Were Tabled: Indian Matters (HR21A-H1.1), 21st Congress, Records of the U.S. Senate, Record Group 233, National Archives, Washington, D.C.
64. Petition of Ladies of the Town of Huntsburgh for the Protection of Indian Rights (no endorsement date), Committee of the Whole House: Removal of Indians, Petitions and Memorials Referred to Committees (HR21A-G23.3), 21st Congress, Records of the U.S. House of Representatives, Record Group 233, National Archives.
65. Berlant, *The Female Complaint*, 145.
66. Male leaders of the anti-removal movement typically aligned with Whig Party politics. While Evarts distrusted motives of "party spirit," he welcomed the support of Whig leaders like Henry Clay. Andrew, *From Revivals to Removals*, 70, 248.
67. Beecher, "Circular Addressed to the Benevolent Ladies of the U. States," 65.

68. Petition of the Female Inhabitants of the Township of Lewis and the State of New York (no endorsement date), Committee on Indian Affairs: Removal of Indians, Petitions and Memorials (HR21A-G.2), 21st Congress, Records of the U.S. House of Representatives, Record Group 233, National Archives.
69. Memorial of the Ladies of Steubenville, Ohio.
70. Petition of Massachusetts Ladies of [Monson, County of] Hamden—Relative to Removal of Indians (endorsed February 1, 1831), Committee on Indian Affairs: Removal of Indians, Petitions and Memorials Referred to Committees (HR21A-G8.2), 21st Congress, Records of the U.S. House of Representatives, Record Group 233, National Archives.
71. "Letter to the Delegation of the State of Connecticut."
72. Strand, *Language, Gender, and Citizenship in American Literature,* 44.
73. Memorial of the Ladies of Steubenville, Ohio; Petition of Massachusetts Ladies.
74. Portnoy, *Their Right to Speak,* 49.
75. Beecher, "Circular Addressed to the Benevolent Ladies of the U. States," 65.
76. Ibid.
77. Ibid.
78. Ibid.
79. Ibid. The speaker is Col. David Folsom, principle chief of the Choctaw Nation, who responds here to a U.S. government communication urging the Choctaws to relocate to territories west of the Mississippi. A transcription of the speech appeared in the *Cherokee Phoenix,* November 18, 1829.
80. Beecher, "Circular Addressed to the Benevolent Ladies of the U. States," 65.
81. Ibid.
82. Memorial of the Ladies of Steubenville, Ohio.
83. Petition Protesting Indian Removal from Inhabitants of Hadley, Massachusetts (endorsed February 15, 1831), Petitions and Memorials Referred to Committees (HR21A-G8.2), 21st Congress, Records of the U.S. House of Representatives, Record Group 233, National Archives; Petition on Behalf of Cherokee Rights from New England Women, Abington, Mass. (endorsed May 21, 1838) (HR25A-H1.3), 25th Congress, Records of the U.S. House of Representatives, Record Group 233, National Archives.
84. Petition on Behalf of Cherokee Rights from New England Women, Newburyport, Mass. (endorsed May 5, 1838), Petitions and Memorials Referred to Committees (HR21A-G8.2), Records of the U.S. House of Representatives, Record Group 233, National Archives.
85. Memorial of the Ladies of Steubenville, Ohio.
86. "Letter to the Delegation of the State of Connecticut."
87. Berlant, *The Female Complaint,* 22.
88. Catharine E. Beecher, *An Essay on Slavery and Abolitionism, with Reference to the Duty of American Females,* 2nd edn. (Philadelphia: Perkins and Marvin, 1837), 104.
89. Kilcup, *Fallen Forests,* 48.
90. Beecher, *Educational Reminiscences and Suggestions,* 62–63; Kathryn Kish Sklar, *Catharine Beecher: A Study in American Domesticity* (New Haven, Conn.: Yale University Press, 1973), 99. Some scholars identify Sigourney as co-

author of the "Circular," among them Neil Schmitz, *White Robe's Dilemma: Tribal History in American Literature* (Amherst: University of Massachusetts Press, 2001), 87; Melanie Susan Gustafson, *Women and the Republican Party, 1854–1924* (Urbana: University of Illinois Press, 2001), 15; and Kilcup, *Fallen Forests,* 44. On the question of authorship, see Hershberger, "Mobilizing Women, Anticipating Abolition," 27.

91. Given the letter's Hartford, Connecticut, dateline and its conjunction with the poem, it makes sense to attribute authorship to Sigourney, as Bennett does. Bennett, ed., *Nineteenth-Century American Women Poets,* 7n1.
92. Lydia Huntley Sigourney, "Remonstrance of the Creek Indians against Being Removed from Their Own Territory," in *Poems: By the Author of "Moral Pieces in Prose and Verse"* (Boston: S. G. Goodrich, 1827), 76, 77.
93. Ibid, 77.
94. Lydia Huntley Sigourney, *Letters of Life* (New York: D. Appleton, 1866), 327.
95. On the place of *Traits of the Aborigines of America* within the tradition of white-authored epics on Native themes, see Christopher N. Phillips, *Epic in American Culture: Settlement to Reconstruction* (Baltimore: Johns Hopkins University Press, 2012), 189–90. Both *Ouabi* and *Yamoyden* tell New World love stories in which a Native man voluntarily withdraws or sacrifices himself, symbolically clearing the way for white settlement of the continent.
96. [Lydia Huntley Sigourney], *Traits of the Aborigines of America* (Cambridge, Mass.: University Press, Hilliard and Metcalf, 1822), 18, canto I, lines 244–45; 32, canto II, lines 38–40. Subsequent references to page, canto, and line of this edition are cited parenthetically as, for example, 18, I:244–45.
97. For example, Sigourney cites Elias Boudinot's *A Star in the West; or, A Humble Attempt to Discover the Long Lost Ten Tribes of Israel* (1816), a book that made the case for Native rights based on a theory of their origins. (Boudinot, a white congressman, should not be confused with his Cherokee namesake, editor of the *Cherokee Phoenix.*) Sigourney, *Traits of the Aborigines of America,* 252, II, note 36.
98. Miles, "Circular Reasoning," 232–34.
99. A footnote to these lines quotes in full (without attribution) Henry Rowe Schoolcraft's "Geehale: An Indian Lament," a poem unique among other Indian laments in its pointed refutation of the natural extinction narrative. A bereft Native speaker insists his kindred "fell not by hunger, or lingering decay, / The steel of the white man hath swept them away." Sigourney, *Traits of the Aborigines of America,* 232, III, note 1.
100. In her memoirs, Sigourney recalls that she wrote the poem in 1817, though given the inclusion of the Chehaw massacre, it is clear she was still adding to it in 1818. Sigourney, *Letters of Life,* 327.
101. On the Chehaw massacre and its aftermath, see David Stephen Heidler and Jeanne T. Heidler, *Old Hickory's War: Andrew Jackson and the Quest for Empire* (Baton Rouge: Louisiana State University Press, 2003), 159–76. In a footnote, Sigourney describes then General Jackson leading the attack on the Chehaw, but Jackson was fighting the Seminoles in Florida at the time. Sigourney, *Traits of the Aborigines of America,* 254, III, note 40.

102. Baym, "Reinventing Lydia Sigourney," 399.
103. L. H. Sigourney, "Pocahontas," in *Pocahontas, and Other Poems* (New York: Harper and Brothers, 1841), 13–37, lines 172–73. Subsequent references are indicated parenthetically by line number.
104. Phillips calls attention to the fact that when Sigourney made the same comparison early in her career in *Traits of the Aborigines of America,* she underlined this irony: as unsuspecting as Pharaoh, Pocahontas's father, Powhatan, does not imagine that "his child's weak arm / Fostered that colony, whose rising light / Should quench his own forever" (78, I:1094–96). Phillips, *Epic in American Culture,* 192, 194.
105. Portnoy, *Their Right to Speak,* 82–83.
106. On the proliferation of representations of Pocahontas in the nineteenth century, see Robert S. Tilton, *Pocahontas: The Evolution of an American* Narrative (New York: Cambridge University Press, 1994); Frances Mossiker, *Pocahontas: The Life and Legend* (New York: Da Capo Press, 1996); and Ann Uhry Abrams, *The Pilgrims and Pocahontas: Rival Myths of American Origins* (Boulder, Colo.: Westview Press, 1999).
107. Robert Dale Owen, *Pocahontas: A Historical Drama, in Five Acts* (New York: George Dearborn, 1837), 21.
108. Thomas L. M'Kenney, *Memoirs, Official and Personal* (New York: Paine and Burgess, 1846), 231.
109. Ruricola, "Mr. Wirt and the Indians," *Cherokee Phoenix, and Indians' Advocate,* December 17, 1831. The connection between the Pocahontas story and political disputes over removal could be less deliberately drawn as well. An 1836 Washington, D.C., performance of George Washington Custis's play *Pocahontas; or, The Settlers of Virginia: A National Drama* was rumored to have included a dance by a visiting delegation of Cherokee chiefs led by the activist John Ross. The Cherokee group was indeed in the city at the time of the performance, but it was there to protest removal. Susan Scheckel, *The Insistence of the Indian: Race and Nationalism in Nineteenth-Century American Culture* (Princeton, N.J.: Princeton University Press, 1998), 58.
110. On Hemans's influence on Sigourney, see Lootens, "Hemans and Her American Heirs," and Janet Dean, "'Exil'd Murmurings': 'The American Hemans' and the Politics of Displacement," in *Reconsidering Sigourney,* ed. Mary Louise Kete and Elizabeth Petrino (Amherst: University of Massachusetts Press, forthcoming).
111. The kidnapping is described in John Frost, *History of the United States; for the Use of Common Schools* (Philadelphia: Thomas Cowperthwait and Company, 1839), 47, and George S. Hillard, *Life of and Adventures of Captain John Smith* (New York: Harper and Brothers, 1839), 189. Hillard's text was one of Sigourney's sources (33n3).
112. Baym, "Reinventing Lydia Sigourney," 403.
113. Philip Young, "The Mother of Us All: Pocahontas Reconsidered," *Kenyon Review* 24, no. 3 (Summer 1962), 391–415.
114. Lydia Huntley Sigourney to Dr. Sprague, Hartford, July 13, 1836, Lydia Huntley Sigourney Papers, Connecticut Historical Society, Hartford.

115. Bennett, *Poets in the Public Sphere,* 52.
116. Ibid., 60.
117. Sigourney, *Letters of Life,* 327.

3. Reading Lessons: Sentimental Critique in S. Alice Callahan's *Wynema: A Child of the Forest*

1. S. Alice Callahan, *Wynema: A Child of the Forest,* ed. A. LaVonne Brown Ruoff (1891; reprint, Lincoln: University of Nebraska Press, 1997), 23; hereafter cited parenthetically as *W.*
2. A. LaVonne Brown Ruoff, "Editor's Introduction," in Callahan, *Wynema,* xxviii.
3. Jaime Osterman Alves, *Fictions of Female Education in the Nineteenth Century* (New York: Routledge, 2009), 100.
4. James H. Cox, *Muting White Noise: Native American and European American Novel Traditions* (Norman: University of Oklahoma Press, 2006), 33.
5. Craig S. Womack, *Red on Red: Native American Literary Separatism* (Minneapolis: University of Minnesota Press, 1999), 114, 120.
6. Melissa Ryan, "The Indian Problem as a Woman's Question: S. Alice Callahan's *Wynema: A Child of the Forest,*" *American Transcendental Quarterly* 21, no. 1 (2007), 23–45.
7. Cari M. Carpenter, *Seeing Red: Anger, Sentimentality, and American Indians* (Columbus: Ohio State University Press, 2008), 29–53.
8. Susan Bernardin, "On the Meeting Grounds of Sentiment: S. Alice Callahan's *Wynema: A Child of the Forest,*" *American Transcendental Quarterly* 15, no. 3 (2001), 209. See also Kara Mollis, "Teaching 'Dear Mihia': Sentimentalism and Cross-Cultural Education in S. Alice Callahan's *Wynema: A Child of the Forest,*" *MELUS* 33, no. 3 (2008), 111–29, and Siobhan Senier, "Allotment Protest and Tribal Discourse: Reading *Wynema*'s Successes and Shortcomings," *American Indian Quarterly* 24, no. 3 (2000), 420–40.
9. Beth Piatote, *Domestic Subjects: Gender, Citizenship, and Law in Native American Literature* (New Haven, Conn.: Yale University Press, 2013), 64–65.
10. Laura Wexler, *Tender Violence: Domestic Visions in an Age of U.S. Imperialism* (Chapel Hill: University of North Carolina Press, 2000), 10.
11. Cox and Alves also explore the ways Callahan critiqued reading practices, but they see her as more complicit with than resistant to the dominant culture. In Cox's words, *Wynema* is "a part of, rather than a challenge to, colonial literary traditions." Cox, *Muting White Noise,* 35–36. Alves demonstrates how Callahan encouraged a critical reading of both newspaper reports and school lessons, but she sees such reading as a process of mediation rather than resistance. Alves, *Fictions of Female Education,* 7.
12. James L. Machor, "Introduction: Readers/Texts/Context," in *Readers in History: Nineteenth-Century American Literature and the Contexts of Response,* ed. James L. Machor (Baltimore: Johns Hopkins University Press, 1993), xi.

13. Zitkala-Ša, "The School Days of an Indian Girl," in *American Indian Stories, Legends, and Other Writings,* ed. Cathy N. Davidson and Ada Norris (New York: Penguin, 2003), 97, 99.
14. This phrase originated with Richard Henry Pratt, founder of the Carlisle Indian Industrial School, where Zitkala-Ša later taught. David Wallace Adams, *Education for Extinction: American Indians and the Boarding School Experience, 1875–1928* (Lawrence: University Press of Kansas, 1995), 52.
15. On Zitkala-Ša's critiques of education for assimilation and sentimentalism, see Susan Bernardin, "The Lessons of a Sentimental Education: Zitkala-Ša's Autobiographical Narratives," *Western American Literature* 32, no. 3 (1997), 212–38.
16. Frederick E. Hoxie, *A Final Promise: The Campaign to Assimilate the Indians, 1880–1920* (1984; reprint, Lincoln: University of Nebraska Press, 2001), 53.
17. T. J. Morgan, "Supplemental Report on Indian Education," in *Documents of United States Indian Policy,* ed. Francis Paul Prucha, 3rd edn. (Lincoln: University of Nebraska Press, 2000), 177.
18. Amelia V. Katanski, *Learning to Write "Indian": The Boarding-School Experience and American Indian Literature* (Norman: University of Oklahoma Press, 2005), 48, 85–89.
19. W. T. Harris, "The Relation of School Education to the Work of Civilizing Other Races," in *Report of the Secretary of the Interior,* vol. 2, *Report of the Commissioner of Indian Affairs* (Washington, D.C.: Government Printing Office, 1896), 1016.
20. Michael C. Coleman, *American Indian Children at School, 1850–1930* (Jackson: University Press of Mississippi, 1993), 112–15; Ruth Spack, *America's Second Tongue: American Indian Education and the Ownership of English, 1860–1900* (Lincoln: University of Nebraska Press, 2002), 69–70.
21. Homi K. Bhabha, *The Location of Culture* (1994; reprint, New York: Routledge, 2005), 128. It is important to acknowledge objections to the application of postcolonial theory to Native texts. Arnold Krupat reminds us, to begin with, that there is no "post" in the colonial status of Native Americans. Arnold Krupat, *Turn to the Native: Studies in Criticism and Culture* (1996; reprint Lincoln: University of Nebraska Press, 1998), 30. Nonetheless, Bhabha's theories help explain how in colonized subjects' adoption of white literary modes, important differences—such as shifting perspectives and revised subject positions, or the incorporation of multiple rhetorical forms—call attention to the constructed nature of "colonial" readings. Callahan's adoption of a conventionally white, middle-class idiom makes particularly useful Bhabha's concept of mimicry as "at once resemblance and menace." Bhabha, *The Location of Culture,* 123.
22. Myriam Vučović, *Voices from Haskell: Indian Students between Two Worlds, 1884–1928* (Lawrence: University Press of Kansas, 2008), 103.
23. Harriet Beecher Stowe, *Uncle Tom's Cabin; or, Life among the Lowly,* in *Three Novels* (New York: Library of America, 1982), 515.
24. Elizabeth Fekete Trubey, "'Success Is Sympathy': *Uncle Tom's Cabin* and the Woman Reader," in *Reading Women: Literary Figures and Cultural Icons from the Victorian Age to the Present,* ed. Janet Badia and Jennifer Phegley (Toronto:

University of Toronto Press, 2005), 55. While Stowe's work makes a useful point of comparison, I do not mean to suggest it defines sentimental writing in the nineteenth century. Rather, my argument underlines the diversity and complexity of texts we define as sentimental literature. On nineteenth-century African American writers' use of literary sentimentalism, see Sarah Robbins, *Managing Literacy, Mothering America: Women's Narratives on Reading and Writing in the Nineteenth Century* (Pittsburgh: University of Pittsburgh Press, 2004), 157–93. On sentimentalism in writing by nineteenth-century Native women writers, including Callahan, E. Pauline Johnson (Mohawk), and Sarah Winnemucca (Paiute), see Carpenter, *Seeing Red.*

25. Wexler, *Tender Violence,* 105.
26. Ibid., 109–10, 112, 113.
27. Katanski, *Learning to Write "Indian,"* 64–65.
28. Embe [Marianna Burgess], *Stiya: A Carlisle Indian Girl at Home* (Cambridge, Mass.: Riverside Press, 1891), 20, hereafter cited parenthetically as *S.* "Embe" is a pseudonym for Marianna Burgess (M.B.). Jacqueline Fear-Segal, "Eyes in the Text: Marianna Burgess and *The Indian Helper,*" in *Blue Pencils and Hidden Hands: Women Editing Periodicals, 1830–1910,* ed. Sharon M. Harris (Boston: Northeastern University Press, 2004), 136.
29. Tsisnah, whose first name is also recorded as Loisah and Lozah, was a prisoner of the Apache War taken to Carlisle in 1886. Janice Gould, "Telling Stories to the Seventh Generation: Resisting the Assimilationist Narrative of *Stiya,*" in *Reading Native American Women: Critical/Creative Representations,* ed. Inéz Hernández-Avila (Lanham, Md.: AltaMira Press, 2005), 19n3. Tsisnah's work placements in homes in Maryland and Pennsylvania are recorded in Alicia Delgadillo, *From Fort Marion to Fort Sill: A Documentary History of the Chiricahua Apache Prisoners of War, 1886–1913* (Lincoln: University of Nebraska Press, 2013), 261.
30. Another scholar reads this photograph as an illustration of the industry and order required of the assimilated subject, but this does not explain Burgess's emphasis on the institutional buildings rather than the people who have been assimilated within them. Jane E. Simonsen, *Making Home Work: Domesticity and Native American Assimilation in the American West, 1860–1919* (Chapel Hill: University of North Carolina Press, 2006), 91.
31. Leslie Marmon Silko, *Yellow Woman and a Beauty of the Spirit: Essays on Native American Life Today* (New York: Simon and Schuster, 1996), 163.
32. Wexler, *Tender Violence,* 105.
33. Fear-Segal, "Eyes in the Text," 117.
34. A key feature of the newspaper fulfilled this function. The "Man-in-the-Bandstand," a persona of Burgess's creation with a regular column in the paper, functioned as an invisible but always vigilant authority, ostensibly keeping students under surveillance from the bandstand on the campus grounds. Ibid., 108–19; Katanski, *Learning to Write "Indian,"* 45–59; Jessica Enoch, "Resisting the Script of Indian Education: Zitkala-Ša and the Carlisle Indian School," *College English* 65, no. 2 (2002), 122–23.
35. Katanski, *Learning to Write "Indian,"* 65; Ruoff, "Editor's Introduction," xvi–xvii.

36. Ruoff, "Editor's Introduction," xv, xvi.
37. Quoted in Carolyn Thomas Foreman, "S. Alice Callahan: Author of *Wynema A Child of the Forest,*" *Chronicles of Oklahoma* 33, no. 3 (1955), 312.
38. *Annual Report of the Commissioner of Indian Affairs to the Secretary of the Interior* (Washington, D.C.: Government Printing Office, 1878), 153. On other ways *Wynema* supports alternative educational initiatives for Native Americans, see Mollis, "Teaching 'Dear Mihia'," 123–24.
39. Wexler, *Tender Violence,* 104, 105.
40. As critics note, the reference to tepees seems particularly calculated to evoke white readers' romanticized images of Native people, as such structures were unknown among the Muscogee. Ruoff, "Editor's Introduction," xxxiv; Womack, *Red on Red,* 115; Lisa Tatonetti, "Behind the Shadows of Wounded Knee: The Slippage of Imagination in *Wynema: A Child of the Forest,*" *Studies in American Indian Literature* 16, no. 1 (2004), 3.
41. Womack, *Red on Red,* 115.
42. Ryan, "The Indian Problem as a Woman's Question," 27.
43. Ibid., 30–31. See also Mollis, "Teaching 'Dear Mihia'," 121.
44. Senier, "Allotment Protest and Tribal Discourse," 432.
45. Womack, *Red on Red,* 108–9.
46. Piatote, *Domestic Subjects,* 64.
47. Ibid., 67. Piatote notes that the polyvocality of accounts reflects a complex political landscape and a dynamic Native public sphere. In the next chapter, I address the inter- and intratextual debates in a Native magazine that likewise reflect the Native public sphere.
48. Alves, *Fictions of Female Education,* 96.
49. The name "Wynema" recalls a third tale of female sacrifice: the Modoc woman Toby (or Tobey) Riddle, also known as Winema, risked her life to protect Indian Commissioner Alfred B. Meacham during the Modoc War of 1873 and dramatized her rescue in a popular lecture-play. Ruoff, "Editor's Introduction," xliv, note 1.
50. Charlotte J. Rich, *Transcending the New Woman: Multiethnic Narratives in the Progressive Era* (Columbia: University of Missouri Press, 2009), 49.
51. Ann Douglas, *The Feminization of American Culture* (1977; reprint, New York: Farrar, Straus, and Giroux, 1998), 254.
52. Elizabeth Cook-Lynn, *Why I Can't Read Wallace Stegner and Other Essays* (Madison: University of Wisconsin Press, 1996), 80.
53. Womack, *Red on Red,* 118.
54. Jane Tompkins, *Sensational Designs: The Cultural Work of American Fiction, 1790–1860* (New York: Oxford University Press, 1986).
55. Gillian Brown, *Domestic Individualism: Imagining Self in Nineteenth-Century America* (Berkeley: University of California Press, 1990), 39–60; Richard Brodhead, *Cultures of Letters: Scenes of Reading and Writing in Nineteenth-Century America* (Chicago: University of Chicago Press, 1993), 18; Amy Kaplan, *The Anarchy of Empire in the Making of U.S. Culture* (Cambridge, Mass.: Harvard University Press, 2002), 29.
56. Cindy Weinstein, *Family, Kinship, and Sympathy in Nineteenth-Century American Literature* (New York: Cambridge University Press, 2006), 7.

57. Paul Ricoeur, *Freud and Philosophy: An Essay on Interpretation,* trans. Denis Savage (New Haven, Conn.: Yale University Press, 1970), 32. Ricoeur famously describes Marx, Nietzsche, and Freud as founders of the "school of suspicion" that shapes modern interpretative practices.
58. Rita Felski, "Suspicious Minds," *Poetics Today* 32, no. 3 (Summer 2011), 216. See also Rita Felski, "Critique and the Hermeneutics of Suspicion," *M/C Journal* 15, no. 1 (2012), http://journal.media-culture.org.au, and "After Suspicion," *Profession* (2009), 28–35.
59. Eve Kosofsky Sedgwick, *Touching Feeling: Affect, Pedagogy, Performativity* (Durham, N.C.: Duke University Press, 2003), 125.
60. Michael Warner, "Uncritical Reading," in *Polemic: Critical or Uncritical?* ed. Jane Gallop (New York: Routledge, 2004), 13–38; Sianne Ngai, *Ugly Feelings* (Cambridge, Mass.: Harvard University Press, 2007); Michael Millner, *Fever Reading: Affect and Reading Badly in the Early American Public Sphere* (Durham: University of New Hampshire Press, 2012).
61. Sedgwick, *Touching Feeling,* 150–51.
62. Ruoff, "Editor's Introduction," xxvi; Bernardin, "On the Meeting Grounds of Sentiment," 219; Annette Van Dyke, "An Introduction to *Wynema, A Child of the Forest,*" *Studies in American Indian Literature* 4, nos. 2–3 (Summer–Fall 1992), 126.
63. Sedgwick, *Touching Feeling,* 126, 149.
64. Ibid., 128.
65. Paul Kelleher, "If Love Were All: Reading Sedgwick Sentimentally," in *Regarding Sedgwick: Essays on Queer Culture and Critical Theory,* ed. Stephen M. Barber and David L. Clark (New York: Routledge, 2002), 150.
66. Sedgwick, *Touching Feeling,* 145.
67. Tatonetti, "Behind the Shadows of Wounded Knee," 10; Senier, "Allotment Protest and Tribal Discourse," 434.
68. Callahan's depiction of events is historically inaccurate, especially where she characterizes the victims of the massacre as rebels "on the war path" (*W,* 74). But as Tatonetti points out, this representation reflects inaccuracies circulating in the popular press when Callahan was writing. Tatonetti, "Behind the Shadows of Wounded Knee," 13.
69. While the story of Wildfire and Miscona is fictional, the account of Few Tails is historically based, though the ambush took place after the massacre. N. Scott Momaday, *The Man Made of Words: Essays, Stories, and Passages* (New York: St. Martin's Press, 1997), 100.
70. This lesson carries over to another white character, Robin, who sees in the slaughter at Wounded Knee evidence of the U.S. government's murderous intentions (*W,* 101).
71. On the adoption of Wounded Knee orphans as a reflection of a pan-Indian ethic, see Piatote, *Domestic Subjects,* 60–62.
72. Tatonetti argues that the end of the novel shows Callahan's "personal struggle to balance the injustice of the massacre with the romance of her original story and the privileged narrative of her life, which, like Wynema's, was a picture of 'successful' assimilation." I would argue instead that Chikena's and Carl's statements leave a lingering sense of apocalypse that anticipates

contemporary Native novels like Leslie Marmon Silko's *Almanac of the Dead.* Tatonetti, "Behind the Shadows of Wounded Knee," 26.

4. Talking Back: Ora Eddleman's "Indian Magazine" and Native Publicity

1. "Indian Woman as Editor," *Pittsburgh Press,* February 8, 1902. Eddleman's work sometimes appeared under the pseudonym Mignon Schreiber and, later, her married name, Ora Eddleman Reed. I use Ora Eddleman because it is the name most connected with her writing and editing career.
2. The Ojibwe writer Jane Johnston Schoolcraft produced much of the content for the broadly distributed literary magazine *The Muzzinyegun; or, Literary Voyager,* launched in 1826, but that manuscript was overseen by Schoolcraft's husband, the white ethnologist Henry Rowe Schoolcraft. Other early Native magazines such as *A Wreath of Cherokee Rose Buds* and *The Sequoyah Memorial* were sponsored by mission schools.
3. Daryl Morrison, "*Twin Territories: The Indian Magazine* and Its Editor, Ora Eddleman Reed," *Chronicles of Oklahoma* 60, no. 2 (1982), 143. No library or archive holds all issues of *Twin Territories.* Selections of Eddleman's contributions to *Twin Territories, Sturm's Statehood Magazine,* and *Sturm's Oklahoma Magazine* are reprinted in *Native American Women's Writing, 1800–1924,* ed. Karen L. Kilcup (Malden, Mass.: Blackwell, 2000), 350–95, and in *Native American Writing in the Southeast: An Anthology, 1875–1935,* ed. Daniel F. Littlefield, Jr., and James W. Parins (Jackson: University Press of Mississippi, 1995), 134–52.
4. "A Cherokee City Editor," *Kansas City Journal,* July 12, 1898; "An Indian Woman Editor," *New York Times,* December 8, 1901; James T. Elliott, "Proofreaders' Societies and Their Doings," *Inland Printer* 28 (October 1901–March 1902), 769; "An Indian Magazine," *Timely Topics,* February 7, 1902, 367; "A Magazine for Indians," *Harper's Weekly,* March 29, 1902, 413; C[harles] F[letcher] L[ummis], "That Which Is Written," *Out West Magazine,* May 1902, 534.
5. "A Cherokee City Editor," 10.
6. C. F. L., "That Which Is Written," 534.
7. Ora V. Eddleman, "Our Indian Cousins: Not to Be Considered in Connection with Domestic Service," *Good Housekeeping,* December 1902, 396–97; "Modern Mistress Lo," *Harper's Bazaar,* October 1908, 1002–4.
8. Juan González and Joseph Torres, *News for All the People: The Epic Story of Race and the American Media* (New York: Verso, 2011), 243. Here and elsewhere in this chapter I depend on biographical information from Morrison, "*Twin Territories: The Indian Magazine,*" 136–66; Mark Trahant, *Pictures of Our Nobler Selves: A History of Native American Contributions to News Media* (Nashville: Freedom Forum First Amendment Center, 1995), 25–26; and James W. Parins, *Literacy and Intellectual Life in the Cherokee Nation, 1820–1906* (Norman: University of Oklahoma Press, 2013), 240–45.
9. Eddleman is only starting to gain recognition in our own day. *Twin Territories* is described in Parins, *Literacy and Intellectual Life in the Cherokee Nation,* 240–43; Daniel F. Littlefield, Jr., and James W. Parins, eds., *American*

Indian and Alaska Native Newspapers and Periodicals, 1826–1924 (Westport, Conn.: Greenwood Press, 1984), 366–69; and Patricia Okker, *Our Sister Editors: Sarah J. Hale and the Tradition of Nineteenth-Century American Women Editors* (Athens: University of Georgia Press, 1995), 12–13. Alexia Kosmider provides the most extensive critical analyses of Eddleman's writing and editing. Kosmider, " 'What the Curious Want to Know': Cherokee Writer, Ora Eddleman Reed Writes Back to the Empire," *Literature and Psychology* 41, no. 4 (1995), 51–72; "Strike a Euroamerican Pose: Ora Eddleman Reed's 'Types of Indian Girls,' " *American Transcendental Quarterly* 12, no. 2 (June 1998), 109–31; and *Tricky Tribal Discourse: The Poetry, Short Stories, and Fus Fixico Letters of Creek Writer Alex Posey* (Moscow: University of Idaho Press, 1998), 21–31.

10. Ella Robinson, "Interview with Mary Eddleman of Muskogee. Life and Experiences of an Indian Pioneer Woman," *Indian Pioneer Collection* 27, interview no. 7888, 128–36, Western History Collections, University of Oklahoma, Norman, http://digital.libraries.ou.edu; Ora Eddleman Reed, "Pioneer Publisher, First Daily Newspaper in Indian Territory," *Chronicles of Oklahoma* 23, no. 1 (1945), 38.
11. "In the matter of the application of Mary Eddleman, et als, to be enrolled as citizens of the Cherokee Nation," case no. 11, Northern District, Indian Territory (December 10, 1896), U.S. National Archives and Records Administration, Southwest Region, Fort Worth, Texas.
12. Jamaica Kincaid, *My Garden (Book)* (New York: Farrar, Straus and Giroux, 1999), 114.
13. *Twin Territories* 3, no. 3 (March 1902), 89.
14. Except in quotations, I follow Beth Piatote's practice of omitting letters in this word, both to denaturalize its use and to call attention to the violence of its utterance. Beth Piatote, "A Note on Terminology," in *Domestic Subjects: Gender, Citizenship, and Law in Native American Literature* (New Haven, Conn.: Yale University Press, 2013), ix. On the connotations of sq—w, which became increasingly pejorative in the late nineteenth century, see Nancy J. Parezo and Angelina R. Jones, "What's in a Name? The 1940s–1950s 'Squaw Dress'," *American Indian Quarterly* 33, no. 3 (Summer 2009), 379–80, and Debra Merskin, "The S-Word: Discourse, Stereotypes, and the American Indian Woman," *Howard Journal of Communications* 21, no. 4 (2010), 348.
15. "Tucheta" is the name Eddleman used in joining the Indian Territory Press Association when she was sixteen years old, and it appears under her photograph in *Good Housekeeping*. "A Cherokee City Editor"; Eddleman, "Our Indian Cousins."
16. Blood quantum remains a primary standard for enrollment according to the federal government and many tribes, and Native writers and activists continue to challenge and complicate its meanings. For a summary of critical debates surrounding tribal membership, see Pauline Turner Strong, *American Indians and the American Imaginary: Cultural Representation across the Centuries* (Boulder, Col.: Paradigm, 2012), 59–60. On present-day conflicts over enrollments within Eddleman's tribe, see Circe Sturm, *Blood Politics:*

Race, Culture, and Identity in the Cherokee Nation of Oklahoma (Berkeley: University of California Press, 2002).

17. Parins, *Literacy and Intellectual Life in the Cherokee Nation*, 127.
18. *Twin Territories* 1, no. 1 (December 1898), 2.
19. "A Talk with Our Subscribers," *Twin Territories* 4, no. 1 (January 1902), 14.
20. Chauncey Yellow Robe, "The Menace of the Wild West Show," *Quarterly Journal of the Society of American Indians* 2, no. 1 (January–March 1914), 224.
21. "Then and Now," *Twin Territories* 1, no. 9 (November 1899), 9.
22. Morrison, "*Twin Territories: The Indian Magazine*," 144.
23. Kent Carter, *The Dawes Commission and the Allotment of the Five Civilized Tribes, 1893–1914* (Orem, Utah: Ancestry, 1999), ix.
24. Yellow Robe, "The Menace of the Wild West Show," 224–25.
25. Quoted in Jace Weaver, Craig S. Womack, and Robert Allen Warrior, *American Indian Literary Nationalism* (Albuquerque: University of New Mexico Press, 2006), 13.
26. Nancy Bentley, *Frantic Panoramas: American Literature and Mass Culture, 1870–1920* (Philadelphia: University of Pennsylvania Press, 2009), 179–80, 175.
27. Cheryl Walker, *Indian Nation: Native American Literature and Nineteenth-Century Nationalisms* (Durham, N.C.: Duke University Press, 1997), 108–26.
28. Dee Garceau, "Mourning Dove: Gender and Cultural Mediation," in *Sifters: Native American Women's Lives*, ed. Theda Perdue (New York: Oxford University Press, 2001), 108–26.
29. Carol Batker, *Reforming Fictions: Native, African, and Jewish American Women's Literature and Journalism in the Progressive Era* (New York: Columbia University Press, 2000), 15.
30. *American Indian Magazine* was distributed to Native and associate (non-Native) members of the Society of American Indians. Zitkala-Ša, *American Indian Stories, Legends, and Other Writings*, ed. Cathy N. Davidson and Ada Norris (New York: Penguin, 2003), 163.
31. "What the Curious Want to Know," *Twin Territories* 4, no. 1 (January 1902), 27.
32. "What the Curious Want to Know," *Twin Territories* 4, no. 11 (November 1902), 340.
33. Kosmider, " 'What the Curious Want to Know,' " 63.
34. *Twin Territories* 4, no. 1 (January 1902), 15.
35. Siobhan Senier, *Voices of American Indian Assimilation and Resistance: Helen Hunt Jackson, Sarah Winnemucca, and Victoria Howard* (Norman: University of Oklahoma Press, 2001), 12.
36. Robert Allen Warrior, *Tribal Secrets: Recovering American Indian Intellectual Traditions* (Minneapolis: University of Minnesota Press, 1995), 9.
37. Jace Weaver, *Other Words: American Indian Literature, Law, and Culture* (Norman: University of Oklahoma Press, 2001), 39.
38. Jürgen Habermas, *The Structural Transformation of the Public Sphere: An Inquiry into a Category of Bourgeois Society*, trans. Thomas Berger with the assistance of Frederick Lawrence (Cambridge, Mass.: MIT Press, 1991), 42–43.

39. Ibid., 170–71.
40. For example, Bentley, *Frantic Panoramas;* Miriam Hansen, *Babel and Babylon: Spectatorship in American Silent Film* (Cambridge, Mass.: Harvard University Press, 1994); and Michael Millner, *Fever Reading: Affect and Reading Badly in the Early American Public Sphere* (Durham: University of New Hampshire Press, 2012).
41. Studies that analyze the post-bourgeois counterpublicity of periodicals include Mark Morrison, *The Public Face of Modernism: Little Magazines, Audiences, and Reception, 1905–1920* (Madison: University of Wisconsin Press, 2001); Brita Ytre-Arne, "Women's Magazines and the Public Sphere," *European Journal of Communication* 26, no. 3 (2011), 247–61; and Teresa Zackodnick, *Press, Platform, Pulpit: Black Feminist Publics in the Era of Reform* (Knoxville: University of Tennessee Press, 2011).
42. Jean Marie Lutes, "Beyond the Bounds of the Book: Periodical Studies and Women Writers of the Late Nineteenth and Early Twentieth Centuries," *Legacy* 27, no. 2 (2010), 336.
43. Frankie Hutton and Barbara Straus Reed, eds., *Outsiders in 19th-Century Press History: Multicultural Perspectives* (Bowling Green, Ohio: Bowling Green State University Press, 1995); Okker, *Our Sister Editors;* Aleta Feinsod Cane and Susan Alves, eds., *"The Only Efficient Instrument": American Women Writers and the Periodical, 1837–1916* (Iowa City: University of Iowa Press, 2001), 1–19; Sharon M. Harris, ed., *Blue Pencils and Hidden Hands: Women Editing Periodicals, 1830–1910* (Boston: Northeastern University Press, 2004); James P. Danky and Wayne A. Wiegand, eds., *Print Culture in a Diverse America* (Urbana: University of Illinois Press, 1998); González and Torres, *News for All the People.*
44. Matthew Schneirov, *The Dream of a New Social Order: Popular Magazines in America, 1893–1914* (New York: Columbia University Press, 1994), 1–4.
45. Nancy Fraser, "Rethinking the Public Sphere: A Contribution to the Critique of Actually Existing Democracy," in *The Phantom Public Sphere,* ed. Bruce Robbins (Minneapolis: University of Minnesota Press, 1993), 14, 20, 15.
46. Catherine R. Squires, "Rethinking the Black Public Sphere: An Alternative Vocabulary for Multiple Public Spheres," *Communication Theory* 12, no. 4 (November 2002), 446–47.
47. Fraser, "Rethinking the Public Sphere," 13; Squires, "Rethinking the Black Public Sphere," 447.
48. Margaret Beetham, *A Magazine of Her Own: Domesticity and Desire in Women's Magazines, 1800–1914* (London: Routledge, 1996), 11.
49. The problem of defining interpretive parameters of a multiauthored, multigenre serial publication—of determining what constitutes "the text" under question—has been posed in Lyn Pyket, "Reading the Periodical Press: Text and Context," in *Investigating Victorian Journalism,* ed. Laurel Brake, Aled Jones, and Lionel Madden (New York: St. Martin's Press, 1990), 11; Ann Ardis, "Staging the Public Sphere: Magazine Dialogism and the Prosthetics of Authorship at the Turn of the Twentieth Century," in *Transatlantic Print Culture,* ed. Ann Ardis and Patrick Collier (New York:

Palgrave Macmillan, 2008), 32; and Susan Belasco Smith and Kenneth M. Price, "Introduction: Periodical Literature in Social and Historical Context," in *Periodical Literature in Nineteenth-Century America,* ed. Kenneth M. Price and Susan Belasco Smith (Charlottesville: University Press of Virginia, 1995), 9. I adopt Beetham's intertextual approach of treating all components of the magazine "as part of a field of other texts as well as a field of power relations." Beetham, *A Magazine of Her Own,* 5.

50. Margaret Beetham, "Towards a Theory of the Periodical as a Publishing Genre," in *Investigating Victorian Journalism,* ed. Laurel Brake, Aled Jones, and Lionel Madden (New York: St. Martin's Press, 1990), 24, 27.
51. Chas. [Charles] Gibson, "The Passing of the Indian," *Twin Territories* 4, no. 4 (April 1902), 94.
52. Montague Chamberlain, "The Passing of the Indian," *Twin Territories* 4, no. 10 (October 1902), 317.
53. Mon Torkin, "The Comanches, or 'Prairie Indians,'" *Twin Territories* 2, no. 2 (February 1900), 34. The essay is serialized in *Twin Territories* 2, nos. 2–5 (February–May 1900).
54. Michael Warner, *Publics and Counterpublics* (New York: Zone Books, 2002), 90.
55. *Twin Territories* 5, no. 1 (January 1903), 24.
56. Mignon Schreiber [Ora V. Eddleman] and Barton Langford, "Only an Indian Girl," *Twin Territories* 2, no. 3 (March 1900), 55. The story is serialized in *Twin Territories* 2, nos. 2–7 (February–July 1900). It bears Eddleman's pseudonym in all but the last installment, which is credited to Langford.
57. The story describes the contested 1887 election for Cherokee chief in which the anti-allotment National Party challenged the accommodationist Downing Party.
58. Mignon Schreiber [Ora V. Eddleman] and Barton Langford, "Only an Indian Girl," *Twin Territories* 2, no. 5 (May 1900), 101.
59. Morrison, "*Twin Territories: The Indian Magazine,*" 150.
60. Belasco Smith and Price, "Introduction," 3.
61. On community and proto-feminist agency in correspondence departments of women's magazines, see Margaret Beetham, "Periodicals and the New Media: Women and Imagined Communities," *Women's Studies International Forum* 29, no. 3 (2006), 235, and Kristin Mapel Bloomberg, "Cultural Critique and Consciousness Raising: Clara Bewick Colby's *Woman's Tribune* and Late-Nineteenth-Century Radical Feminism," in *Women in Print: Essays on the Print Culture of American Women from the Nineteenth and Twentieth Centuries,* ed. James P. Danky and Wayne A. Wiegand (Madison: University of Wisconsin Press, 2006), 37. On the construction of a pan-Indian community in the correspondence department of a Native monthly started in 1916, see Rochelle Raineri Zuck, "'Yours in the Cause': Readers, Correspondents, and the Editorial Politics of Carlos Montezuma's *Wassaja,*" *American Periodicals* 22, no. 1 (2012), 81.
62. "What the Curious Want to Know," *Twin Territories* 4, no. 7 (July 1902), 215. Correspondents are identified in the column with initials or a pseud-

onym followed by location. I have found only one inquiry denoted as originating within Indian Territory.

63. For example, the June 1900 issue solicits reader photographs of territory farmhouses and announces a contest in which a winning reader would supply the final chapter in a serial written by Eddleman. "Pictures of Territorial Farm Houses" and "Are You Interested in This?" *Twin Territories* 2, no. 5 (May 1900), 132.
64. "What the Curious Want to Know," *Twin Territories* 4, no. 1 (January 1902), 26.
65. "What the Curious Want to Know," *Twin Territories* 2, no. 12 (December 1900), 245.
66. The two responses to white women looking for Native husbands are in "What the Curious Want to Know," *Twin Territories* 4, no. 4 (April 1902), 118, and "What the Curious Want to Know," *Twin Territories* 4, no. 7 (July 1902), 214.
67. See, e.g., "What the Curious Want to Know," *Twin Territories* 4, no. 7 (July 1902), 204.
68. "What the Curious Want to Know," *Twin Territories* 4, no. 4 (April 1902), 118; "What the Curious Want to Know," *Twin Territories* 4, no. 5 (May 1902), 146.
69. "What the Curious Want to Know," *Twin Territories* 4, no. 1 (January 1902), 26.
70. "What the Curious Want to Know," *Twin Territories* 4, no. 2 (February 1902), 58.
71. "What the Curious Want to Know," *Twin Territories* 4, no. 1 (January 1902), 27.
72. Ibid., 26.
73. "What the Curious Want to Know," *Twin Territories* 4, no. 2 (February 1902), 58.
74. Ibid.
75. "What the Curious Want to Know," *Twin Territories* 4, no. 1 (January 1902), 27.
76. "What the Curious Want to Know," *Twin Territories* 4, no. 11 (November 1902), 340.
77. "What the Curious Want to Know," *Twin Territories* 2, no. 12 (December 1900), 256.
78. Allan Sekula, "The Body and the Archive," *October* 39 (1986), 6.
79. Shawn Michelle Smith, *Photography on the Color Line: W. E. B. Du Bois, Race, and Visual Culture* (Durham, N.C.: Duke University Press, 2004), 3.
80. Ibid., 63–65.
81. On photography of Native Americans in the late nineteenth century, see Alfred L. Bush and Lee Clark Mitchell, *The Photograph and the American Indian* (Princeton, N.J.: Princeton University Press, 1994), xv–xxiii; Martha A. Sandweiss, *Print the Legend: Photography and the American West* (New Haven, Conn.: Yale University Press, 2002), 155–206; and Susan Bernardin et al., *Trading Gazes: Euro-American Women Photographers and Native North Ameri-cans, 1880–1940* (New Brunswick, N.J.: Rutgers University Press, 2003), 11–12.

82. Ben Maddow, *Faces: A Narrative History of the Portrait in Photography* (Boston: Little, Brown, 1977), 16–18.
83. Shawn Michelle Smith, *American Archives: Gender, Race, and Class in Visual Culture* (Princeton, N.J.: Princeton University Press, 1999), 61.
84. Sekula, "The Body and the Archive," 6.
85. Theodore Roosevelt, "Foreword," in Edward Curtis, *The North American Indian,* vol. 1 (Cambridge, Mass.: The University Press, 1907), xi. Curtis crystalizes this notion in his well-known elegiac photograph *The Vanishing Race.*
86. Nancy Hathaway, *Native American Portraits, 1862–1918* (San Francisco: Chronicle Books, 1990), 11.
87. Nigel Russell, "Process and Pictures: The Beginnings of Photography and Photographing American Indians," in *Spirit Capture: Photographs from the National Museum of the American Indian,* ed. Tim Johnson (Washington, D.C.: Smithsonian Institution Press, 1998), 131, 122.
88. Richard W. Hill, Sr., "Developed Identities: Seeing the Stereotypes and Beyond," in Johnson, ed., *Spirit Capture,* 141.
89. My thinking here is inspired by Shawn Smith's analysis of Thomas Askew's portraits of children in Du Bois's archive. Noting that a larger array of props is used in these portraits than in portraits of adults, Smith surmises that the not fully developed narrative of the subject's young lives "needs some formal scripting in order to be communicated to the viewer." Smith, *Photography on the Color Line,* 71.
90. "A Very Grave Error," *Twin Territories* 1, no. 3 (March 1899), 72.
91. Ibid.; "Types of Indian Women," *Twin Territories* 1, no. 1 (December 1898), 17.
92. Kosmider, "Strike a Euroamerican Pose," 109–31.
93. "Types of Indian Girls," *Twin Territories* 4, no. 7 (July 1902), 204.
94. Ibid.
95. Rose Stremlau, *Sustaining the Cherokee Family: Kinship and the Allotment of an Indigenous Nation* (Chapel Hill: University of North Carolina Press, 2011), 143–44. A transcription of testimony in an enrollment hearing is available in Carter, *The Dawes Commission and the Allotment of the Five Civilized Tribes,* 120.
96. Stremlau, *Sustaining the Cherokee Family,* 143–44.
97. David A. Chang, *The Color of the Land: Race, Nation, and the Politics of Landownership in Oklahoma, 1832–1929* (Chapel Hill: University of North Carolina Press, 2010), 94.
98. Eddleman, "Our Indian Cousins."
99. Kosmider, "Strike a Euroamerican Pose." The photograph, which appears in the March 1903 issue of *Twin Territories* without identifying Eddleman, is reproduced on the cover of this book, courtesy of the Research Division of the Oklahoma Historical Society.
100. "Types of Indian Girls." *Twin Territories* 4, no. 3 (March 1902), 69.
101. Irwin's photographs of Annie Berry are in the William E. Irwin Photograph Collection at Yale University, New Haven, Conn.
102. David Treuer, "How Do You Prove You're an Indian?" *New York Times,* December 20, 2011.

103. Stremlau, *Sustaining the Cherokee Family,* 14, 185. See also Sturm, *Blood Politics,* 79–81; Angie Debo, *And Still the Waters Run: The Betrayal of the Five Civilized Tribes* (Princeton, N.J.: Princeton University Press, 1973), 179; and Carter, *The Dawes Commission and the Allotment of the Five Civilized Tribes,* 170–73.
104. *Twin Territories* 2, no. 6 (June 1900), 112.
105. Mignon Schreiber [Ora V. Eddleman], "Lucy and I as Missionaries," *Twin Territories* 2, no. 3 (March 1900), 43. The story is serialized in *Twin Territories* 2, nos. 3–8 (March–August 1900).
106. Mignon Schreiber [Ora V. Eddleman], "Lucy and I as Missionaries," *Twin Territories* 2, no. 4 (April 1900), 83.
107. Mignon Schreiber [Ora V. Eddleman], "Aunt Mary's Christmas Dinner," *Twin Territories* 2, no. 12 (December 1900), reprinted in Kilcup, ed., *Native American Women's Writing,* 369–72.
108. Mignon Schreiber [Ora V. Eddleman Reed], "A Pair of Moccasins," *Twin Territories* 2, nos. 8–12 (August–December 1899), reprinted in Kilcup, ed., *Native American Women's Writing,* 364.
109. "The Honor of Wynoma," *Twin Territories* 4, no. 11 (November 1902), reprinted in Kilcup, ed., *Native American Women's Writing,* 372–76. Subsequent references are to the reprinted version. The story is unsigned; however, I agree with Kilcup that its plot and style justify attribution to Eddleman.
110. Gayle Wald, *Crossing the Line: Racial Passing in Twentieth Century U.S. Literature and Culture* (Durham, N.C.: Duke University Press, 2000), 30, 187.
111. "The Honor of Wynoma," 373, 374.
112. Ibid., 374, 375.
113. Ibid., 375.
114. Ibid., 376.
115. Ibid.
116. Ibid.
117. Ibid.
118. For objections to Momaday's concept, see Arnold Krupat, *The Voice in the Margin: Native American Literature in the Canon* (Berkeley: University of California Press, 1989), 14. For a cogent rejoinder, see Strong, *American Indians and the American Imaginary,* 62–63.
119. Chadwick Allen, *Blood Narrative: Indigenous Identity in American Indian and Maori Literary and Activist Texts* (Durham, N.C.: Duke University Press, 2002), 178.

Epilogue: Toward a Theory of Feminist Indigenist Reinvention

1. Valerie S. Mathes, "Nineteenth Century Women and Reform: The Women's National Indian Association," *American Indian Quarterly* 14, no. 1 (Winter 1990), 4.
2. Joy Harjo and Gloria Bird, "Introduction," in *Reinventing the Enemy's Language: Contemporary Native Women's Writings of North America,* ed. Joy Harjo and Gloria Bird (New York: Norton, 1997), 21, 22, 23–24.

3. Elizabeth Archuleta, "'I Give You Back': Indigenous Women Writing to Survive," *Studies in American Indian Literature* 18, no. 4 (2006), 89–90.
4. Laura Cotelli, "*Almanac of the Dead:* An Interview with Leslie Marmon Silko," in *Conversations with Leslie Marmon Silko,* ed. Ellen L. Arnold (Jackson: University of Mississippi Press, 2000), 125; Thomas Irmer and Matthias Schmidt, "An Interview with Leslie Marmon Silko," in Arnold, ed., *Conversations with Leslie Marmon Silko,* 154.
5. For example, Melody Graulich finds in the novel "little of the sensuous lyricism of Silko's early work or its rich treatment of tradition." Melody Graulich, "Introduction: Remember the Stories," in *"Yellow Woman": Leslie Marmon Silko,* ed. Melody Graulich (New Brunswick, N.J.: Rutgers University Press, 1993), 24n7.
6. Irmer and Schmidt, "An Interview with Leslie Marmon Silko," 154; Cotelli, "*Almanac of the Dead,*" 122.
7. Dean Rader, *Engaged Resistance: American Indian Art, Literature, and Film, from Alcatraz to the NMAI* (Austin: University of Texas Press, 2011), 132–37, 146.
8. "Comic book" refers to a print or digital text that tells a story serially in words and pictures and is inexpensively produced in medium-length, standalone form. Comic books are distinct from comic strips (which are shorter and typically appear as a small component of a magazine or newspaper) and graphic novels or memoirs (which are longer and more highbrow). On terminology, see Charles Hatfield, *Alternative Comics: An Emerging Literature* (Jackson: University of Mississippi Press, 2005), 4–6.
9. "A Chat with Arigon Starr, Creator of 'Super Indian' Comics," *Indian Country Today Media Network,* June 14, 2012, http://indiancountrytoday medianetwork.com.
10. R[achel] J[ames] M[cCarthy], "Beyond the Panel: An Interview with Arigon Starr of Super Indian, Part Two," *Bitch Media,* March 2, 2012, http://bitchmagazine.org.
11. On the commercial comic book representations of Native people, see Cornel D. Pewewardy, "From Subhuman to Superhuman: Images of First Nation Peoples in Comic Books," *Simile: Studies in Media and Information Literacy Education* 2, no. 2 (May 2002), 1–9; Michael A. Sheyahshe, *Native Americans in Comic Books: A Critical Study* (Jefferson, N.C.: McFarland, 2008); and C. Richard King, "Alter/native Heroes: Native Americans, Comic Books, and the Struggle for Self-Definition," *Cultural Studies↔ Critical Methodologies* 9, no. 2 (April 2009), 214–23. On the handful of "superheroes of color" in mainstream commercial comics, see Frederick Luis Aldama, "Multicultural Comics Today: A Brief Introduction," in *Multicultural Comics from Zap to Blue Beetle,* ed. Frederick Luis Aldama (Austin: University of Texas Press, 2011), 1–25.
12. Hillary L. Chute, *Graphic Women: Life Narrative and Contemporary Comics* (New York: Columbia University Press, 2010), 9.
13. Hatfield, *Alternative Comics,* x.
14. Darth Anexandros, interview with Arigon Starr, Arizona Latin Arts and Culture Center, June 6, 2014, www.youtube.com.

15. Arigon Starr, *Super Indian: Volume One,* ed. Janet Miner (West Hollywood, Calif.: Wacky Productions Unlimited, 2012).
16. Ibid.
17. This conspiratorial relationship between the comic book creator and the reader may be intrinsic to the form itself, as the fracturing of time and space created by the multipanel format of comics requires the reader to connect discrete moments and construct a unified reality, making her the writer-artist's "silent accomplice." Scott McCloud, *Understanding Comics: The Invisible Art* (New York: HarperCollins, 1994), 68.
18. On the indigenization of the Superman figure by Starr and other Native writers and artists, see Susan Bernardin, "Future Pasts: Comics, Graphic Novels, and Digital Media," in *The Routledge Companion to Native American Literature,* ed. Deborah Madsen (New York: Routledge, 2016), 480–93. Bernardin makes a similar point about the redirection of mainstream comics in *Super Indian: Volume One.* Her essay offers a far more complete analysis of Starr's series than I can accommodate here.
19. Arigon Starr, *Super Indian: Volume Two,* ed. Janet Miner (West Hollywood, Calif.: Wacky Productions Unlimited, 2015).
20. Starr, *Super Indian: Volume One.*
21. Starr, *Super Indian: Volume Two.*
22. Starr, *Super Indian: Volume One.*
23. Quoted in T. V. Reed, *The Art of Protest: Culture and Activism from the Civil Rights Movement to the Streets of Seattle* (Minneapolis: University of Minnesota Press, 2005), 303.

Index

Page numbers in italics refer to illustrations.

JANET DEAN is Professor and Chair of English and Cultural Studies at Bryant University. She previously taught at the State University of New York at Stony Brook and the University of South Dakota. Dean earned a B.A. from Colby College and an M.A., M.Phil., and Ph.D. from Columbia University, where she was nominated for the Bancroft Dissertation Prize. She is winner of the Don D. Walker Essay Prize in Western American Literature and held an Andrew W. Mellon Fellowship at the Library Company of Philadelphia. She currently resides with her husband and two children in Providence, R.I.